BEST OF BAIN

BEST OF BAIN

from the pages of  Harvard Business Review

BAIN & COMPANY ◀

Contents

The Journey to Full Potential

Manny Maceda

E very company faces times in its life when change becomes essential. Its primary business matures and growth begins to slow. Technologies or market dynamics evolve. The competitive landscape tilts. A new CEO brings a fresh leadership team and a new set of priorities.

Great business leaders thrive on this kind of change. They anticipate the challenging questions: Where will this company be in three, four, or five years? Will it succeed in its new situation, or will it struggle in the middle of the pack? Where is the company headed now, and how will we know that it is on the right track?

For 40 years, Bain & Company has worked alongside leaders who recognize what it takes to win. We've helped our clients embrace the opportunities prompted by these kinds of questions and lead successfully through change. We have worked with them to identify a compelling vision of the destination, and we have helped them develop a road map to get there. This *journey to full potential* can raise a company's performance by an order of magnitude and deliver real, sustainable growth. In many respects, a journey to full potential takes the measure of a company and its leaders, and defines their collective success.

To reach its full potential, a company needs five broad capabilities. Most companies have strengths in some of these areas but need help in others. A few find that they require a transformation, and must rebuild in all five.

1. Winning Strategy

At Bain, we think about strategy as "where to play and how to win." The concept forces leadership teams to ask two vital questions. First, where will we compete? This involves tough choices: Once a company's leaders decide where to play—which market segments, product categories, and customers—they must engage in the art of allocating scarce resources to out-invest and out-execute where they have chosen to compete. Second, what's our differentiation against the competition, so that our target customers keep coming back and recommend us to their friends?

It's up to the company's leaders to translate strategy into a mission for the front line. The strategy should be grounded in nonnegotiable principles and embedded in a set of routines that guide people's decisions and behavior on the job. The best strategies are embodied in a few repeatable models. In this way, strategy becomes truly operational—not sitting in the board room but brought to life every day in the actions of the front line.

2. Customer Focus

Every successful company has a set of core customers, individuals or businesses that it can serve better than anyone else. These customers are loyal, committed, and profitable. Winning companies develop a deep understanding of who is in this core group, and who isn't. The key, in our experience, is having a rigorous method for nurturing core customers and turning more and more of them into passionate advocates for the company and its products. An approach like Bain's Net Promoter® system builds this customer focus into everyday operations, channeling customer ratings and comments directly to frontline employees through closed-loop feedback. Another hallmark of the companies that achieve full potential: productive sales forces and effective customer operations.

3. Operational Excellence

Is the company managing its cost structure and assets more efficiently than its closest competitors? Are its products and services consistently superior and more reliable than others in its market segments? Does it have speed and flexibility where it counts? Very few firms can aspire to be lowest cost and highest quality everywhere they operate. The right focus results from aligning its operations with the firm's strategy and becoming a leader in quality, functionality, and cost where customers value it most. Operational excellence—world-class performance in cost, quality, time to market, information systems, and other indicators of efficient and effective operations—is not absolute; it is measured relative to the competition and to a company's own history of performance. But if operations and IT systems do not provide a distinct competitive advantage, a company will find itself at the mercy of more-efficient rivals.

4. High-Performance Organization

Companies facing major change need strong leadership committed to their mission. They need an organizational structure that is properly aligned with the business, and not too complex. They must be able to attract and retain top talent. What many companies overlook is that all these organizational elements have to support fast, effective decision making and execution. Our experience and research have shown that great companies make better decisions than their competitors. Decision roles and methods are clear and well understood, allowing rigorous accountability. Everyone from frontline employees outward knows how to execute decisions—and expects to be held accountable for doing so.

5. Maximum Enterprise Value

Translating a great business into outstanding financial performance is partly a matter of efficient financial processes—budgeting, planning, reporting, and so on. But the greater financial challenge is to maximize the long-term value of the enterprise. That requires sound cash management, building and then exploiting a strong balance sheet, and striking the right balance in managing risks. A thriving company that scores high on all these measures is likely to maximize its stock price and total return to shareholders. Successful private equity firms understand the importance of creating a sound capital structure and a strategy designed to maximize value. So do the companies that we call "disciplined acquirers," those that build up repeatable capabilities in mergers and acquisitions and use M&A to increase their valuation beyond what would be possible through organic growth alone.

Making Change Stick

We don't regard this as one of the five capabilities, because it underlies all of them. Initiatives to create a better strategy, improve the organization, or reach any other objective don't matter much if the company cannot implement lasting change. Ultimately that means encouraging and enabling people throughout the organization to learn new ways of doing things day in and day out.

Lasting change naturally requires sustained commitment, and it requires careful tracking of progress in a form that everyone can see and understand. But in our experience it requires something more: an understanding of the psychological and emotional obstacles to change. A practical set of tools like Bain's Results Delivery® methodology can help companies anticipate and compensate for the predictable mood swings, from initial skepticism and fear to boundless excitement and back again, that accompany—and often undermine—every major change effort.

Getting Started

Every journey begins with determining the point of arrival. What is our mission? What kind of company do we want to be? A point of arrival isn't just for the board or the annual report: It's a set of objectives for the entire organization, well known to people in every unit and at every level. Its goal is to get people fired up, excited about the future, ready to roll up their sleeves and go to work. It says, "This is where we are headed—and you can gauge our success by our progress toward that goal."

Some companies find themselves in unusually difficult straits, with weaknesses in nearly every capability we have outlined. For them, the task is how best to move through the full list of capability improvements that are required. More commonly, full potential efforts start with a dominant theme. A manufacturer assessing its capabilities, for example, concluded that everything needed attention except its organization, which was stronger than that of competitors. A high-tech company with the largest global market share in its industry determined that its organization was weaker than its other capabilities—it had grown bureaucratic and complacent. A third company, in the financial services industry, decided that it needed to focus both on cost competitiveness (to fend off attacks from lower-end competitors) and customer service (to hold off higher-end competition). A fast-growing specialty retailer recognized, with more than $1 billion in sales, that it needed more systematic operations and professional functions.

Establishing a company's point of departure requires thorough, data-based diagnoses of its strengths and weaknesses. Bain's approach relies on information from executive and employee surveys and interviews, from financial analysis, from customer responses, and from competitor analysis. Our Performance Improvement Diagnostic℠ and its 12 "must-have facts" enable a CEO or general manager to identify a business's most important priorities and thereby to focus on practical change efforts where they will have the greatest effect.

For many business leaders, a journey to full potential becomes a major milestone in their careers and shapes the destiny of their companies. The results speak louder than any words: The manufacturer we mentioned above revamped its strategy, its customer focus, and its operations—and then embarked on a major capital restructuring designed to accelerate the creation of value. The high-tech company eliminated much of its bureaucracy, regained its nimbleness, and solidified its #1 position. The financial services firm earned a profitable leadership role in the broad middle of its market. And the retailer survived its growing pains to become a global leader in its industry.

In many respects, the articles in this book reflect our own journey, as our thinking and practice have evolved during our 40-year history. But they also show how many high-potential companies have confronted wide-ranging challenges over the years, how those companies have learned from their experience—and how they have realized, in the end, the greatness that is the hallmark of business success.

Winning Strategy

Your Brand's Best Strategy

What really drives profit? In consumer goods, market share alone is not the answer.

Vijay Vishwanath and Jonathan Mark

We updated the analysis in this article several years after it was published and found some intriguing developments, such as new potential in low premium categories. But the underlying analysis and conclusions presented here remained much the same. Profitability in consumer products certainly depends on market share—but also, more importantly, on the nature of a product's category. If a company fails to understand the opportunities and constraints each category presents, it will not realize a brand's full potential.

This construct has helped consumer goods companies take specific actions. Some have realized that their best move was to divest dead-end brands, those with low share in a low premium category. Many companies realized that they had "hitchhiker" brands that were seriously undermanaged, and took measures to increase these brands' profitability. Some category leaders have discovered how they can increase the "premiumness" of entire categories, thus raising profitability for all players. In emerging markets, where some categories are starting to mature, this has been a key strategy. In all these moves, the patterns of high road/low road strategy have played a guiding hand.

During the 1970s, Procter & Gamble moved aggressively to gain market share in the coffee business. Freed from a consent decree that had restrained its ability to grow geographically, Folgers, a P&G subsidiary, came east from its western stronghold and took on Maxwell House in a clash of the coffee titans. After the dust settled, Folgers indeed had moved to a new plateau of market share—from which it has not retreated. But its victory had a decidedly bitter taste. In committing to and achieving major gains in market share through its pricing actions, P&G effectively eliminated the industry profits of the entire "roast and ground" segment—a situation that persisted until the early 1990s.

HBR May–June 1997

What had gone wrong? Once Folgers had achieved its goal of gaining market share, why didn't significant profitability follow? Could Folgers have known in advance that its plan wasn't necessarily the best strategic move?

We believe that the answer is yes. Conventional wisdom holds that market share drives profitability. Certainly, in some industries, such as chemicals, paper, and steel, market share and profitability are inextricably linked. But when we studied the profitability of premium brands like Folgers—brands that sell for 25% to 30% more than private-label brands—in 40 categories of consumer goods, we found some surprising results. Chief among them, we discovered, was that market share alone does not drive profitability. In fact, market share explains only about half of the differences in profitability among brands; in some categories, there is hardly any correlation at all.

Instead, a brand's profitability is driven by *both* market share *and* the nature of the category, or product market, in which the brand competes. A brand's relative market share (RMS) has a different impact on profitability depending on whether the overall category is dominated by premium brands or by value brands to begin with. That is, if a category is composed largely of premium brands, then most of the brands in the category are—or should be— quite profitable. If, on the other hand, the category is composed mostly of value and private-label brands, then returns will be lower across the board. When we compared the actual profitability of the 40 premium brands we studied with

What Explains a Brand's Profitability?

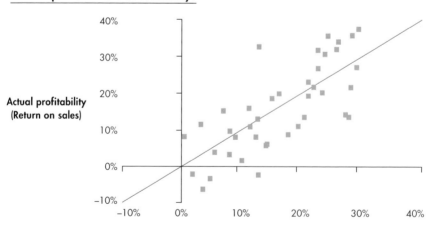

Actual profitability (Return on sales)

Predicted profitability (Return on sales)
based on relative market share and the "premium" degree of a category

their predicted profitability, using as variables RMS and the "premium" degree of a category, we found a strong correlation. (See the exhibit "What Explains a Brand's Profitability?")

The facial-skin-care category is filled largely with premium brands, and most players earn more than 15% pretax operating profit, or return on sales (ROS). What's more, even brands with market share one-fifth to one-tenth that of the category leader, Oil of Olay, have operating profits only slightly lower than Oil of Olay's. But processed meats, in which market leader Oscar Mayer and other premium competitors account for less than 40% of the category, are a different story. The brands with high relative market share earn about 10% ROS; those with low relative market share usually earn less than 5%. The category is what makes the difference.

Developing the most profitable strategy for a premium brand, therefore, means reexamining market share targets in light of the brand's category. In other words, managers must think about their brand strategy along two dimensions at the same time. First, is the category "premium" or "value"? (Is it dominated by premium brands or by value brands?) Second, is the brand's relative market share low or high?

If we visualize a matrix with those two dimensions, we can map the position of any premium brand within one of four quadrants. Each quadrant has different implications for a brand's profit potential. And each requires a different strategy. (See the exhibit "Two Dimensions, Four Strategies.")

Two Dimensions, Four Strategies

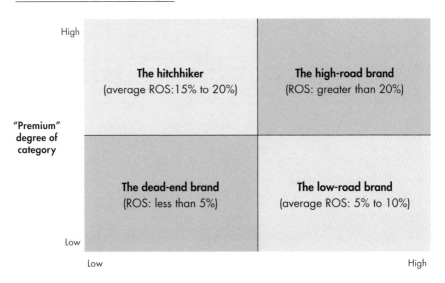

Procter & Gamble's strategy for Folgers was based on the implicit notion that greater RMS always means greater profits. But when the company went after share, it started a price war. Competitors responded, and a category that had once been premium became value. All players suffered. Given the quadrant that Folgers had originally occupied—a market share follower in a premium category—did P&G pursue the optimum strategy?

The Hitchhiker: Premium Category, Low RMS

Folgers was what we call a *hitchhiker*. And for hitchhikers—whose average ROS is generally between 15% and 20%—gaining share by lowering prices is dangerous. Hitchhikers shouldn't rock the boat; it is usually in their best interest to follow the leader's pricing moves.

What brands in this quadrant *should* focus on is innovation coupled with niche marketing or variations on niche marketing. Successful hitchhiker brands either attract and keep a narrow base of loyal users, as Neutrogena does in the facial-bar-soap category, or lead the market in a subsegment of a larger category, as Post does in shredded-wheat and banana-nut cereals. The common theme is an innovative brand for which consumers are willing to pay a premium price.

Cereal, in fact, is a good example of a category in which the hitchhiker strategy can pay off. More than 60% of the category is made up of premium, or high-end, products, and consumers pay at least 30% more for those brands than they do for value brands, despite the recent price cuts. Kellogg is the clear market leader, but Post and General Mills each control certain subsegments and do very well following Kellogg in overall RMS.

For an interesting variation on hitchhiking, the automobile industry is worth a look. Over the past 10 years, the category as a whole has become increasingly premium and profitable. Why? Automakers have figured out that it is far more rewarding to target specific customer groups with innovations—highly stylized vehicles—than to compete at the low end of the market with a high RMS. As a result, the average price of an automobile sold in the United States has risen much faster than the rate of inflation. Entire segments—such as sport utility vehicles and minivans—are continually being created and redefined; and the traditional four-door family sedan now accounts for only a small portion of the automobile category. Chrysler has been a primary driver—and the largest beneficiary—of this change. The company, which had long been a weak player in the market, now offers many niche vehicles and earns more than $1,000 in profit for each one it sells.

Brands that occupy the premium-category, low-RMS quadrant can maintain healthy profit levels for long periods. But the hitchhiker position is vulnerable—in particular to pricing moves by the market leader. If the market leader in a premium category lowers prices—as Marlboro did in the cigarette industry in 1993—the hitchhiker's profits can erode overnight, especially if the price gap between premium and value brands was wide to begin with. It's true that many premium categories sustain large price gaps for years. But managers of hitchhiker brands must recognize and evaluate the risks.

The High Road: Premium Category, High RMS

When a brand leads the market in a premium category, we call it a *high-road brand*. High-road brands generally earn more than 20% ROS. The keys to success in this quadrant are innovation, innovation, and innovation. Consumers of high-road brands tend to be loyal and willing to pay premium prices. In return, they continually demand improvements and changes—in form, size, and function—that deliver real value.

Kraft Macaroni & Cheese is a good example of a brand that has successfully sustained its position in the high-road quadrant. Building on its original product, Kraft constantly engages existing customers and attracts new ones with its innovations. For example, over the past 15 years, the company has introduced spiral pasta, pasta in the shape of cartoon characters, and several different cheese flavors—all selling at premium prices in what has remained a premium category. Clorox is another good example. Not only has it innovated in its original category, household bleaches; it has also used innovation as a way to trade on strong customer equity and to muscle into ancillary categories, such as all-purpose cleaners and toilet bowl cleaners.

Gillette is a third good example. When Gillette's main competitor introduced low-cost disposable razors sold by the bag, the dynamics of the razor category began to shift. At first, Gillette's managers responded in kind by introducing their own packages of low-cost disposable razors. Realizing, however, that a dominant share in a value-oriented category would confine the company to an ROS of 5% to 10%, they also began to consider other paths to profitability. As a result, Gillette poured more than $200 million into R&D and introduced the Sensor shaving system. The Sensor sold at a 25% price premium over Atra, another Gillette brand, which until then had been the highest-priced system on the market.

Gillette successfully made consumers "trade up" to a new spending level—and a new set of performance expectations. What's more, 15% of Sensor sales came from people who had formerly bought competitors' disposable razors. Instead of paying roughly 40 cents per razor, they began to pay $3.30 for a shaving system that required 70-cent replacement cartridges. The Sensor and its succeeding generations of products—along with the innovations of other companies that followed suit—restored the razor category to premium status.

When managers of high-road brands are confronted with a price war or a threat from a private label, it is critical for them to think through the consequences of their reactions. Kimberly-Clark and Procter & Gamble have long faced a private-label threat to their premium products in the diaper category. Kimberly-Clark has always responded to that threat with new technologies and applications. The result? Innovations such as Ultratrim and Pull-Ups, which allow the company to continue charging a price premium. P&G's early efforts to fight private labels, on the other hand, seemed more focused on reducing prices and repositioning its products downward. Only when that strategy failed to produce the desired results did P&G turn to innovation to sustain profitability. Pampers Baby-Dry Stretch diapers, which have a superabsorbent core, and Pampers Premium diapers, which boast "breathable" side panels, are two innovations that have helped P&G strengthen its position as a high-road brand.

If innovation is the most important component of a successful high-road strategy, judicious pricing is second in importance. Educated consumers will pay more for innovation, trading up to higher-priced products. But there's a limit. Extremely high prices can produce mind-boggling returns over the short term, but such profits are not sustainable. If there is a substantial price gap between premium brands and value brands in a category, someone will fill the breach. Our research suggests that consumers are more loyal to premium brands that are only somewhat more expensive than value brands.

If there is a considerable price gap within a category, high-road brands can maintain a pricing edge for a longer time by innovating profusely. Advil's prices are 100% higher than those of equivalent private-label analgesics; but Advil's innovations have been limited, and the brand has continued to lose share to private-label offerings. Tylenol has also lost share to private-label brands, but its prolific innovation—different strengths, different forms, different formulations for specific ailments—has proved a more effective strategy than Advil's.

Raising entry barriers is the third key ingredient of a successful high-road strategy. One way to do that is through product (or stock-keeping-unit) proliferation, as Tylenol has done. Not only does such proliferation signify the brand's growth, but it also acts as a line of defense against lower-priced alternatives. Retailers would rather stock a variation on a leading brand than an alternative that cannot command proportional shelf space and hasn't been proven to turn over at a rapid rate.

Managers also can block new entrants to a category by using proprietary delivery systems, such as direct store delivery (DSD)—a program through which manufacturers deliver directly to stores rather than through retailers' warehouses. If the product is perishable, a DSD program ensures freshness. DSD also gives the manufacturer enormous merchandising power. Because the person stocking the shelves is employed by the manufacturer, not only can the manufacturer control how the product is displayed, but it also knows firsthand what is selling and how fast. Programs like these tend to have high fixed costs; minor players find it difficult to respond effectively.

Coca-Cola, Frito-Lay, and Nabisco are all good examples of high-road food brands that have erected those kinds of barriers. Frito-Lay has expanded its product line to the point where—given shelf-space constraints—competitors simply cannot keep up. What's more, its DSD system ensures that anyone who wants to compete must first confront a massive investment hurdle. Witness the demise of Eagle Snacks. Eagle simply was unable to match Frito-Lay's investments.

Finally, managers of high-road brands must be certain that their spending on support activities—such as marketing, R&D, and capital improvements—is consistent with their strategy. That's good advice in any case, but for high-road brands it is critical. Building brand equity and reinforcing the brand's image must be primary concerns; hence spending on media advertising should be a dominant part of the marketing mix. And R&D, as we've said, should focus on innovation rather than on reducing costs.

Can high-road brands fall from grace? Certainly. If managers succumb to the temptation to "milk" the brand—scaling back innovations or raising prices without offering commensurate increases in value—consumers will balk. What's more, over time such actions will reduce the premium nature of the category as a whole. Managers then will confront the two-fold task of turning around a flagging brand and trying to increase profits in an area that is no longer primed to encourage higher levels of profitability.

The Low Road: Value Category, High RMS

When a brand competes in a value category and has a high RMS, we call it a *low-road brand*. Most low-road brands do not realize significant profits as a result of their price premiums; they earn an average ROS of only 5% to 10%. That's because many low-road price premiums reflect bloated cost structures, not differentiated or more valuable products. In this quadrant, then, the primary goal should be cutting costs and plowing back the savings into lower prices. Managers should take a hard look at their cost structures and eliminate steps that do not add value. That way, they can free up resources to devote to building brand equity. The strategy is to encourage consumers who are buying value brands to purchase the premium brand by reducing the price gap between the two and by boosting the brand's equity—in effect, giving consumers "permission" to pay the higher price.

Managers can cut costs in many areas. One option is reducing stock-keeping units. Many low-road brands sport large numbers of SKUs because their managers believe that consumers value the variety. But in this quadrant, such proliferation does not ensure greater profits; often, it simply leads to more complex manufacturing and delivery systems, which in turn lead to higher overhead costs. High-road brands, with their strong customer equity and their position in a premium category, require the variety; low-road brands do not.

Other cost-cutting measures—to round up the rest of the usual suspects—include rationalizing capacity (closing facilities), consolidating suppliers, and standardizing components. Managers also should scrutinize the designs of their products and packages. Over time, many manufacturers tend to develop an almost slavish regard for the "gold standard" and, as a result, build additional costs into their products or packages. They need to examine whether those extra costs are justified: Do value-oriented consumers really appreciate the additional features?

Oscar Mayer occupied the low-road quadrant in the processed-meats business in the early 1990s and pursued a low-road strategy. The company attacked costs aggressively, eliminating more than half of its SKUs, closing plants, getting out of raw material vertical integration, and consolidating suppliers. Then it used the savings to lower prices.

Oscar Mayer benefited greatly from its strategy: Over a three-year period, profits improved significantly. But the entire category is benefiting as well: It is taking on more of a premium flavor. Now the challenge is increasingly about brand equity; profits for all competitors that can strengthen equity should rise.

Oscar Mayer is beginning to behave like a high-road brand, and because its category is shifting, that strategy should work well. The company is devoting more money to reinforcing its brand image. For the past two years, for instance, it has sponsored the Super Bowl halftime show—traditionally the bailiwick of high-road products. And it is putting more effort into innovation. Consider the Lunchables product line—a premium convenience product designed for a specific meal. After a slow start, Lunchables has taken off and has been copied by competitors.

In most cases, premium brands competing in value categories do so against a host of regional value brands. Such was the case for Anheuser-Busch, which pursued a low-road strategy during the 1970s and 1980s. In the early 1970s, the beer market sported a number of small, regional value brands. Then, over a 15-year period, Anheuser-Busch reduced its costs and plowed the savings into advertising and lower prices, and consumers began to "trade up" to Budweiser. The once-regional beer market began to consolidate, eventually becoming a national business.

If a low-road strategy is successful, the category as a whole may slowly begin to change, as has happened with beer. New, high-end players have entered the market. Several market leaders—including Anheuser-Busch—are now concentrating on innovation. New consumers are being drawn to the category as they become aware of product variations. And increasingly, value-conscious consumers are willing to buy premium brands because they find the higher prices acceptable. Today the entire beer category is becoming more premium: A larger number of companies are competing on brand equity rather than on price.

It may be useful to reiterate the major differences between the high-road and low-road quadrants because, too often, managers of brands with high market share do not differentiate among brands in what are two fundamentally different situations. They pursue the same strategy in both cases and then wonder why their actions are not always rewarding. For low-road brands, cost reduction is critical, SKUs should be reduced, and R&D investments should be aimed at making the manufacturing process more efficient and reducing waste. In the high-road quadrant, cost reduction is not nearly as important, SKU proliferation is desirable, and R&D should focus on product innovation and manufacturing flexibility.

The Dead End: Value Category, Low RMS

Finding a winning strategy in the value-category, low-RMS quadrant is tough, even for those brands that command more than a minimal share of the market. That's why we call them *dead-end brands*. Premium products in this position simply don't make money: They generally earn an ROS of less than 5%. And, unfortunately, many managers of such brands are perennial optimists. "The brand isn't making money today, but it will in the future" is a common, but often misguided, refrain.

The fact is, dead-end brands will never make money. So the choices for managers are limited: Either get out of the business or commit to a massive turnaround project, which will move the brand into another quadrant.

One way to "get out of the box" is to slash prices with an eye toward taking share from the market leader (the low-road brand). Such drastic price reduction is usually possible only if the brand is part of a portfolio of products that share internal costs. For example, a dead-end brand can gain ground if managers consolidate package suppliers across an entire portfolio. Another option is out-sourcing in areas where the brand isn't large enough to command economies of scale. Or managers might consider bringing together a number of smaller brands in order to gain scale—a move that is commonly called a "string of pearls" strategy.

Heinz Nine Lives canned cat food is one of the best examples we know of a dead-end brand that turned its business around in that manner. Heinz is well known in general for its disciplined approach to cost reduction, but the managers of Nine Lives elevated cost cutting to an art form. After reducing prices several times in the 1980s to compete for share, and after unsuccessfully trying to break the price-war cycle by raising prices in 1991, the managers turned their attention inward. Deciding on a price per can that they believed would be acceptable to consumers, they set out to cut internal costs to meet that goal. They closed eight plants, integrated some of the business vertically (they now make their own cans), and began forming alliances with suppliers.

Heinz Nine Lives already had strong brand equity and access to some inexpensive materials (tuna from the company's Star-Kist business). But it was the dramatic cost reduction that really turned the product around. The brand has been transformed from an also-ran to probably the most profitable product in the category. And Heinz didn't stop there. Once the Nine Lives cost-cutting process was complete, the company went on a pet-food-acquisition binge that more than doubled the size of its business.

Another way to leave the dead-end quadrant—albeit an even more difficult one—is to "trump" the category by introducing a superpremium product that completely resets consumers' expectations. Most often, it takes a new entrant to shake up a category to that extent. Witness how Häagen-Dazs introduced superpremium ice cream into what had been a low-cost, regional market. It is very hard even for established players to follow suit because of the ingrained images of their brands.

The coffee category is also worth another look in this context. Many established manufacturers have recently launched highly differentiated products such as coffee singles and premium roasts. They also are trying to brand coffee sources, such as Java and Colombian, for the first time. Interestingly, such retailers as Starbucks, the Coffee Connection, and Peet's provided the catalyst for change: In effect, they played the role of new entrant to the market, and the credit for resetting expectations lies with them. It remains to be seen whether the established manufacturers can successfully follow their lead.

The biggest mistake that managers make in the dead-end quadrant is hanging on to a brand for years without seriously asking the following questions:

Can I become the low-road player through scale and cost reduction? Do I have a prayer of "trumping" this category? If the answers are no, the managers should sell or shut down the brand.

Managing a Portfolio of Premium Brands

In addition to setting strategic imperatives for individual brands, our matrix can help managers better understand the dynamics of a portfolio of products. By plotting their portfolio on the matrix, managers can see which brands are performing up to potential and adjust their expectations for individual brands—and their overall resource allocation—accordingly.

For example, R&D funds should be heavily skewed toward high-road and hitchhiker businesses and should focus on innovation. Often, managers who are overseeing a portfolio spend a disproportionate amount of R&D money on dead-end brands, believing that they can spark a turnaround. Usually, such spending is futile; the money is better spent in areas that promise a decent investment return.

Big-ticket media campaigns that are designed to build equity should be saved for high-road and hitchhiker brands as well. For low-road brands, spending on marketing should be limited largely to trade and consumer promotions—activities that lower a product's price. Of course, if managers are trying to change a category's dynamics and turn a low-road brand into a high-road brand, spending more to build equity can be justified. It's a judgment call, and it's all about timing. The important thing is to be aware of the implications of any action—and to resist the urge to spend money where it won't do any good. When considering a portfolio of brands, managers will be tempted to spend too much on marketing for dead-end brands. But throwing promotional money at the trade—offering discounts to supermarkets in exchange for product promotion, for example—simply won't work. It's far better to limit spending on dead-end products and move funding to brands in other quadrants.

Capital spending for dead-end products should be limited as well. As we've said, for low-road and dead-end brands, the focus should be on cost reduction. It would be better to use capital resources to bolster innovation for high-road and hitchhiker brands. Spending money on reducing a product's time-to-market and on flexible manufacturing to churn out short-run SKUs is also worthwhile for high-road and hitchhiker brands. Again, managers must be aware of the possible consequences of any investment.

As we've stressed throughout, category dynamics can change. One of the brands in a portfolio may be a classic hitchhiker, and a competitor's move may cause the entire category to shift from premium to value almost overnight. Beer, once a value category, is now premium. The same goes for athletic footwear. Sneakers were once a value buy; now the category is solidly premium.

The matrix is not meant to be a onetime tool. Managers must reexamine individual brands and entire portfolios on a regular basis. Only by doing so can they successfully prepare for or initiate category shifts and, in the process, help their organizations maximize profitability by coalescing around innovation- and cost-driven businesses.

How to Map Your Industry's Profit Pool

Do you know where the money's being made in your industry?

Orit Gadiesh and James L. Gilbert

People used to know what business they were in. They were manufacturers, or distributors, or service companies. If you asked them about their business definition, they wondered why you questioned anything so obvious. The work represented in this article helped to reshape these conventional ways of thinking. It showed, for example, that most of a vehicle manufacturer's profit might come from financing customer purchases—which meant that automakers needed to rethink their entire business models.

Since the article was written, technology, new competitors, and new customer expectations have reshaped virtually every industry. Profit pools have grown far more fluid than they used to be. So our clients find they must continually reevaluate the business they are in. Is an Internet company primarily a search engine, a social network, or a media company? Should a maker of heavy equipment focus its efforts on developing after-sale services such as installation and maintenance? You can't answer these questions unless you are able to map the profit pool—and it will not be standing still.

M any managers chart strategy without a full understanding of the sources and distribution of profits in their industry. Sometimes, they focus their sights on revenues instead of profits, assuming that revenue growth will eventually translate into profit growth. In other cases, they simply lack the data or the analytical tools required to isolate and measure variations in profitability. Whatever the cause, an incomplete understanding of profits can create blind spots in a company's strategic vision, leading it to overlook attractive profit-building opportunities or to become trapped in areas of weak or fading profitability.

In this article, we will describe a useful framework for analyzing how profits are distributed among the various activities that form an industry's value chain.

HBR May–June 1998

15

Such an analysis can provide a company's managers with a rich understanding of their industry's profit structure—what we call its *profit pool*—enabling them to identify which activities are generating disproportionately large or small shares of profits. Even more important, a profit-pool map opens a window onto the underlying structure of the industry, helping managers see the economic and competitive forces that are determining the distribution of profits. As such, a profit-pool map provides a solid basis for strategic thinking. (See our article "Profit Pools: A Fresh Look at Strategy," HBR, May–June 1998.)

Mapping a profit pool is, in one sense, a straightforward exercise: you define the value chain activities and then you determine their size and profitability. But while the goal is simple, achieving it can be complicated. Why? Because in most industries, financial data are not reported in nice, neat bundles corresponding to each value-chain activity. Detailed data may be available on individual companies, but those companies will often participate in many different activities. Similarly, there may be good information on product sales or customer purchases or channel volumes, but the products, customers, and channels will rarely line up cleanly with the boundaries of a particular activity. Translating the available data into accurate estimates of an activity's size and profitability requires considerable creativity.

Although no two companies will perform the analysis in precisely the same way, it is possible to describe a broadly applicable process for getting the answers—a process that lays out the tasks that need to be accomplished, the questions that need to be asked, the types of data that need to be collected, and the types of analyses that need to be done.

A Four-Step Process

Mapping a profit pool involves four steps: defining the pool's boundaries, estimating the pool's overall size, estimating the size of each value-chain activity in the pool, and checking and reconciling the calculations. (See the exhibit "Mapping a Profit Pool.") We will describe each step and then provide an example of how the entire process is applied. Finally, we will look at ways of organizing the data in chart form as a first step toward plotting a profit-pool strategy.

Define the Pool

Before you can start analyzing your industry's profit pool, you need to define its boundaries by identifying the value-chain activities that are relevant to your own business. Where, for purposes of developing strategy, should the value chain be said to begin and to end? At the conclusion of this step, you should

Mapping a Profit Pool

Step 1 Define the pool	Step 2 Determine the size of the pool	Step 3 Determine the distribution of profits	Step 4 Reconcile the estimates
Task			
Determine which value-chain activities influence your ability to generate profits now and in the future	Develop a baseline estimate of the cumulative profits generated by all profit-pool activities	Develop estimates of the profits generated by each activity	Compare the outputs of steps 2 and 3 and, if necessary, reconcile the numbers
Guidelines			
Take a broad view of the value chain; look beyond traditional industry definitions	Seek a rough but accurate estimate	Shift between aggregation and disaggregation in your analysis	If the numbers don't add up, check all assumptions and calculations
Examine your industry from three perspectives: your own company's, other players', and the customer's	Take the easiest analytical routes available; go where the data are	Look at your own company's economics first, then look at large mixed players, then at a sample of smaller players	Collect additional data if necessary
Talk to industry players and analysts to uncover new or emerging business models	Try to take at least two different views of pool size—for example, company-level and product-level	If relevant company data are unavailable, use proxies such as product-level or channel-level sales	Resolve all inconsistencies; don't ignore them
Don't disaggregate activities more than necessary	Focus on the largest components—for example, large companies, high-volume products; extrapolate smaller components from a sample	Think creatively	
Output			
List of all value-chain activities in your profit pool (in sequential order)	Estimate of total pool profits, usually expressed as a range	Point estimates of profits for each value-chain activity	Final estimates of activity and total pool profits

have a clearly defined list of the individual value-chain activities that make up your profit pool.

The key is to define the value chain broadly enough to capture all the activities that have a meaningful influence on your ability to earn profits—not just today but in the future as well. You should begin by taking a close look at your own business, breaking it down into its discrete value-chain activities. But you shouldn't stop there. Because there are many ways to compete in any industry—and new ways are being thought up all the time— you should also look at the activities of your competitors and potential competitors. Have other companies in your industry adopted business models that involve different sets of activities? Might you have opportunities to perform new activities in your industry or in other industries? Are there activities being performed in other industries that could displace or substitute for the activities you are performing?

A company that operates call centers to handle telephone orders for catalog retailers, for example, may in the future be able to fulfill customer service functions for electric utilities or transportation carriers. And, just as important, it may one day face a competitive threat from companies in other industries, such as telephone companies, cable television operators, or even Internet service providers. The call-center operator should, therefore, define its profit pool to include not only those value chain activities traditionally associated with direct-mail retailing but also activities in other industries that could influence its future creation of profits.

Finally, you should take a step back to look at your industry through the eyes of the customer. How would the customer define the life cycle of the product or service you produce? Often, a customer will define your industry to include activities that you would consider peripheral. If a paint manufacturer, for example, asks homeowners about the experience of buying and using paint, it may find that the disposal of leftover paint is an important activity from their perspective. Disposal requirements may influence the kinds of paint they buy and thus may have a direct impact on the paint industry's profit pool. The manufacturer would be wise to include paint disposal as part of its value chain.

In addition to deciding which activities to include, a company needs to decide the proper level of aggregation for each activity. In the automotive industry, for example, financial service activities, such as lending, leasing, and renting, make up an important part of the profit pool. Do you define those activities as a single value-chain segment or do you look at them individually? The answer depends on the business you're in. A chain of auto parts stores would probably not need to divide the financial service segment into its component activities— after all, the company would not be likely to participate in any of those activities. A used car dealer, however, might well want to break down the financial services segment into the narrower segments of lending, leasing, and renting. Because the dealer controls an important point of customer contact, it may decide to enter one or more of these activities in the future. It may also find itself competing with a participant in one of these activities—say, a new car dealer that needs to sell used cars coming off their leases.

Defining the bounds of a profit pool requires, in short, not just analytical skills but also good, basic business judgment. The pool you draw must be tailored to fit the strategic questions you face.

Determine the Size of the Pool

Once you have defined the profit pool, you need to determine its overall size. What is the total amount of profits being earned in all the value chain activities? At this point, all you need is a rough estimate of total industry profits. The idea is to establish a baseline against which you can check the reliability of the more detailed, activity-by-activity calculations you will make later.

If you're lucky, you may be able to estimate the size of the pool by reading a few industry reports from stock analysts or other researchers. Or you may be able to find a reliable estimate of overall industry revenues and then apply an assumed industry-average margin to it. Usually, though, developing this estimate will not be so straightforward. The way you define your profit pool is unlikely to coincide precisely with any traditional industry definition. Moreover, the financial data you require may not be readily available in the form you need.

A good idea in these situations is to try to build up estimates of the total pool based on the profitability of individual companies, products, channels, or regions. You should always try to focus first on the biggest pieces—the largest companies or the highest-volume products, for example. If there are large public companies that account for a significant proportion of industry profits, use their financial statements as a starting point. To gauge the profits of the smaller players, you adjust the leaders' margins—to reflect the smaller players' competitive advantages or disadvantages—and then apply the adjusted margin to the remaining industry revenues. You then add the leaders' actual profits to your estimate of the total profits of the smaller companies to gain an overall estimate of industry profits. (See the sidebar "What Is 'Profit' Anyway?")

While a high degree of precision isn't necessary at this point, you do need to have confidence in the general accuracy of the estimate. Therefore, it is always advisable to develop estimates based on at least two different views of an industry. Try to develop estimates based, for example, on players and products. You can then compare the estimates to ensure they're in the same ballpark. The more data you have and the more analytical approaches you take, the more accurate your estimate will be.

Determine the Distribution of Profits

Determining the way profits are distributed among different value-chain activities is the core challenge of profit-pool mapping. There are two general analytical approaches to this task: aggregation and disaggregation. If you are in an industry in which all the companies focus on a single value-chain activity—in which all are, in other words, "pure players"—you will calculate activity profitability by aggregating the profits of all the pure players. If, by contrast, all the companies

What Is "Profit" Anyway?

Today there are almost as many ways to define *profit* as there are to make it. For practical purposes, though, managers tend to think about profit in one of three ways: as *accounting profit,* as *return on investment,* or as *cash-flow contribution.* Because each of the measures can be used as the basis for management decisions, they all can be important in profit-pool mapping.

Accounting profit represents a company's earnings as formally reported. It is the measurement method underlying net-income and earnings-per-share calculations in shareholder reports and other official filings. Its precise method of calculation can vary, depending on the accounting standards specific to a given industry or country.

Return on investment represents a company's earnings after taking into account the cost of capital invested in the business. Because ROI represents the true profit associated with investment in an industry, it is an essential measure for evaluating potential new investments. It can be measured using a number of different methodologies, which all have advantages and disadvantages. One of the most useful ROI measures is economic value-added (EVA), which equals after-tax operating profits minus the cost of all invested capital. Because EVA expresses returns as an absolute profit value rather than as a percentage, it lends itself well to profit-pool mapping.

Cash-flow contribution is, in general, a company's earnings before taking fixed-asset and capital costs into account. It is frequently expressed as earnings before income taxes, depreciation, and amortization (EBITDA). In some cases, fixed operating costs, such as overhead, are also subtracted. An incremental measure, it represents the amount of cash left from a sale after subtracting the variable costs associated with that sale. Cash-flow contribution is frequently used as the basis for management decision making in mature, high-fixed-cost, and cyclical industries, particularly during down cycles. It is also a useful profit measure for companies that are investing to gain market share and for those that are engaged in leveraged buyouts.

Developing detailed profit-pool maps using all three measures would be a forbiddingly complex undertaking. In most cases, fortunately, it is sufficient to use just one basis of measurement for in-depth mapping. Other relevant measures can then be roughly estimated as needed. Most companies will use accounting profit as their basic measure because that's the form in which profit data are generally reported. However, when a company's profit pool extends across industries or countries, managers need to be aware of and take into account possible differences in accounting standards. The goal should always be to measure profit consistently across the entire pool.

in your industry are vertically integrated "mixed players," each performing many different activities, you will need to disaggregate each company's financial data to arrive at estimates for a specific activity.

In reality, of course, most industries include a combination of pure players and mixed players. Your analysis, therefore, will likely include both aggregation and disaggregation. At some stages, you'll be tearing data apart. At others, you'll be building it up.

You start, once again, by looking at the economics of your own company, examining revenues, costs, and profits by activity. If you're a pure player, this won't take much work—all your revenues and costs will be allocated to the same activity. If you're involved in many activities and your financial-reporting system does not clearly distinguish among them, you will need to disentangle your revenues and costs. In companies whose fixed costs are shared by a number of different activities, as is the case in many financial-services institutions, allocating costs will likely require not only careful analysis but also some in-depth thinking about the structure of the business.

Now you look outside your company to examine the economics of other players in the industry. Although the sources of company data will vary by industry, there are some common places to look. You will draw on annual reports, 10-K filings, and stock-analyst reports (for public companies), as well as company profiles by research organizations such as Dun & Bradstreet, reports by industry associations, and trade magazines. For regulated industries, the government can be a good source. And in some industries, there are companies that specialize in collecting and reporting detailed financial information. If data are unavailable on a company, you may need to estimate its profitability based on the performance of a similar company for which data are available.

You should always look first at any pure players. Once you know their revenues, costs, and profits, you'll have an economic yardstick for measuring the activity in which they specialize. You can then look at the mixed players. In some cases, they will report their financial information by activity, making your work easier. In other cases, however, the information they report will be aggregated—you'll need to break it down by activity. To accomplish that, you can often use what you learned about the margins and cost structure of the pure players to make accurate assumptions about the mixed players' economics for a given activity, taking into account their particular competitive advantages and disadvantages. For activities in which your company participates, you may also be able to use your own economics as a yardstick.

You won't need to collect data on all the companies participating in all the value chain activities. In most industries, the 80/20 rule will apply: 20% of the companies will account for 80% of the revenues. By collecting data on the largest companies, you will likely have covered most of the industry. You can then extrapolate the economic data for the smaller companies by collecting data on a sample of them. Once you have the data on your own company, the large pure players, the large mixed players, and a sample of the smaller companies, you add up the figures, activity by activity, to arrive at overall estimates.

Sometimes, it will actually be easier to gather financial data on products, customers, or channels than on companies. This is often the case in industries characterized by a high degree of vertical integration. In such cases, you should go where the data are. If you can get detailed data on the economics of different product types, for example, you can allocate costs, revenues, and profits to different activities at the product level. Then you add up the numbers, activity by activity, to arrive at total estimates. As with company data, the process is a matter of aggregating and disaggregating.

At the end of this step, the shape of your profit pool should be clear. You will know the profits—as well as the revenues, costs, and margins—of each value-chain activity. And you will know how your own economics stack up to the averages, activity by activity.

Reconcile the Estimates

The fourth and final step in the analysis serves as a reality check. You add up the profit estimates for each activity, and you compare the total with the overall estimate of industry profits you developed earlier. If there are discrepancies, you need to go back and check your assumptions and calculations and, if necessary, collect additional data. Don't be surprised if you have to spend considerable time reconciling the numbers. Because you will often have made your estimates in an indirect way, based on fragmented or incomplete data, discrepancies will be common.

Applying the Process: The RegionBank Case

To show how a company would actually use this process, let's put ourselves in the shoes of the managers of RegionBank, a hypothetical retail bank based in the midwestern United States. RegionBank is in a tight spot. Fundamental changes in the financial services industry have undermined the traditional advantages of its vertically integrated, regionally focused business model. Powerful national product specialists—MBNA in credit cards, Fidelity in mutual funds, Countrywide Mortgage in mortgage lending—are stealing away many of its best customers. New distribution channels, such as telephone and online banking, threaten to render its expensive network of local branches obsolete. Even its back-office transactional functions, like credit card processing, are under attack from highly efficient specialists such as First Data Corporation.

As RegionBank's management team, we know we cannot simply stay the course, hoping for the best. As margins narrow, our current business model seems unsustainable. But to develop a new model—one that will allow us to carve out and hold on to a substantial piece of the banking industry's rapidly shifting profit pool—we need to have a thorough understanding of the industry and its patterns of profit creation. Where in the banking value chain are attractive profits being generated? Why is the profitability of some banking activities rising while the profitability of others is falling? Which companies are capturing the profits? What are their business models? Only after we know where and how profits are being made—and by whom—will we be in a position to think about the forces shaping our industry and to make rational decisions about our strategic direction.

Define the Pool

We start by setting the bounds of our profit pool. After looking at the activities we perform, the activities performed by current and potential competitors, and the ways customers perceive our business, we see that our industry is broader than the regional banking industry as traditionally defined. It encompasses the entire U.S. consumer-financial-services industry, which can be viewed as including three core activities: acquiring customers through branches or other channels (acquisition); lending and managing money (for simplicity, we'll call this activity *funding*); and delivering a variety of related backroom services, such as transactions and reporting (servicing). These activities define RegionBank's playing field, and by focusing on them we will have the necessary breadth of vision to answer the question on which all our strategic decisions turn: Where in consumer financial services will companies be able to make money?

Determine the Size of the Pool

To develop a rough but accurate estimate of our profit pool, we undertake two different analyses. We determine the cumulative profits generated by all the industry's major products, and then we determine the cumulative profits earned by all the companies competing in the three industry activities. We choose products and players for a simple reason: those are the ways financial data are typically reported in the industry.

First, we examine products. We know that the consumer-financial-services industry, as we have defined it, has five major product categories: credit cards, mortgages, deposits, mutual funds, and consumer loans. Sales and profitability data for each of these categories are reported regularly by the federal government as well as by private data-reporting companies, making data collection a simple exercise.

Similarly, when we turn to the players, we know that companies in the industry are required to report their financial information in considerable detail. By looking at the largest players individually and extrapolating from a sample of the smaller players, we are able to quickly estimate total profits. Both methodologies yield a similar range of estimates for the size of the profit pool—between $60 billion and $70 billion—so we are confident that we have a reliable estimate.

Determine the Distribution of Profits

Now we have an estimate of the size of RegionBank's current industry profit pool—in total and by product and player. What we don't have, however, is an understanding of how the pool is distributed among the three value-chain activities: acquisition, funding, and servicing. This leads to our first major analytical problem. In consumer financial services, revenue and profit information simply isn't available for individual value-chain activities. Rather, as we saw before, financial information is organized by company and by product type. We will not, therefore, be able to measure value chain activities directly. Instead, we will have to construct five different profit pools—one for each major product category—and divide each pool into the three activities. We will then be able to add up the activity data for each product to gain an industrywide measure of activity profitability.

For the sake of illustration, let's take one product—credit cards—and walk through the way we determine the distribution of its profit pool. We start by gathering profit and revenue data for all the key players in the credit card business: card issuers, subscriber and merchant acquirers, and customer and account servicers. Because RegionBank is itself an issuer of credit cards, we can use our internal financial data as a benchmark for credit card profitability.

Since there are literally thousands of credit card issuers, it would not be practicable to collect financial information on all of them. We therefore pursue an 80/20 approach, collecting data on all the major industry players but analyzing only a sample of the smaller players. To ensure that we don't overlook any important competitors, we take the time to talk to people representing different aspects of the industry, including leading banks in overseas markets

Untangling the Credit-Card Value Chain

The credit-card value chain encompasses three business activities. As a result of variations in the type of data available, the profits generated in each activity need to be calculated in very different ways.

Acquisition		Funding		Servicing		
$80	value of a subscriber	$279	average annual revenues per subscriber	$60	annual payments to servicer per subscriber	
−$64	cost of acquiring a subscriber	−$235	average annual costs per subscriber	x .17	average servicer margin	
$16	acquisition profit per subscriber	$44	annual funding profit per subscriber	$10	annual servicing profit per subscriber	
amortized over five years	average life of subscriber account					
$3.20	annual acquisition profit per subscriber					
x 260 million	total number of subscribers	x 260 million	total number of subscribers	x 260 million	total number of subscribers	Total credit-card profits
$800 million	acquisition profits	+ $11.4 billion	funding profits	+ $2.6 billion	servicing profits	= $14.8 billion

and companies in related industries such as home equity lending. We need to remember, as we pull together the information, that competition in our industry is shifting rapidly, with many kinds of new players entering the fray. As the strategic landscape evolves, new competitors and new services could present threats or opportunities to RegionBank. Failing to consider them now could be costly.

Once we have profit data for all the relevant players in the credit card industry, we need to disaggregate the data by value chain segment. (See the exhibit "Untangling the Credit-Card Value Chain.") We use a different calculation method for each segment:

Servicing. Because there are several large, public companies that specialize in credit card servicing—pure players—servicing is the easiest of the three segments for which to estimate profits. So it's a good place to start. We know, from our own experience as a card issuer, that a typical issuer pays approximately $60 per subscriber per year to third-party processors to handle transaction processing, statement generation, and all the other back-office tasks associated with that subscriber. By studying the financial statements of the pure players, we find that their average pretax margin for servicing is 17%, indicating that about $10 per year in servicing profits are generated per subscriber ($60 X .17). Given the roughly 260 million credit-card subscribers in the United States, this works out to $2.6 billion in annual servicing profits.

Acquisition. There are no pure players in credit card acquisition, so we need to be a little more creative here. By examining recent purchases of credit-card-subscriber portfolios, we find that the price paid, per subscriber, is approximately $80. We also know, from our own experience and from general industry studies, that the average cost of gaining a new card subscriber is in the neighborhood of $64, which indicates that the acquisition profit per card is $16. Amortizing this figure over the average life of a subscriber account (five years) yields $3.20 in annual acquisition profits per subscriber, or $800 million for the entire credit-card business.

Funding. Finally, to estimate funding profits, we detail all the revenues and costs associated with funding a credit card—in other words, we create a profit and loss statement for a card. The data required for this exercise are reported in the secondary markets where card portfolios are bought and sold. First, we add up all the annual revenues accruing to a typical card from interest, annual fees and other charges, and merchant payments ($279), and then we subtract all the costs associated with that card ($235), many of which, such as acquiring and servicing, we have already detailed. We arrive at an annual funding profit of $44 per subscriber, or $11.4 billion in total.

We now have categorized the credit card profit pool by value chain activity: $800 million for acquisition, $11.4 billion for funding, and $2.6 billion for servicing. We make similar calculations for each of the other four product categories—mortgages, deposits, mutual funds, and consumer loans—and we add up the totals to establish estimates for the size of each activity in the consumer-financial-services industry: $10.0 billion in acquisition, $42.4 billion in funding, and $10.4 billion in servicing. We now know the current shape of our profit pool.

Reconcile the Estimates

As a reality check, we add up the activity totals ($63 billion) and compare the sum with our initial estimate of the industry profit pool (between $60 billion and $70 billion). The numbers jibe, so we are confident that our estimates are reasonable.

RegionBank's Profit-Pool Map

A profit-pool map compares a value chain activity's revenues with its profitability. By developing a map of the current U.S. consumer-financial-services industry, RegionBank is able to see the profits being generated by acquisition, funding, and servicing activities. By comparing this map with a map from an earlier point in time, the company will be able to spot trends in profit distribution.

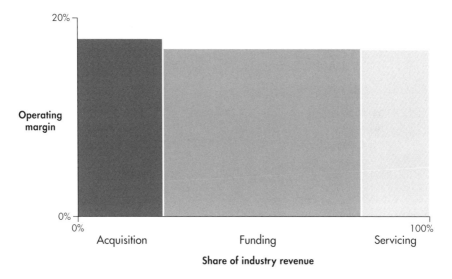

Visualizing the Profit Pool

As the end product of profit-pool mapping—and the starting point of strategy development—you will want to portray the data you've collected in a series of charts. Visualizing the profit pool makes it easier to spot areas of disproportionately large and disproportionately small profits and to identify trends influencing the distribution of profits. The resulting insights can form the basis for the development of a strategy that will enable a company to capitalize on or even control the direction of profit-pool shifts.

There are several different ways to chart a profit pool, each of which provides different insights. One of the simplest but most useful charts is what we call a *profit-pool map*, in which profit distribution is compared with revenue distribution. (See the exhibit "RegionBank's Profit-Pool Map.") The map takes the form of a series of building blocks—each representing a value chain activity—plotted on a graph. The horizontal axis of the graph represents the percentage of industry revenues, and the vertical axis represents operating margins. Thus the width of each block indicates the activity's share of total

RegionBank's Profit-Pool Mosaic

A profit-pool mosaic reveals the distribution of an industry's profits along two dimensions. RegionBank uses a mosaic to see the profits being earned by different types of companies within each of the three core value-chain activities in its industry.

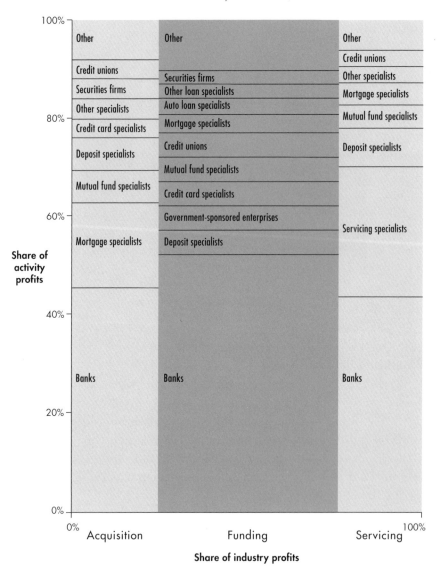

industry revenues, its height indicates the activity's profitability, and its area indicates the activity's total profits.

The profit-pool map portrays the distribution of profits and revenues along a single dimension: value chain activity. It will often be useful, however, to chart the profit pool along two dimensions simultaneously. In RegionBank's case, for example, we know that many new players—product specialists, servicing specialists, and various other nontraditional competitors—have entered the industry in recent years. It would therefore be illuminating to see how industry profits are distributed among different types of companies as well as among different value-chain activities. To visualize a profit pool in two dimensions, we can create a graph that we call a *profit-pool mosaic*. (See the exhibit "RegionBank's Profit-Pool Mosaic.")

In a profit-pool mosaic, the total area of the chart equals 100% of industry profits (in RegionBank's case, $63 billion). The horizontal axis indicates the percentage of total industry profits created in each activity—roughly 67% in funding, 17% in servicing, and 16% in acquisition—and the vertical axis shows the percentage of profits created by company type *within* an activity. (Depending on a company's particular situation and challenges, other dimensions, such as products, channels, and geographic regions, can be plotted in a mosaic.) By looking at the mosaic, we can see not only how much money is being made, activity by activity, but also who's making it.

Profit-pool maps and mosaics are only snapshots, of course. They show us the shape of the pool as it exists today, but they don't show us how the pool has been changing. To get a more dynamic view—which is essential for strategy development—we need to plot similar charts for the profit pool at earlier points in time. To develop such comparison charts, we go through the same steps of data collection and analysis; we just use data from an earlier year. By seeing how the pool's shape has changed—where profits have increased or diminished, who's been gaining or losing profits—we can often infer which competitive, economic, and other forces have been shaping the industry's profit structure.

In turn, we can project how these forces might reshape the pool in the future. It is often a useful exercise, in fact, to plot a projected profit pool. If your industry is stable, with no major uncertainties on the horizon, you will probably need to develop only a single view of the future, projecting future profit data based on current trends. If there's a lot of uncertainty in your industry, you should develop a range of possible views of the future. For instance, RegionBank might create a series of mosaic charts representing different scenarios for how its industry might look in five years. Practically speaking, you won't be able to chart all the possible future permutations of a profit pool. We have found, though, that plotting three to five scenarios, representing a range of possibilities, is enough to provide valuable guidance in strategy development.

A Foundation for Strategy

Profit-pool mapping reveals the location and size of profit concentrations within an industry and sheds light on how those concentrations might shift. We have focused on analyzing the pool in terms of value chain activity. Knowing the distribution of profits along the value chain provides you with the broadest view of profit trends in your industry. Such a view is essential for identifying structural shifts that could influence the profits available to you and your competitors in the future. It is important to note, however, that profits concentrate not just in particular value-chain activities but also in particular product types, customer segments, distribution channels, and geographic regions. To develop the fullest possible understanding of your profit pool, you will want to map the pool along some, if not all, of these dimensions as well.

As even our simplified RegionBank case indicates, profit-pool mapping often requires a considerable investment of time. And, since every business situation is unique, tough questions about scope and methodology will need to be answered at every step of the analysis. But mapping your profit pool will provide you with important benefits. You'll gain a new store of strategic information and, even more important, a more creative approach to strategy formulation.

The sheer act of defining, categorizing, and mapping a pool can stir the thinking of your management team, leading it to challenge old assumptions and to generate valuable new business insights. When you define the shape of today's profit pool, you refine and deepen your knowledge of the mechanics of your industry—where profits are created, how they're created, and who's creating them. And when you think through the forces shaping the pool, you identify and isolate the most critical drivers of future industry profitability. Ultimately, the discipline of profit-pool mapping rewards you with a richer view of your business and where you might lead it.

Desperately Seeking Growth: The Virtues of Tending to Your Core

Even in the best of times, nine out of 10 management teams fail to sustain profitable growth.

Chris Zook

The 1990s brought the world a remarkable economic boom. Yet Bain research showed that only 9% of large companies in developed nations hit even their low-end growth targets. Since that time, companies have found it still more challenging to sustain profitable growth. The world is globalized. Technologies evolve faster than ever. Strong new competitors are emerging in the developing world. Companies that rely on the competitive advantages of the past are likely to find themselves left behind in this new environment.

This short article's message—focus on your core—thus seems even more relevant today than when it was written. For many of our clients, the primary challenge is to capitalize on the hidden assets and capabilities of the core business itself—in other words, to strengthen and develop the core so that it can reach its full potential. The most successful companies in today's world, from TetraPak to Toyota, from Enterprise to Nike, are those that have strong, focused cores. Conversely, many of the past decade's corporate meltdowns can be traced to a failure to tend to or adapt the core.

I f you believe that Internet companies distinguish themselves from the rest of the economy by failing to turn a profit, consider this: Even in the best of times, nine out of 10 management teams fail to sustain profitable growth. In our 10-year study of 1,854 public companies from the seven largest industrial countries, only 9% achieved their bottom-end growth targets, despite one of the greatest economic booms in business history. In the old economy as in the new, most bursts of growth do not translate into sustained value creation. But when we compared companies that succeeded in growing profitably—specifically,

Harvard Management Update June 2001

the subset of firms that sustained growth for a decade—with those that didn't, some intriguing patterns emerged:

1. The long-term winners narrowed their focus instead of widening it.

Nearly 80% of these growing companies had one or more core businesses with clear market leadership. They did not allow themselves to be distracted by buying insufficiently related businesses. For example, the advertising firm Saatchi & Saatchi bought the Gartner Group in 1988 in a misguided effort to become a one-stop shop for media and consulting services. Disappointed in Gartner's 10% margins and slower-than-industry growth, Saatchi resold Gartner in 1990 to private equity investors Information Partners. By focusing on collecting, packaging, and distributing high value, syndicated data, Gartner developed a deep subscriber base. Sales rose from $55 million under Saatchi to $734 million in 1999; margins tripled to 30%.

2. Winning companies showed disciplined thinking.

Defining the competitive, customer, and product borders of your core business is vital to choosing the right related opportunities. Amazon.com began as a successful bookseller, but then prematurely stretched its definition to include all consumer retail, taking on industry giants by expanding aggressively into power tools, cosmetics, and consumer electronics. The results have been gloomy: Amazon is now like a young chess player in a high school auditorium—running from table to table, trying to beat a grand master at every game.

3. Profitably growing companies tapped the full potential of their core businesses.

Unsuccessful companies routinely set performance targets that were too low. They underinvested. They abandoned their core businesses prematurely, searching for new opportunities that only eroded their core. Data from 185 companies in 33 industries show that market leaders earned a 25.4% return on capital, compared with 14.3% for companies in a weaker market position. Many firms fail to recognize this power that market leadership provides for launching highly related lines. Grainger, the leader in industrial-products distribution, hit a slump in the 1980s and assumed it had reached the limits of expansion. But when it charted the true boundaries of its core, Grainger found it had underestimated its growth potential: A market originally valued at $3 billion was actually worth closer to $30 billion.

4. Companies that underexploited their core failed to appreciate the importance of reinvestment.

Companies with long-term growth and profits invested at a rate of 15.3%, nearly twice that of rivals. In 1980, Intel was smaller in total market value than either Advanced Micro Devices or National Semiconductor. But by reinvesting with a narrow focus on digital logic chips for PCs, Intel today dwarfs those two firms, which spread their R&D funds over a range of businesses.

Profitable growth is rarer than you think, but there are a handful of steps you can take to help your company achieve it:

Narrow your focus. Instead of trying to be all things to all people, concentrate on what you do profitably and best.

Think *inside* the box. Don't try to erase boundaries in hopes of becoming the next big thing. Only by knowing exactly where the boundaries lie can you identify profitable opportunities inside—and outside—those borders.

Assume that a strong core is underperforming. Set stretch targets and then mine the core for all it's worth.

Reinvest. Pumping money into your core may seem counterintuitive in a climate in which companies are looking to cut costs wherever they can. But it will be money well spent.

Growth Outside the Core

Expanding into adjacent markets is tougher than it looks; three-quarters of the time, the effort fails. Here's how to change those odds dramatically.

Chris Zook and James Allen

When a company has reached the full potential of its original core business, it must expand the core's boundaries in order to grow. An athletic equipment company, for example, might move into adjacent markets such as sports apparel, and of course it can enter one new sport after another. But all such expansionary moves are risky. In today's hypercompetitive marketplace, the odds of a successful adjacency move have declined to perhaps one in five.

The decision about where to expand is thus one of the toughest a company must make, and in the past it was often left to the senior team's intuition and judgment. This article helped to provide a scientific basis for the decision. The data, the framework for mapping out growth opportunities, the hedging strategies and the idea of multiple, sequential adjacency moves—all these have become increasingly central to effective strategy, and have been put to work by clients around the globe. The article laid the groundwork for the 2004 book Beyond the Core, *and the idea of making similar moves into one adjacent market after another was one seed that led to the 2012 book* Repeatability.

Golf ranks as one of the most brutal and demanding markets in the sports business. So, despite its fabled swoosh, Nike was regarded as an amateur when it decided in 1995 to branch out from shoes to golf apparel, balls, and equipment. Four years later, however, Nike had scored priceless marketing victories—not once, but three times running. First, the British Open champ wore Nike's golf shoes in 1999. Next, Tiger Woods switched from Titleist golf balls, the leading brand, to Nike golf balls in 2000. And, finally, David Duval won his first major tournament just after switching to Nike golf clubs in 2001.

HBR December 2003

Nike's entry into the golf market appeared to be the business equivalent of sinking three successive holes in one. But those who had followed the company closely over the previous decade were not surprised. They recognized the formula that Nike has applied and adapted successfully in a series of entries into sports markets—from jogging to volleyball to tennis to basketball to soccer. Nike begins by establishing a leading position in athletic shoes in the target market. Next, Nike launches a clothing line endorsed by the sport's top athletes—like Tiger Woods, whose $100 million deal in 1996 gave Nike the visibility it needed to get traction in golf apparel and accessories. Expanding into new categories allows the company to forge new distribution channels and lock in suppliers. Then it starts to feed higher-margin equipment into the market—irons first, in the case of golf clubs, and subsequently drivers. In the final step, Nike moves beyond the U.S. market to global distribution.

This formula, we would argue, is the reason that Nike pulled away from Reebok as leader in the sporting goods industry. In 1987, Nike's operating profits were $164 million to Reebok's $309 million, and Nike's market valuation was half the size of Reebok's. By 2002, Nike had grown its profits to $1.1 billion, while Reebok's had declined to $247 million. Both companies had started out in the same business with the same manufacturing technology and comparable brand names. Yet Nike found a formula for growth that it used successfully again and again, while Reebok seemed to pursue a different source of growth every year with uneven results.

To learn more about how to sustain profitable growth, we recently conducted a five-year study of corporate growth involving 1,850 companies. We tracked specific growth moves and linked them back to individual company performance. Our research yielded two major conclusions. One was that most sustained, profitable growth comes when a company pushes out the boundaries of its core business into an adjacent space. We identified six types of adjacencies, ranging from adjacent links in the value chain to adjacent customers to adjacent geographies. (For the complete list, see the exhibit "Six Ways to Grow into an Adjacent Space.")

Our second finding was that companies like Nike consistently, profitably outgrow their rivals by developing a formula for expanding those boundaries in predictable, repeatable ways. The average company succeeds only 25% of the time in launching new initiatives. Companies that have hit upon a repeatable formula have success rates of twice that, and some drive their rates up to 80% or higher. That's because growing a business is normally a complex, experimental, and somewhat chaotic process. Repeatability allows the company to systematize the growth and, by doing so, take advantage of learning-curve effects.

Companies that master repeatability work within any number of adjacencies. Some companies make repeated geographic moves, as Vodafone has done in expanding from one geographic market to another over the past 13 years, building revenues from $1 billion in 1990 to $48 billion in 2003. Others apply a superior business model to new segments. Dell, for example, has repeatedly adapted its direct-to-customer model to new customer segments and new product categories. In other cases, companies develop hybrid approaches. Nike, as noted above, executed a series of different types of adjacency moves. It expanded into adjacent customer segments, introduced new products, developed new

Six Ways to Grow into an Adjacent Space

In our recent study of the drivers of profitable, sustainable corporate growth, we analyzed 181 adjacency moves that took place between 1995 and 1997 (recent enough to have data but before the Internet era of more reckless investing). We excluded growth through diversification, which leads a company far away from its core business. We also excluded inside-core growth moves, like accelerating innovation in R&D, investing in corporate ventures, and stepping up the company's metabolism by, say, speeding up operations or hiring more salespeople. What we found were six types of adjacencies that successful companies used to outperform their competitors.

Expand along the value chain. This is one of the most difficult adjacency moves.
De Beers extended its diamond business from wholesaling into retailing.

Grow new products and services.
IBM moved into global services, which now constitutes 50% of the company's revenue and pretax profits.

Use new distribution channels.
EAS, a leading sports supplement company, made minor changes in formulation, packaging, and celebrity sponsorship of its Myoplex sports bar and moved from a niche position in specialty nutrition stores to become the leader in its category, selling to Walmart.

Enter new geographies.
Vodafone expanded from the U.K. to Europe, the United States, Germany, and Japan.

Address new customer segments, often by modifying a proven product or technology.
Charles Schwab expanded its advisory services for discount brokerage customers to target high-net-worth individuals.

Move into the "white space" with a new business built around a strong capability. This is the rarest and most difficult adjacency move to pull off.
American Airlines created the Sabre reservation system, a spin-off now worth more than the airline itself. Sabre, in turn, went on to create a new business adjacency of its own in the online travel agent Travelocity.

distribution channels, and then moved into adjacent geographic markets. The first time Nike did this, it undoubtedly struggled with the inherent complexity of making so many moves, but as it repeated the process again and again, managers learned to execute consistently.

The successful repeaters in our study had two common characteristics. First, they were extraordinarily disciplined, applying rigorous screens before they made an adjacency move. This discipline paid off in the form of learning-curve benefits, increased speed, and lower complexity. And second, in almost all cases, they developed their repeatable formulas by studying their customers and their customers' economics very, very carefully. These capabilities may seem basic and unglamorous, yet companies that excel at them set the stage for industry-leading growth.

The Discipline Needed

We focused our study on 25 companies that achieved sustainable growth performance far in excess of their peer groups. This diverse set of companies ranged from retailers like PetSmart to banks like Lloyds to consumer electronics companies like Legend. Typically, these companies grew revenues three times faster than did the average company in their respective industries. Collectively, their revenues rose from $107 billion to $276 billion in the last 10 years, while earnings increased from $7 billion to $23 billion during that period. Together, they created more than half a trillion dollars of shareholder value that has largely persisted despite the market collapse of recent years. On average, they returned 22% annually to shareholders. The majority of these standouts have one or two powerful, repeatable formulas that generate successive waves of new growth, allowing them to push beyond the boundaries of their core businesses.

Typically these formulas are applied by CEOs who approach growth strategy with a strong sense of discipline and restraint. Many of them have well-defined rules about which opportunities to pursue. We heard over and over in interviews, "Never put the core business at risk." These executives also wouldn't make a move unless they had a good shot at being one of the top three players in a new space. And although they constantly scanned for opportunities, they pursued only one at a time. Says Peter Burt, the former deputy chairman of U.K.-based financial services leader HBOS, "The most important screen for new adjacencies is to limit the number of new variables we are managing to a small number: one."

To get a sense of how effective this disciplined approach can be, consider the story of Olam, a Nigeria-based start-up that went from distributing one product in one country to building a $1.9 billion multinational business in only 13 years. Today, Olam supplies cocoa, coffee, cashews, sesame, and other food commodities to global packaged food companies including Kraft, General Foods, Sara Lee, and Nestlé. The company's activities have expanded to the point where it now manages the complete supply chain for agricultural raw materials in some of the most challenging markets in the world, including Ivory Coast, Gabon, and Uzbekistan.

Olam was launched in 1989 as an intermediary between local Nigerian producers of cashews and shea nuts, an ingredient in chocolate, and big food processors like Mars and Planters. Large customers had previously been dealing with an array of poorly capitalized local exporters, who would sell forward contracts for commodities and simply default if the price turned unfavorable at delivery time. Olam created its own vehicles for hedging commodity price risks and foreign currency risks in currencies where there are no forward-exchange markets, offering a better security proposition to customers. Solving this problem created a competitive advantage for Olam that became the kernel of its repeatable formula.

The young company quickly became a reliable source of Nigerian cashews, establishing a strong presence in its core market. Olam's CEO, Sunny Verghese, insisted that each of his executives spend a lengthy term living in the supply areas to absorb the details of bringing commodity products out of unruly, developing markets safely and profitably. Verghese himself lived in rural Nigeria for three and a half years.

Customers, recognizing Olam's growing expertise in distribution in developing markets, began asking the company to handle cashew producers in Burkina Faso, Ivory Coast, Ghana, and Cameroon. Olam was able to make this adjacency move with little risk: It was simply changing a single variable—geography—but continuing to sell the same product to the same customers using the same formula. Not long after the geographical expansion was under way, customers wanted Olam to move other commodities—coffee, cocoa, sesame, and shea nuts—through its infrastructure of buyers, quality laboratories, and warehouses. Again, these adjacency moves varied a single step—the commodity product—but did not change customers, supply chain, geography, or channels. Verghese is convinced that Olam's success in these moves stemmed from its ability to change a single variable at a time—a management feat that requires an exquisite degree of control.

As Olam repeated the process with new products and new markets, other growth opportunities emerged. The company, once a middleman, now controls most of the supply chain for existing products in the countries where it operates. From its core business of trading in raw cashews, for instance, the company moved into shelling and blanching cashews. Similarly, its strength as a trader of cocoa, coffee, cotton, and sesame enabled the company to build businesses in hulling, sorting, and processing those crops as well. From its strong position in sourcing and processing, Olam moved into even higher-value adjacencies, including marketing, distribution, and risk management. Olam now operates in 35 countries and handles 12 agricultural commodities.

Not all of Olam's moves worked out. When the company entered the black pepper and rubber markets, for example, both commodities seemed promising. But Olam quickly realized that differences in industry regulations and trading norms across Africa and Asia would make it difficult and expensive for the company to expand beyond one key producing country—Nigeria in the case of rubber and India for black pepper. So Olam exited the markets. These experiences helped tighten Olam's investment criteria for making adjacency moves. When evaluating a new opportunity, the management team whittles each potential move down to its essence and ensures that it meet three defining criteria. First, the team asks, will the opportunity allow Olam to function as supply chain manager, not simply as intermediary? Second, will the company be dealing in agricultural raw materials—the products it knows best? Third, will it be operating on the ground in emerging markets—the terrain it understands well?

Even with those questions answered, Olam still isn't ready to move. The company applies additional screens to assess whether it should repeat its formula in an adjacent market. The company must have a good shot at being in the top three in terms of global market share in that product, and it must have a physical presence in all the key processing countries. The adjacency move must also provide clear opportunities to expand into higher-value processing. And each new product must have strong end-market customers—big players willing to enter long-term contracts.

These rules give Verghese and his team the game plan for repeating adjacency moves. But the discipline required to apply the formula successfully can't be overemphasized. Now based in Singapore, Olam is the leading global supplier of cashews and shea nuts, the original core business, and ranks among the top six suppliers worldwide in its other key products. Olam has relied on organic growth to expand at a pace that far outstrips the industry average of 2%. From 1997 to 2003, the company grew revenues at 84% and earnings at 28%, with a return on capital of 35%. While most producers of agricultural raw materials plod along, Verghese says Olam's repeatable adjacency formula "makes it pretty clear where our next $1 billion will come from."

The Benefits Gained

Olam and Nike have little in common. Yet both companies have been extremely disciplined at finding one formula for incremental growth and repeating it over and over again. That repetition appears to create real, interconnected strategic benefits, each of which contributes to competitive advantage.

Learning-Curve Effects

A repeatable model allows managers to refine skills and systematize processes that are developed mostly through guesswork the first time. GE Capital, for example, built expertise in evaluating and executing deals on its way to becoming a serial acquirer. A Bain study of 1,700 acquirers found that companies doing more than three relatively small deals per year achieved 25% higher returns than companies doing fewer, but larger, acquisitions. One reason: better organizational capability gained through experience.

Reduced Complexity

When we asked A.G. Lafley, the CEO of Procter & Gamble, how the consumer goods company had managed to consistently outperform its industry, he talked about the importance of managing complexity. "Complexity is the bane of a large organization," Lafley said. "It strangles growth." When P&G's legendary Crest brand was flagging in the late 1990s, the company sparked a growth revival by expanding into two large adjacencies—teeth whitening and brushing. Two innovative products led the charge—Crest Whitestrips and the SpinBrush. Using the same Crest brand, the same P&G marketing infrastructure, and the same channels to reach the same set of customers, P&G quickly launched the two adjacent products—adding more than $200 million of new sales apiece in one year. By holding other variables constant and changing one thing at a time, P&G dramatically reduces complexity, which allows it, in turn, to make adjacency moves one after the other without straining the system.

Speed

When a company has mastered a repeatable formula for adjacency moves, it can successfully start—and finish—a number of moves faster than a competitor would. Vodafone, for example, is able to collect high-potential properties in wireless communications, thanks to a rigorous formula for evaluating and acquiring regional cellular phone service companies. A well-honed process for rapidly teasing out key criteria, mapping market boundaries, and calculating the profit potential of future add-on services enabled Vodafone to snap up the number one or number two wireless players in quick succession in markets across Europe, North America, and parts of Asia, while competitors gave chase.

Strategic Clarity

A surprising number of chief executives fail to communicate a clear growth strategy to the investment community—and they pay a high price. Compaq failed to convince investors that its superscale growth rationale could work, whereas Dell's direct model resonated with investors. Employee loyalty also hinges on understanding and believing in the company's strategy for the future, according to a recent Bain survey. Companies savvy enough to identify and execute a repeatable formula for growth have the advantage of strategic clarity: Repeatable formulas are compelling, and they are easy to understand.

Even when competitors work in the same geographic markets, seek the same customers, and are affiliated with the same channels, the company with a repeatable formula will typically grow faster and more profitably than its rivals. To see this principle in action, let's return to Nike and compare its growth path with Reebok's. The handicap for Reebok was its undisciplined approach to growth. Reebok veered from one adjacency to the next without a clear plan. The company sought to position itself as a sports and performance company, not a fashion and fitness company, for example—but undercut that approach with such brand additions as Ralph Lauren and Polo footwear. Unrelated investments like the acquisition of the Boston Whaler boat company also sapped Reebok at the same time that its core shoe business was under severe attack.

Nike, meanwhile, was refining its repeatable formula. The company had been selling shoes for 22 years when it broke into basketball with Michael Jordan's 1985 endorsement, followed by its entry into tennis in 1986 with John McEnroe as its brand star. Throughout the 1990s, the company picked up speed as it moved into baseball, football, cycling, volleyball, hiking, soccer, and then golf. Shoes drove the business, but increasingly Nike replicated its success with adjacency moves into apparel and hard goods. The star power of its endorsers made international expansion a logical next step. Having started out neck and neck with Reebok, Nike ended up increasing its global market share from 22% in 1990 to 38% in 2002, four times the share of its nearest competitor.

What's in this story for the typical company? First, repeatability doesn't happen overnight. Nike took a while to find its repeatable pattern. Second, a repeatable formula for adjacency expansion is practically imitation proof. Nike's formula helped it pull away from competitors that were watching its success but unable to match it. Indeed, Nike's ability to replicate success was a siren song that lured competitors to Nike's own game, where their efforts foundered. Reebok's efforts to duplicate Nike's "Air Jordan" halo, for instance, led to the "Shaq Attack" sneaker. But copying one move in Nike's pattern gave Reebok little traction, and by the time Reebok figured out Nike's game, Nike had pulled too far ahead to catch. Finally, repeatability is about strategic focus. Nike accomplished its expansion without displacing its core athletic shoe business. Indeed, the company increased the strength of the original business, then drove that market power into new adjacencies just a step or two away from the core.

By definition, however, there is always an adjacency too far removed for successful repeaters. As companies get better at rapid adjacency expansion, opportunities proliferate. Along with the confidence to follow customers aggressively into new adjacencies, companies need to develop the confidence to say no when the organization is stretched. Golf clubs, for instance, may turn out to be one step too far for Nike at this stage. Tiger Woods seems to think so. Woods's recent decision to swap Nike clubs for an older set as he tried to regain his winning form suggests that Nike still has work to do in expanding the business to include golf clubs.

Indeed, every successful repeater we examined in our study has entered adjacencies that didn't pan out—Lloyds pulled back from California's big financial services market, Staples withdrew from selling insurance products, Olam, as

The New Math of Profitable Growth

A company that develops a method for repeatable adjacency moves has many advantages in terms of speed and transparency, organizational efficiency, mastery of hidden detail, and reduced complexity. The result is often a breakthrough in performance; executives make relatively modest adjustments and improvements that drive significant increases in growth and valuation. One might call it the new math of profitable growth.

Consider a simulated scenario of a company in a 3% growth market. Let's see what the company would be worth if it achieved just half of the average benefits captured by the most successful repeaters in our study. Using its repeatability formula, the firm:

- cuts 30% off the time it takes to realize the growth benefits from its adjacency moves;
- handles three instead of two adjacency initiatives per year because of its superior organizational knowledge; and
- boosts its success rate from 30% to 55% because it reaps learning-curve benefits from its repeatable formula.

That firm can grow revenue much faster—by 6.4% per year as opposed to 3.9% (the average performance in a 3% growth market). Compounded over five years at a constant margin and price-to-earnings ratio, this higher growth rate leads to a 50% improvement in value creation over competitors by the end of the period. If the higher growth rate leads also to a much higher P/E, as is likely, the increase in value creation could be much larger.

Companies that make such substantial improvements in the timing, quantity, and success rate of their adjacency moves see the benefits magnified by stock market valuations. Clearly, disproportionate advantage accrues from successful, repeatable growth versus moderately successful, "hunt and peck" growth, allowing companies to significantly distance themselves from their competitors.

we've seen, exited from black pepper and rubber. In each instance, the companies have used their setbacks to become more closely acquainted with the tastes and habits of their customers and the companies' own limitations.

The Sources of Repeatability

Of course, failed experiments aren't the only way to figure out what works. In our interviews with CEOs, we heard strikingly similar observations about the process for developing a repeatable formula for adjacency expansion. Nearly 80% of the successful adjacency formulas we studied were built around insights about customer behavior. It's a logical connection for companies to make: The more attuned a company is to its customers' preferences the more readily it can spot untapped opportunities.

Segmenting Customers

For many companies, the foundation for a repeatable formula is effective customer segmentation. This may come as a surprise, particularly among CEOs who have grown disillusioned with conventional techniques used to group customers into logical clusters. Over the last 10 years, segmentation has come to be seen by some senior executives as the domain of marketers and ad agencies—useful for marketing campaigns but not as a lever of growth strategy. The rap against segmentation is that it's not practical enough to use for allocating resources, particularly when delineations among customers are based too heavily on lifestyles and psychological motivations.

Structured properly, however, with pragmatic segments that illuminate how customer behavior leads to purchasing decisions, customer segmentation becomes a seedbed of repeatable adjacency moves. Companies can develop a more thorough understanding of customer needs. Perhaps even more valuable is the framework such analysis provides for making very large-scale investment decisions to pursue new adjacencies. Identifying the lifetime value of each segment, and determining a company's market share within each, allows the management team to rank the attractiveness of new adjacency opportunities. The same tools help spot patterns of success, reinforcing repeatable formulas when they emerge.

Dell, for instance, has used this approach to enter one adjacency after another. With its direct-to-customer model, Dell communicates with end user customers regularly and feeds that information into deep and detailed segments. Dell then subdivides existing customer segments, making slight adjustments to its direct model to tap sources of new growth. Dell first split its public sector activities into education and government, for example; then it segmented education by primary and secondary schools; higher education was further divided into colleges and universities. For each segment, Dell changed its product focus, rewired its sales force training, and—most important—modified its sales force cost structure. This approach enables Dell to lock on to high priority segments and control its margins with remarkable precision. As a result, the company has developed a strategy where competitive advantage is based not on volume alone, but on knowledge of its customers and ability to serve them efficiently.

Growing Share of Wallet

Selling related products to customers you know intimately—in other words, growing share of wallet—is another highly successful expansion strategy, according to our study. Yet plenty of firms get it wrong—Saatchi & Saatchi in consulting, Sears in financial services, and Allegis in travel, to name a few. Success depends on understanding your customers' behavior and following familiar pathways to build the new business.

Over the last 14 years, American Express has exemplified the power of a repeatable formula based on selling related products to customers it knows. In the 1970s, the switch from checks to "plastic" was in full swing, propelling the growth of AmEx's basic green and gold cards. As market momentum slowed in the 1980s, the management team decided to assemble a "financial supermarket" of products around the core credit card business. The strategy spawned a series of acquisitions—seven in six years— starting with brokerage firm Shearson Loeb Rhodes in 1981 and concluding with E.F. Hutton in 1987. The company grew dramatically in size, but profitability suffered and the stock price dropped by more than 50% from 1987 to 1991, when top management was replaced.

The new team quickly divested all but one of the acquired businesses and then set about strengthening the original core business of charge cards. They started by analyzing the detailed microeconomic buying behavior reflected in the millions of transactions that poured in each day. The data contained patterns of opportunity—expanding from individual consumers to corporate cardholders, for instance, or from a focus on business-travel to retail and everyday spending. From a couple of cards with no add-on services, AmEx managers created a family of cards with varied interest rates, terms, services, and reward programs. In the process, they uncovered four repeatable formulas: finding new customer segments; creating new, more precisely targeted charge- and credit-card products, including popular reward programs; expanding the types of merchants where cardholders can use their cards; and selling additional services to existing card customers.

Each time AmEx considers a new product, teams first scrutinize market data to see if existing buying behavior supports the move. "We're often serving the same customers," says Alfred E. Kelly, Jr., group president of consumer and small business services. "They just might be in different segments depending on whether they are at work, on vacation, or shopping on the weekend."

Mirroring Customer Adjacencies

Other companies uncover opportunities by tracking their customers' expansion plans and anticipating their needs.

In the mid-1990s, for example, STMicroelectronics' search for new opportunities led the European microprocessor company to map out key customer segments where it could become number one in the world. Wireless phones were just beginning to take off, and handset manufacturers, including ST's customer Nokia, wanted to load their phones with new services and features without taxing the batteries. ST saw an adjacency opportunity: Its leading technology in power management for microprocessors could be adapted to grow with the capabilities of wireless handsets. Today, ST is Nokia's leading supplier of a one-chip system capable of driving the entire phone. Building on that success, ST has gone on to supply the system to wireless handset manufacturers in the United States and Asia. Similarly, when ST's customers in the computer industry began expanding into disk drives, printers, and monitors, the company saw an opportunity to grow with its customers in a market largely ignored by its rival, Intel. ST invested to adapt its logic chips, and today is the world's leading supplier to computer peripheral companies.

ST's growth pattern has been to adapt a core technology prompted by insights from its dozen largest customers, apply the technology to new segments, expand into new geographies, then start the cycle again. The formula has proven highly resilient in a volatile industry. CEO Pasquale Pistorio stays in close contact with key account managers at ST's largest customers, often joining them on visits to their own customers. More than 95% of ST's R&D budget goes to developing new capabilities for existing customers, rather than making bets on future technologies that look generally promising.

The STMicroelectronics story illustrates the two key principles of repeatability. First, adjacency expansion succeeds only when built around strong core businesses that have potential for leadership economics. Second, the best place to look for adjacency opportunities is inside a company's strongest customers.

Repeatability is just one formula for profitably outstripping the average growth rate in your sector. There are others: Investing in faster product innovation or cornering market power, to name a couple. But focused companies with a strong core that hit upon a formula for repeatedly expanding their strengths to new arenas have it made for the long term. Such repeatability becomes a source of growth and value year after year. The formula for repeatability is already lodged in your experience—you just need to look for it.

The Great Repeatable Business Model

Leveraging a simple formula allows corporations to create new and more-lasting differentiation.

Chris Zook and James Allen

This article focuses on differentiation, which is one of the three pillars of a great repeatable model. The companies we work with have found that differentiation is essential—but so are the other two pillars. One of these is working with people on the front line to create a set of nonnegotiable principles. Nonnegotiables make the strategy real; they enable frontline people to incorporate it into their everyday actions and decisions. The other pillar is the ability to learn and adapt as the world changes. Only companies with robust learning systems can stay on top of the marketplace's inevitable evolution.

Some companies seem to understand these principles intuitively, particularly the importance of nonnegotiable principles. It's a hallmark, for instance, of companies that are still led by their founders—the founders themselves have a gut-level ability to establish and communicate these principles to people throughout the organization. But even a giant corporation can get its mojo back when the senior team begins to understand that strategy doesn't exist in the abstract—it is a social contract that has to be cocreated with the front line, and it has to be reflected in how people act every day on the job.

Differentiation is the essence of strategy, the prime source of competitive advantage. You earn money not just by performing a valuable task but by being different from your competitors in a manner that lets you serve your core customers better and more profitably.

The sharper your differentiation, the greater your advantage. Consider Tetra Pak, a company that in 2010 sold more than 150 billion packages in 170 markets around the world. Tetra Pak's carton packages extend the shelf life of

HBR November 2011

products and eliminate the need for refrigeration. The shapes they take—squares and pyramids, for example—stack more efficiently in trucks and on shelves than most cans or bottles. The packaging machines that use the company's unique laminated material lend themselves to high-volume dairy operations. These three features set Tetra Pak well apart from its competitors and allow it to produce a package that more than compensates for its cost.

In studying companies that sustained a high level of performance over many years, we found that more than 80% of them had this kind of well-defined and easily understood differentiation at the center of their strategy. Nike's differentiation resides in the power of its brand, the company's relationships with top athletes, and its signature performance-focused product design. Singapore Airlines' differentiation comes from its unique ways of providing premium service at a reasonable cost on long-haul business flights. Apple's differentiation consists of deep capabilities in writing easy-to-use software, the integrated iTunes system, and a simplicity of design and product line (Apple has only about 60 main SKUs).

You can find high performers like these in most industries. The cold truth about hot markets is this: Over the long run, a company's strategic differentiation and execution matter far more to its performance—our research suggests at least four times as much—than the business it happens to be in. Every industry has leaders and laggards, and the leaders are typically the most highly differentiated.

But differentiation tends to wear with age, and not just because competitors try hard to undermine or replicate it. Often the real problem is internal: The growth generated by successful differentiation begets complexity, and a complex company tends to forget what it's good at. Products proliferate. Acquisitions take it far from its core. Frontline employees, more and more distant from the CEO's office, lose their sense of the company's strategic priorities. A lack of consistency kills economies of scale and retards the company's ability to learn. Small wonder that "reinvention" and "disruption" have become leading buzzwords; companies struggling with complexity and fading differentiation come to believe they must reimagine their entire business models quickly and dramatically or else be overwhelmed by upstarts with disruptive innovations.

Most of the time, however, reinvention is the wrong way to go. Our experience, supported by more than 15 years of research into high performance, has led us to the inescapable conclusion that most really successful companies do not reinvent themselves through periodic "binge and purge" strategies. Instead they relentlessly build on their fundamental differentiation, going from strength to strength. They learn to deliver their differentiation to the front line, creating an organization that lives and breathes its strategic advantages day in and day out. They learn how to sustain it over time through constant adaptation to changes in the market. And they learn to resist the siren song of the *idée du jour* better than their less-focused competitors. The result is a simple, repeatable business model that a company can apply to new products and markets over and over again to generate sustained growth. The simplicity means that everyone in the company is on the same page—and no one forgets the sources of success.

Let's look in more detail at what this involves.

Sources of Differentiation

Opportunities for differentiation are rich and varied in virtually every industry. To examine them more closely, we built a database of 8,000 global companies and tracked their performance over 25 years. We created another database of 200 global companies, which we studied in detail. We supplemented that research with two other data sets: a survey conducted with the Economist Intelligence Unit of nearly 400 global executives, and 50 interviews with chief executives around the world. Building on the data, we cataloged 250 assets or capabilities that can contribute to differentiation and sorted them into three major clusters of five categories each. (See the exhibit "The Differentiation Map.")

The most enduring performers, we found, built their strategy on a few vivid, robust forms of differentiation that acted as a system, reinforcing one another. To illustrate, let's examine the factors that make the mutual fund company Vanguard one of the most consistently high-performing businesses in our study.

Ever since its founding, in 1974, Vanguard has been a different kind of company. Its founder, John Bogle, believed passionately in the value of index funds. He saw that a company based on them would need few fund managers and researchers and could therefore charge considerably less than companies with actively managed funds. Bogle also felt he should deal directly with customers and offer them highly responsive service, thus building loyalty. These characteristics are at the core of Vanguard's differentiation today, as can be seen in "The Differentiation Map." The company has the lowest-cost mutual fund "engine," a distribution system that avoids middlemen and allows direct contact with customers, and the highest level of customer loyalty in the industry.

The strongest sources of differentiation in a company's strongest businesses are its crown jewels. Yet our research shows that most management teams spend little time discussing or measuring them and therefore don't agree on what they are. This lack of clarity permeates entire organizations. For instance, more than half of frontline employees say in surveys that they are not clear on their companies' strategic tenets and differentiators. Customers are even more mystified: Although 80% of managers told us they thought their companies were strongly

The Differentiation Map

We cataloged 250 assets or capabilities that can make up a company's differentiation. We then sorted them into three major clusters, each with five categories, to create the Differentiation Map. Assuming that four or five categories are required to achieve differentiation, these 15 basic categories generate more than 5,000 distinct ways in which a company can differentiate itself. (It is possible, however, to break the categories down further, in which case the number of ways to differentiate explodes into more than a million.)

Vanguard's differentiating strengths are highlighted below.

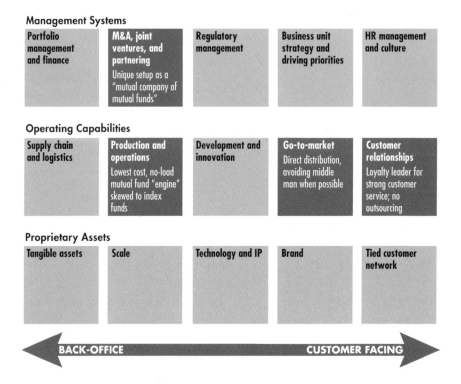

Management Systems

Portfolio management and finance	M&A, joint ventures, and partnering	Regulatory management	Business unit strategy and driving priorities	HR management and culture
	Unique setup as a "mutual company of mutual funds"			

Operating Capabilities

Supply chain and logistics	Production and operations	Development and innovation	Go-to-market	Customer relationships
	Lowest cost, no-load mutual fund "engine" skewed to index funds		Direct distribution, avoiding middle man when possible	Loyalty leader for strong customer service; no outsourcing

Proprietary Assets

Tangible assets	Scale	Technology and IP	Brand	Tied customer network

◄ **BACK-OFFICE**   **CUSTOMER FACING** ►

differentiated, fewer than 10% of customers agreed. Yet understanding and agreeing about differentiation, where it can be applied, and how it must evolve is what makes a strategy work.

A systematic approach to understanding your sources of differentiation is key to rectifying this situation. It enables you to have a meaningful discussion of what distinguishes your company from competitors and what you can build on. When we ask each of a company's top 15 managers privately what he or she feels are the most differentiated and important assets and capabilities, we often find a surprising lack of agreement.

One way to bring data to bear on this range of views is to rate the success of your company's past 20 growth investments and determine what they have in common. This is a starting point for mapping the company's differentiation. Discussions of what really differentiates a business from its competitors are, however, often based on past beliefs more than on current data. As you deliberate about your own key differentiators, you might consult these criteria: Are they (1) truly distinctive? (2) measurable against competitors? (3) relevant to what you deliver to your core customers? (4) mutually reinforcing? (5) clear at all levels of the company? Though each of the five seems obvious, reaching agreement on your differentiation and testing it against these criteria is not as easy as it sounds. The harder it proves, the more valuable the exercise. In our experience, many companies fail these tests—but the most successful ones pass them every time.

The ability to recognize and test the sources of your differentiation in this way is important for focusing innovation. Most innovations, even disruptive ones, affect only one part of a business model, leaving the rest intact. The shift from glasses to contact lenses, for example, had little effect on the basic customer need for vision correction, the industry's distribution system, or the network of eye doctors. The shift from wired to wireless telephony caused chaos for many incumbents, yet some used their infrastructure, customer access, brand, and ability to work with regulatory organizations to prevail. The more precise your understanding of your model and the sources of its success, the more precisely you can focus innovation resources on the areas where the threats and the need for change are greatest.

Growth Based in Differentiation

The best way to grow is usually by replicating your strongest strategic advantage in new contexts. Companies typically expand in one or more of four ways: They create or purchase new products and services, create or enter new customer segments, enter new geographic locations, or enter related lines of business. A company can pursue each of these strategies in various ways—for example, adding new price points or finding new uses for a product or service that will appeal to new customers.

The power of a repeatable model lies in the way it turns the sources of differentiation into routines, behaviors, and activity systems that everyone in the organization can understand and follow so that when a company sets out on a particular growth path, it knows how to maintain the differentiation that led to its initial success. The global agribusiness Olam is a case in point. The company began as a cashew trader. It purchased nuts directly from farmers in Nigeria and sold them to a dozen customers in Europe, managing a supply chain from the farm gate to the shop door. This approach was unusual for the industry. It cut out middlemen, safeguarded Olam's access to products, and increased the company's market intelligence and speed of reaction. To do this well, of course, Olam had to learn to work closely with small farmers. It also had to develop a risk management system that drew on information garnered from farmers, customers, and commodities and foreign exchange markets to minimize the risks of crop problems, price and currency volatility, and supply disruption.

Making Your Differentiation Easier to Repeat

Replicating your greatest successes means deeply understanding their root causes, maintaining a 360-degree view of where they could be adapted, and ensuring that the entire organization internalizes the strategy and the differentiation on which they are built.

Here are six actions to consider:

1. Make sure that you and your management team agree on your differentiation now and in the future. You may want to ask each person to write it down; then you can collate the results in advance for discussion. At a minimum, consider three questions: (a) What do our core customers see as our key sources of competitive differentiation? (b) How do we know? (c) Are these sources becoming more or less robust?

2. See whether the front line of your organization agrees with what you come up with. Can employees and supervisors describe the strategy and the areas of differentiation as you do? Do they feel that they understand the strategy? Is it simple and clear? Online surveys, anonymously tabulated, can be a big help with this task.

3. Write your strategy on a page, or even on an index card. Does your description of it center on the key sources of differentiation? Is your page sharp and convincing to others, including customers and investors, and backed by data?

4. Conduct a postmortem of your 20 most recent growth investments and initiatives. Are your greatest successes or disappointments explained, in part, by the central differentiators that were transferred?

5. Translate your strategy into a few nonnegotiables. Can you describe simple principles that the organization believes in and that define the key behaviors, beliefs, and values needed to drive the strategy? Are they embedded in day-to-day routines, or are they simply words on a page?

6. Review how you monitor the most important health indicators of your core business and its differentiators, both for short-term adjustment and for long-term investment in new capabilities. Does your method drive learning and adaptation? Is quickness to adapt a competitive advantage? Are you sure?

These capabilities translated into other contexts. Olam realized that its knowledge of small farmers in Nigeria could be applied to small farmers in, say, Burkina Faso. Its risk management skills could be applied to peanuts or coffee beans as well as to cashews. The company accordingly added both farmers and customers in new countries and new products. It now sources 20 agricultural products from farmers in 65 countries and delivers them to more than 11,000 customers across the world.

Of course, Olam's differentiation evolved as the company grew. For instance, as it expanded into certain countries, it found opportunities to acquire and fold in small operations based in those countries. Although Olam had no experience with M&A, its capabilities and assets, including good contacts at the ground level in its countries of operation, gave it an advantage in recognizing promising opportunities and understanding how to negotiate with and integrate acquisitions.

Over time, the company has developed playbooks for M&A and deal integration and now considers them important differentiating features that frontline managers (and everyone else in the organization) understand and value. As Olam's CEO, Sunny Verghese, explains, "Our line managers find and consummate transactions at the local level. It is sort of a hidden asset that we have because our people are in the market at a lower level of contact than anyone else. Our ability in transactions is now part of our core, and we manage it centrally with a unique repeatable formula of clear rules and criteria."

Supporting Your Differentiation

Although differentiation is at the heart of a repeatable model, it needs the support of a rigorously focused yet flexible organization. Our research shows that powerful differentiations create the most enduring profits when a company delivers them to the front line in the form of simple, nonnegotiable principles and when it creates robust learning systems that facilitate constant adaptation. Let's look at these factors in turn.

Nonnegotiable Principles

This is a fundamental building block of repeatability, a way of keeping everyone on the same page. Analysis of our 200-company database reveals that 83% of the best-performing businesses had established explicit, widely understood principles across the organization, while only 26% of the worst performers had done so. Indeed, a link between well-defined, shared core principles and frontline behavior was more highly correlated with business performance than any other factor we studied.

The logic of this connection seems clear. Nonnegotiables translate the most important beliefs and assumptions underlying the company's differentiation into a few prescriptive statements that all employees can understand, relate to, and use as a reference point for making trade-offs and decisions. In effect, they are the headlines of the user's manual for a company's strategy.

To illustrate how companies use nonnegotiables, let's go back to Olam. A key differentiator is that the company manages supply chains right from the farm gate. To support this, Olam requires managers to live in the rural areas of developing countries in order to learn what really goes on at the farms. This nonnegotiable principle is the foundation for hiring criteria, assignments, and the structure and content of training. Another nonnegotiable is that each manager give highest priority to relationships with local farmers. Olam's field operating manual captures many of the routines that support this requirement. The company's principles, and the practices that support them, are central to its culture and provide a bonding experience for managers, who respond to trade-offs and challenges at all levels with remarkable consistency.

Tetra Pak has different but equally powerful nonnegotiables. One of them is that the package must save more than it costs, an idea that originated with the company's founder and was the reason for developing its signature tetrahedron-shaped package for milk or juice. Every major new product, package design, or line of equipment must meet that standard. Tetra Pak has developed sophisticated methods for evaluating the systems cost of packaging, including production costs, spoilage, transportation and storage, and disposal costs. It claims that it can reduce operating costs by as much as 12% for a dairy or juice company.

To understand the power of this consistency, consider that from the moment a business is founded, management becomes increasingly distanced from the customer and the front line. Up and down the organization, information slows and grows distorted—the corporate equivalent of the classic game Telephone, in which a message is relayed around a table in whispers and has become unrecognizable by the time it completes the circuit. When a company internalizes a set of principles, the message no longer gets garbled. A shared point of view, core beliefs, and a common vocabulary improve everyone's ability to communicate and foster self-organization, permitting fewer layers, fewer handoffs, and shorter communication lines. All this increases the speed of a business, which means you can capture more growth opportunities ahead of competitors and accomplish more per unit of time.

Robust Learning Systems

Clear differentiation supported by nonnegotiables confers a competitive advantage—for a while. As markets shift, however, successful organizations must also be able to learn quickly and adapt to new circumstances. Both our research and the recent history of business reflect the importance of supporting your differentiation with rapid learning and adaptation. Some 48% of managers in our top group of performers felt that their companies were characterized by strong learning systems, compared with only 9% among the rest. The travails of Kodak, General Motors, Xerox, Nokia, Sony, Kmart, and many others can be seen as cases of arrested adaptation—great formulas that simply did not change fast enough. Most such cases, we should note, didn't involve disruptive innovations that caught the incumbent flat-footed. Stalls and stagnation stem from a failure to learn much more often than from a hard-to-predict disruption.

The most common method of learning in companies with Great Repeatable Models℠ comes from direct, immediate customer feedback. The most powerful demonstration we have seen is through Net Promoter® systems, which are used at Vanguard, in Apple's retail division, and at many other companies. In this approach, customers are usually asked one or two questions shortly after contact about their satisfaction with the experience and their willingness to recommend the product, service, or company to a friend or colleague. The power of the Net Promoter score lies in its simplicity. Companies that chase more-detailed feedback typically find that customers don't bother to engage, so data are fewer and poorer as a result.

In more-complex environments, companies with direct sales forces have other interesting opportunities to create strong feedback loops with customers. Take the toolmaker Hilti. Founded in 1941 by Martin and Eugen Hilti as a mechanical workshop with five employees in Schaan, Liechtenstein, the company focused on innovative tools for difficult construction jobs. Martin Hilti spent much time at job sites, observing and interacting with customers. This was the start of the Hilti direct sales force. Over the decades, the business grew one tool at a time. The company would develop a basic design and then innovate intensively on the details, using information its salespeople acquired at job sites. Today, in an industry where about 75% of products are sold through indirect channels, this direct customer contact remains a differentiated strength. It accounts in part for Hilti's ability to command significant price premiums over competitors.

Real-time response is a competitive weapon of growing importance in a world of increasing speed and complexity. The companies that move fastest can often operate within competitors' decision cycles, so competitors are always responding to them rather than the other way around. Marcia Blenko, Paul Rogers, and Michael Mankins recently studied 760 companies worldwide through 40 questions regarding perceptions of decision speed, quality, and ability to execute. When they synthesized the responses into an index of decision effectiveness, they found that companies ranked in the top quintile produced, on average, a total shareholder return about 6 percentage points higher than the returns of other companies. Companies with robust learning systems usually score higher than average on all three counts.

A repeatable differentiation can falter and even collapse without nonnegotiable principles and robust learning systems—and without strong management to preserve and protect it. Think of Nokia. Its leaders created a formula for tablet-shaped handsets that allowed it to achieve enormous economies of scale and dominate the market for more than a decade. Yet despite considerable surplus resources during that time, the company's leaders failed to adapt and invest aggressively in the future. As a result, in just a year Nokia lost its market position to Apple, Google, and Research In Motion. This lesson is all the more sobering given that Nokia's R&D and product development teams had many years earlier created some of the basic concepts later used in the iPhone: a large display, a touchscreen, Internet readiness, and an app store.

The search for profitable growth is becoming increasingly difficult. Today fewer than 10% of companies achieve more than a modest level of profitable growth over a decade, and the odds of success are declining. A series of interviews we conducted with CEOs regarding their challenges on the job spotlight two reasons for this state of affairs. One is that companies are forced to adapt faster than ever. The other—and this one was at the top of the list—is the need to control ever-growing levels of complexity. Sluggish, too-complex organizations are the silent killers of corporate growth and profitability. Interestingly, only 15% of executives in our survey cited a lack of attractive opportunities as a major barrier to growth. Internal complexity and barriers to speed of adaptation were far more important.

Our findings show that the simplest strategies, built around the sharpest differentiations, have hidden advantages not only with customers but also internally, with the frontline employees who must mobilize faster and adapt better than competitors. When people in an organization deeply understand the sources of its differentiation, they move in the same direction quickly and effectively, learning and improving the business model as they go. And they turn in remarkable performance year after year.

The Battle for China's Good-Enough Market

Multinationals and local firms are squaring off in
China's critical—and rapidly growing—middle market.

Orit Gadiesh, Philip Leung, and Till Vestring

*This article posed a question: Should large multinationals (MNCs) consider entering
China's midrange or "good-enough" market? Contrary to the prevailing opinion at
the time, the article answered this question with a categorical yes. Today the good-
enough segment is growing larger, usually accounting for most of a category's revenue
and a meaningful share of its profits. Not participating in it is likely to threaten a
company's competitiveness and profitability, both in China and worldwide. Some
Chinese companies that pioneered what once was unoccupied good-enough space
today outperform their Western competitors.*

*So any company that wants to achieve leadership economics has to play in the
good-enough market. Moreover, that market has itself begun to segment in recent
years, so it is no great stretch for a company to move from premium products and services to high-end good-enough. Moving to the lower end is more of a stretch, because
margins there are thinner. But the volume is considerably greater, so many premium
players are beginning to figure out how they can compete there as well. Such moves
are now more challenging, because all these segments and subsegments are getting
crowded. But for most, it is either move or be left behind.*

Caterpillar, the world leader in construction equipment, is having trouble
making deeper tracks in China. The U.S.-based manufacturer of tractors,
backhoes, road graders, and other devices began selling equipment in China
in 1975, a year before the death of Chairman Mao. As the Chinese government
invested massively in infrastructure, Caterpillar helped pave the way, literally,
for economic growth and modernization in the world's fastest-growing market
for construction equipment.

HBR September 2007

Like many foreign players in any number of industries, Caterpillar got its start in China by selling goods to the Chinese government—the only possible customer before the era of economic reform—and then began selling high-quality equipment to the private sector as a premium segment of the market emerged. But it never broadened its focus to include other segments, and by the early 2000s, Komatsu, Hitachi, Daewoo, and other competitors from Japan and Korea were in the middle market with tools and equipment that cost less but were still reliable. Meanwhile, a tranche of local manufacturers that had previously been focused only on the low end of the market were burrowing up to battle the established players, designing and releasing their own products targeted squarely at middle-market consumers.

As the experiences of Caterpillar and other multinationals suggest, a critical new battleground is emerging for companies seeking to establish, sustain, or expand their presence in China: It's the "good-enough" market segment, home of reliable-enough products at low-enough prices to attract the cream of China's fast-growing cohort of midlevel consumers.

Harvard professor Clay Christensen, author of *The Innovator's Dilemma*, has used the phrase "good enough" to suggest that start-up companies developing and releasing new products and services don't necessarily need to aim for perfection to make inroads against established players. The phrase can be similarly applied to middle-market players in China that have been able to steal a march on incumbents by developing and releasing good-enough products that are displacing premium ones.

These forward-thinking companies (multinational and domestic firms alike) are doing more than just seizing share of wallet and share of mind in China's rapidly expanding middle market—in and of itself a major achievement. They are conditioning themselves for worldwide competition tomorrow: They're building the scale, expertise, and business capabilities they'll need to export their China offerings to other large emerging markets (India and Brazil, for instance) and, ultimately, to the developed markets. Given China's share of global market growth (Goldman Sachs estimates that China will account for 36% of the world's incremental GDP between 2000 and 2030) and the country's role in preparing companies to pursue opportunities in other developing regions, it's becoming clear that businesses wanting to succeed globally will need to win in China first.

In the following pages, we'll explore the importance of China as a lead market. We'll describe the surge of activity in China's middle market; when (and whether) multinationals and Chinese companies should enter this vibrant arena for growth; and, most important, how they can compete effectively in the good-enough segment. As Caterpillar and other foreign players have learned, achieving leadership in China's middle market isn't easy.

An Evolving Opportunity

Historically, there has been a simple structure to China's markets: at the top, a small premium segment served by foreign companies realizing solid margins and rapid growth; at the bottom, a large low-end segment served by local companies offering low-quality, undifferentiated products (typically 40% to 90% cheaper than premium ones) that often lose money—when producers do their accounting right. Between the two is the rapidly expanding good-enough segment. (For an example of how one market sector breaks out, see the exhibit "The Structure of China's Market for Televisions.")

The good-enough space in China is growing for many reasons, not the least of which are recent shifts in consumer buying patterns and preferences. These shifts are coming from two directions: Consumers with rising incomes are trading up from the low-end products they previously purchased. At the same time, higher-income consumers are moving away from pricey foreign brands and accepting less expensive, locally produced alternatives of reasonable quality. The same holds true on the B2B front.

Consequently, China's middle market is growing faster than both the premium and low-end segments. In some categories, the good-enough space already accounts for nearly half of all revenues. Eight out of every 10 washing machines and televisions now sold in China are good-enough brands. It should come as no surprise, then, that China—and, in particular, its opportunity-rich middle market—is increasingly capturing multinational executives' resources and attention. As Mark Bernhard, chief financial officer of General Motors' Shanghai-based GM China Group, recently told the *Detroit News*: "For GM to remain a global industry leader, we must also be a leader in China."

The Structure of China's Market for Televisions

Premium (narrow)	Good-enough (rapidly expanding)	Low-end (evolving base)
Definition: High-end products purchased by discerning customers with significant purchasing power.	**Definition:** Products of good quality, produced by local companies for a rapidly expanding group of value-seeking consumers with midlevel incomes.	**Definition:** Products of lower quality, meeting basic needs, produced by local firms for a large group of consumers with low incomes.
Leading vendors: Panasonic, Philips, Sony	**Leading vendors:** Hisense, Skyworth, TCL	**Leading vendor:** Konka
Product features: LCD and plasma screens, many state-of-the-art user features, priced according to their status as international brands.	**Product features:** LCD, plasma, and large cathode-ray tube screens, with limited user features, priced to undercut foreign brands.	**Product features:** Cathode-ray tube screens with basic standard user features and low-cost components, priced to sell.
Share of market in 2005: 13%	**Share of market in 2005: 62%**	**Share of market in 2005: 25%**

The automaker's strategy in China embodies that belief. GM had traditionally been an underperformer in the market for small cars. However, its acquisition of Korea's ailing Daewoo Motor in 2002 enabled it to compete and ultimately take a leadership position in China. The deal allowed GM to develop new models for half what it would cost the company to develop them in the West. Daewoo-designed cars now make up more than 50% of GM's sales in China, currently its second biggest market. What's more, GM is using these vehicles to compete against Asian automakers and sell small cars in more than 150 markets around the world, from India to the United States.

Colgate-Palmolive made similar moves in China. It entered into a joint venture in the early 1990s with one of China's largest toothpaste producers, and it acquired China's market leader for toothbrushes a decade later, allowing it to scale up and then leverage its production processes to compete in other parts of the world. As a result, Colgate more than doubled its oral hygiene revenues in China between 1998 and 2005, and it now exports its China products to 70 countries.

Local Chinese competitors pose the biggest challenge to multinationals seeking to capitalize on their business ventures in China and beyond. In the auto industry, for instance, domestic carmakers like Geely and Chery have eaten away at Western companies' market share in China by introducing good-enough cars for local consumption. Several of these automakers have started exhibiting vehicles at car shows in the United States and Europe, buying available Western brands, and exporting vehicles to other emerging markets. True, these players face enormous challenges in meeting safety and emissions standards and in building up the required distribution networks to compete in Europe and North America. But no Western company should underestimate the determination of Chinese firms to figure out how to meet international quality standards and make their global mark.

European and North American companies producing major appliances, microwaves, and televisions know this all too well. They abdicated China to low-cost local competitors in the 1990s and now find themselves struggling to compete globally against those same Chinese companies. Haier, which started making refrigerators in 1984, went on to become one of China's best-known brands and then used its hard-won scale advantages and manufacturing skills to crack, and then dominate, foreign markets. Today, it is one of the largest refrigerator companies in the world, controlling 8.3% of the highly fragmented global market. The company sells products in more than 100 markets, including the United States, Africa, and Pakistan.

Obviously, the stakes in China have changed. Local companies are using booming domestic markets to hone their strategies at home before taking on the world. Multinationals, therefore, need to defend their positions in China not only to profit from the economic growth in that country but also to prevent local competitors from becoming global threats. The good-enough space is where multinationals and Chinese firms are going head-to-head—and it's the market segment from which the world's leading companies will emerge.

Making an Entrance

It's one thing to recognize the importance of China's middle market; it's another thing entirely to turn that awareness into action. The first step in winning the battle for China's good-enough market is determining when—or when not—to enter the fray. That will depend on the attractiveness of the premium segment: Is it still growing? Are companies still achieving high returns or are returns eroding? Another consideration is your company's market position: Are you a leader or a niche player? (See the exhibit "Should You Enter the Middle Market?")

Should You Enter the Middle Market?

Multinationals deciding whether to move into China's middle market need to first consider the attractiveness of the premium segment and their current market position. If conditions warrant, they can attack aggressively from above. Chinese firms can burrow up from below. Both can acquire their way into the good-enough space.

State of the premium market segment

		Strong	Weak or eroding
Companies' competitive position	**Strong**	**Maintain strong premium status** Hold off on entering the good-enough segment of the market—for now. Drop prices as required to remain competitive; lower costs and innovate to defend premium status and sustain margin. Regularly reevaluate the decision not to enter.	**Attack from above or buy your way in** Premium players employ an offensive-defense approach to enter the middle market. That is, they enter the good-enough segment in order to defend against the rise of local competitors and the erosion of the premium segment.
	Weak or eroding	**Innovate to maintain current premium status** Hold off on entering the good-enough segment of the market—for now. Increase innovation efforts to capture a niche position in the premium segment. Regularly reevaluate the decision not to enter.	**Burrow up from below or buy your way in** Value players enter the good-enough segment using a breakthrough approach—with a merger, for instance, or by developing China-specific products or business models—to steal share from incumbents and attain market leadership.

Foreign companies grappling with the good-enough decision in China will need to consider these factors and perform thorough market and competitor analyses, along with careful customer segmentation and needs analyses—classic strategy tools, of course, but applied in the context of a rapidly changing economy that may lack historical data on market share, prices, and the like. Senior managers will need to establish the factors that are key to success in everything from branding to pricing to distribution. This knowledge will inform important decisions about whether companies should expand organically into the middle market, acquire an existing player in that space, or find a good-enough partner.

Generally speaking, competing in the good-enough space is neither necessary nor wise for multinationals operating in stable premium segments. These companies should instead focus on lowering their costs and innovating to maintain their premium or niche positions and to sustain their margins. We studied one large manufacturer of automation equipment, for example, that wisely decided to stand pat in the premium segment. Market research suggested that its customers were still willing to pay more for reliability, even with a variety of lower-cost choices out there. The company continued to invest in R&D, hoping to further differentiate its products from those of local players; it expanded its distribution and service networks to improve its responsiveness to customers; and it cut costs by taking advantage of local production resources.

Few multinationals find themselves in such a fortunate position, however. If growth in the premium segment is slowing and returns are eroding, multinational corporations will need to enter the good-enough space. Even those companies that because of their strong competitive position initially abstain from entering the middle market should revisit their decision frequently to guard against emerging competitive threats. For their part, Chinese companies will need to move upmarket as the lower-end segment becomes increasingly competitive.

Our research and experience indicate that companies contemplating a move into the good-enough space go about it in one of three basic ways: Leading multinationals in the premium segment *attack from above*. The goal for these organizations is to lower their manufacturing costs, introduce simplified products or services, and broaden their distribution networks while maintaining reasonable quality. Meanwhile, Chinese challengers in the low-end segment tend to *burrow up from below*. These companies aim to take the legs out from under established players by providing new offerings that ratchet up quality but cost consumers much less than the premium products do. And, finally, multinationals that can't reduce their costs fast enough, and domestic players looking for more skills, technology, and talent, *buy their way in*.

Each of these moves comes with its own set of traps. The challenge, then, for companies eyeing the middle market is to understand why those that went before them failed in this space—and how to sidestep the pitfalls they encountered. Let's take a closer look at these three approaches.

Attacking from Above

Whether they're selling toothpaste or power transmission equipment, multinational companies dominate China's small but high-margin premium segment—the only one in which foreign players have traditionally been able to compete successfully. So a move toward the middle certainly holds a fair amount of risk for those already thriving in the premium space. A chief concern is cannibalization. After all, selling to consumers in less-than-premium segments could negatively affect sales of high-end products. These companies also run the risk of fueling gray markets for their wares. If, say, a business sells a T-shirt for $10 in China but $20 in the United States, there's a good chance an enterprising distributor will find a way to buy that T-shirt in China and export it to the United States for sale there.

Multinational managers, therefore, need to conduct careful market analyses to understand the differences between China's premium and good-enough segments. There may be, for instance, strong geographic distinctions a company can capitalize on. Consider the strategy GE Healthcare employed to expand sales of its MRI equipment in China. The company created a line of simplified machines targeted at hospitals in China's remote and financially constrained second- and third-tier cities—places like Hefei and Lanzhou, where other multinationals rarely ventured. That good-enough territory had all the right conditions: It was a fast-growing market whose customers' purchasing criteria weren't likely to change soon. GE's cost structure allowed it to compete with other middle-market players in the industry. And there was little risk that the company would cannibalize its premium line of diagnostic machines; large city hospitals were not keen on downgrading their MRI equipment.

Markets are dynamic, and there's no place on the planet where they are shifting as quickly or as dramatically as in China. So multinational executives also need to think about the degree to which the premium and good-enough segments will converge over time. Managers can use traditional forecasting methods (scenario planning, war gaming, consultations with leading-edge customers, and so on) to pick up on emerging threats and impending opportunities. Which brings us back to GE Healthcare's MRI expansion plans: The company's long-held commitment to health care development in China meshed perfectly with

Chinese leaders' publicly stated desire to improve health services in less-privileged areas of the country. Given the government's aims, GE Healthcare understood there would eventually be some overlap of the premium, middle, and low-end markets—and profitable opportunities in the good-enough space.

After weighing the risks that cannibalization and dynamic markets pose to their company's premium positioning, managers in multinationals need to consider their possible opportunities in the good-enough space: Can they take advantage of their lower purchasing costs, greater manufacturing scale, and distribution synergies? Then they have to determine which capabilities they may need to develop: How adept is their organization at designing products, services, brands, and sales approaches that will attract customers in the middle market without

Penetrating the Good-Enough Market, One County Hospital at a Time

GE Healthcare already had a successful business selling high-end medical equipment in China when the Chinese government set a goal for the next decade of improving the health care available in less-privileged locales. To support the government's efforts and also to break out of the high end of the market, GE developed a business case for manufacturing and selling medical devices for China's good-enough market. CEO Jeff Immelt's visits and conversations with Chinese leaders motivated the company to pursue the opportunity. In the end, GE's research and analysis identified a substantial demand from thousands of midtier and low-end Chinese hospitals in less affluent provinces that were not served by multinationals. GE knew that it could design new products and business models to serve this market. GE also knew that by using techniques like Six Sigma to eliminate manufacturing waste, it could make its costs competitive.

A team was charged with observing operations in the target hospitals and meeting with the hospital administrators and physicians to help determine what sort of medical equipment customers wanted, the specific features they needed, possible price points, and the kinds of distribution and services that would be required. Armed with this information, the fact-finding team considered stripping out some of the expensive equipment features and adding others that these target customers valued more. For instance, doctors in China's high-end hospitals preferred to program the medical equipment themselves, whereas physicians in the midlevel and low-end hospitals, who considered themselves less computer savvy, preferred preprogrammed machines.

The team worked with staffers in GE's R&D and manufacturing groups to build the right products at the right price points for the good-enough market. Because GE's existing sales, distribution, and service systems were not geared to the target customers, the company also had to reconfigure its networks of existing representatives and recruit new ones. This middle-market initiative is still a work in progress, but GE Healthcare has taken an enormous first step in establishing itself—and defending itself against rivals—in the good-enough segment.

diminishing their company's position in the premium space? They may need to convene teams dedicated solely to studying the opportunities and resources required in the good-enough segment, as GE Healthcare did. (See the sidebar "Penetrating the Good-Enough Market, One County Hospital at a Time.") They may also want to recruit local management talent—individuals with experience competing in the middle space—or purchase local companies to gain new technologies or expertise.

Those multinationals that decide to enter the middle market tend to employ an "offensive-defense" strategy—aggressively staking claims in the good-enough space to box out emerging local players and established global competitors seeking to gain their own scale advantages. By entering the good-enough space ahead of the pack, for instance, GE Healthcare was able to defend its position against local upstarts, including Mindray, Wandong, and Anke. The company is still trying to develop the optimal product portfolio and is addressing such issues as how best to service the equipment. Even so, GE captured 52% of the $238 million market in 2004, generating roughly $120 million in sales. Having honed its approach to the good-enough space, GE is replicating the strategy in new markets in several developing countries, including India.

Multinationals are bound to find it tough to jump in from above. Apart from the risks of cannibalization and all the challenges always associated with going down-market, companies will need to adapt fast, as customers' preferences change and competitors react. And they will probably need to tear apart the cost structure of their good-enough competitors to understand how those firms make money while charging such low prices. Just switching to local sourcing, for instance, may not be sufficient for large multinationals to match the lower production costs of their domestic competitors.

Burrowing Up from Below

Multinationals for years underestimated the ability and desire of local players in the low end of the market to move up and compete—a miscalculation that may now be coming home to roost. Recent developments have strengthened local competition in China and facilitated Chinese companies' moves upmarket and beyond.

Let's start with consolidation. For years, there were often hundreds of companies in a single industry catering primarily to customers in the low end of the market and typically focusing on regional needs. Many of those companies operated unprofitably—think of Red Star Appliances or Wuhan Xi Dao Industrial Stock. Because of China's free-market reforms, however, the weakest of those competitors are folding, and industries are experiencing waves of consolidation.

Red Star, Wuhan Xi Dao, and 16 other money-losing concerns shifted and reshifted throughout the 1990s to form appliance maker Haier. A competent player or two, like Haier, have risen in each industry, often benefiting from national support. China's booming economy has enabled these survivors to build scale and develop market capabilities such as R&D and branding. As we have seen, over time, several of these emerging domestic champions have become direct challengers to global companies in a variety of industries.

Next, look at the rapidly expanding customer base in the middle space. Chinese customers—whether individual consumers, businesses, or government agencies—are becoming less willing to shell out 70% to 100% premiums for international products. At most, they may pay 20% to 30% more for world-class brands. The Italian dairy giant Parmalat discovered exactly that when it tried selling fruit-flavored yogurt for the equivalent of 24 cents a cup. Instead, consumers went with local brands at half the price. It seemed that brand, innovation, and quality—the hallmarks of multinationals in China—were no longer critical points of differentiation in customers' minds. This price sensitivity is opening up new ground for ambitious Chinese companies traditionally focused on the low end. These firms are designing and releasing good-enough products that overcome buyers' skepticism about quality at much lower prices, which generate higher margins than their low-end products. The often brutal competitive dynamics in the low-end segment also serve as a huge incentive for the better-managed local companies to move up. Until consumer demand began to explode in China, however, there really wasn't anywhere for these firms to go. Now there is.

The journey from low end to good-enough to global usually takes a decade and then some—but more and more Chinese companies are embarking on it. For instance, Lenovo, founded in 1984, entered the good-enough segment via a joint venture, flourished in the middle market, and then went on to establish its international brand with the purchase of IBM's PC division in 2005 for $1.75 billion. It is currently the world's third-largest PC maker. Similarly, Huawei Technologies has grown since 1988 to the point where 31 of the first 50 firms on Standard & Poor's ranking of the world's top telecom companies are clients of the Chinese maker of mobile and fixed telecommunications networks.

Just as foreign players approaching the market from above come face-to-face with their shortcomings—high costs, limited distribution capabilities, and the possibility of cannibalizing their own products—local companies moving up encounter their own limitations. Foremost is the shortage of managerial talent, especially for international businesses. Growing numbers of Chinese students are pursuing MBAs and studying abroad. They are slowly distinguishing themselves from the large cohort of current Chinese managers, whose command-and-control leadership style dominates local manufacturing houses. But catching up remains difficult, as China's surging economic growth outpaces the country's ability to educate and apprentice twenty-first-century managers.

Another obstacle for Chinese companies is their inability to compete with global players through innovation or by establishing a strong brand because of their limited size and their lack of management tools and experience. A question like "How much should we spend on advertising?" can stymie local managers looking at expansion. Long used to competing solely on price, they have little experience in understanding and addressing segment-specific needs, linking those needs to R&D and brand-building efforts, and creating the required infrastructure in sales and distribution.

Consider the early successes enjoyed by Chinese handset manufacturer Ningbo Bird. It was among a group of small, local companies that took 20% to 30% of the telecom market between 2000 and 2002 from the likes of Nokia and Motorola. Ningbo Bird prevailed by competing on price. But its success was short-lived, its march toward global expansion thwarted. The company just didn't have the expertise and resources the foreign corporations had in customer segmentation, R&D, innovation, and distribution.

By contrast, Huawei has been able to successfully navigate such roadblocks. Initially established as a network equipment distributor, Huawei has built and acquired the technical and managerial capabilities it needed to rise up from the low end of the market. From its inception, Huawei invested 10% of its sales in R&D. It developed its own products to penetrate new segments in China and forged technical alliances to further broaden its product mix. With government support, Huawei prompted consolidation in the domestic market, gaining massive scale in the process. The company now controls 14% of the local market for telecom networks. Firmly established in the good-enough space at home, Huawei built brands to meet the requirements of global customers. It established 12 R&D centers around the world, pioneering next-generation technologies (customized communication networks and voice access systems) and partnering with global brands such as 3Com to build customer awareness of its own brands.

Huawei has broadened its reach in stages over 14 years. The company first focused on establishing itself in developing regions of China, where multinationals had less incentive to compete. It then penetrated countries with emerging economies, such as Russia and Brazil. Finally, it attacked the developed countries. It has expanded internationally through aggressive sales and marketing, by taking advantage of low-cost China-based R&D, and by leveraging its ability to outsource some of its manufacturing processes to other players in China. A little more than a decade ago, Huawei was a regional company in a local market that few multinationals considered important. With 2005 revenues of $8.2 billion, it is now second only to Cisco, according to InfoTech Trends' ranking of the networking hardware industry. It could never have ascended the way it has without using China's good-enough segment as a springboard for growth.

Buying Your Way In

For multinational companies that can't alter their costs or processes quickly enough to compete with local players, and for Chinese firms that lack the production scale, R&D mechanisms, and customer-facing capabilities to compete with foreign players, there is still a breakthrough option for entering the middle market—mergers and acquisitions.

China's entry into the World Trade Organization in 2001 fueled a surge in M&A activity. Now, however, foreign acquirers are facing tougher approval processes. China's public commitment to open markets remains strong, but several high-profile deals have gotten stuck at the provincial or ministerial level, owing to increasing public concerns about selling out to foreign firms. For instance, in its bid to buy Xugong Group Construction Machinery, China's largest construction machinery manufacturer and distributor, the U.S. private equity firm Carlyle Group met with unexpected resistance from the government and ended up twice reducing its stake, ultimately to 45%. In rejecting successive Carlyle bids, officials in Beijing insisted the nation's construction equipment industry should be controlled by "domestic hands."

As the Carlyle Group learned, gaining regulatory and political approval for M&As in China is a major undertaking. Foreign companies seeking such approval may need to draft (and redraft) a compelling business case for the acquisition, one that cites up front the benefits for local companies and authorities. Like Carlyle, they must be willing to adjust (and readjust) the structure, terms, and conditions of a deal to gain government support. They may also need to engage in heavy-duty relationship building, investing the time and resources required to woo critical players in the deal.

As is always the case with M&As the world over, it's all about fit: There should be cost and distribution synergies between the multinational and its target and little chance that the local company's products will cannibalize the multinational's premium brands. Successful acquirers in China—multinationals and Chinese firms alike—use a clear strategic rationale to select the right target. They overinvest in the due diligence process. They take a systematic approach to postmerger integration.

That was the game plan behind Gillette's 2003 acquisition of Nanfu, then China's leading battery manufacturer. Gillette's Duracell division throughout the

1990s was losing market share in China to lower-priced competitors. By 2002, Duracell's share of the Chinese domestic battery market was 6.5%. By contrast, Nanfu controlled more than half the market. After careful analysis, Gillette's management team recognized that its Duracell unit was at a cost disadvantage compared with its rivals and concluded it would be difficult to broaden the brand's market penetration. Facing such odds, Gillette decided to buy into the good-enough market, acquiring a majority stake in Nanfu. But Gillette was extremely careful to protect both Duracell's and Nanfu's brands in their respective segments. Gillette continues to sell premium batteries in China under the Duracell brand and has maintained Nanfu as the leading national brand for the mass market. The dual branding, cost synergies, sales growth, broadened product portfolio, economies of scale, and distribution to more than 3 million retail outlets in China have paid off for Gillette, which has seen significant increases in its operating margins in China.

Buying into the good-enough segment also worked for consumer-goods giants Danone, L'Oréal, and Anheuser-Busch—companies that saw the vast potential in China but couldn't get their costs low enough to compete. For instance, in 2004, Anheuser-Busch outbid its competitor SABMiller to acquire Harbin, the fourth-largest brewer in China. That acquisition allowed Anheuser-Busch to reach the masses while preventing Harbin from swimming upstream. The next year, it increased its stake in Tsingtao Brewery, from 9.9% to 27%. Both moves enabled the global brewer to rapidly increase its share among China's drinkers of less-than-premium beer.

Chinese companies are also wrapping their arms around acquisition strategies, attempting to establish their presence in the middle market by purchasing brands, talent, and other resources from target companies in Europe and North America. To date, they've met with mixed results. On the one hand, Lenovo's acquisition of IBM's PC division turned the Chinese computer maker into the world's third-largest PC company. On the other hand, the acquisition experiences of TCL, a major Chinese consumer electronics manufacturer, have been less successful.

TCL built a strong position in the Chinese market by producing and distributing basic cathode-ray tube TVs at astonishingly low prices. It also engaged in contract and private-label manufacturing for the U.S. and European markets. But TCL realized it would need a strong brand to rise up from the low end of the China market and that growing organically in a mature industry like TV manufacturing would be prohibitively expensive. So TCL acquired French firm Thomson, which owned a number of well-known brands, including RCA. Unfortunately, Thomson also owned some high-cost and unproductive manufacturing facilities in France. TCL has struggled since acquiring Thomson, as the market for TVs has shifted from cathode-ray to plasma and LCD technologies. In 2006, the company lost $351 million from operations. Many Chinese companies believe that in order to play in the global arena, they must simply forge ahead, buying established Western brands and distribution systems—whether or not they have the experience and management tools to handle such acquisitions. But, as TCL's story suggests, executing such a plan is hardly cut-and-dried.

In the 1960s and 1970s, the mantra for many organizations was "Capture U.S. market share, capture the world." Today, China—and its middle market in particular—has become the object of multinationals' ardent pursuit. The enormous market potential of the country's population, the formidable growth of the economy, and China's established position in low-cost sourcing and manufacturing are providing competitive advantages for many companies—benefits these organizations are then leveraging both inside and outside the nation.

Local Chinese companies know their futures depend on entering the good-enough space and attacking global leaders (and their premium positioning) by offering low-cost products of reasonable quality that they can eventually take to the world. Multinationals are beginning to recognize that ceding the middle space to Chinese firms may breed competitors that will ultimately challenge them on a global scale. Ironically, Chinese companies that have already gone global are on the defensive as well. A recent *Forbes Asia* article reported that as Haier has attacked international markets and won share abroad, both local companies and multinationals have been nibbling away at its share of China's middle market—which fell from 29% in 2004 to 25% last year.

The stakes are high. All the more reason, then, for companies that have stumbled in China in the past to redouble their efforts. Danone's high product costs thwarted its early attempts to sell dairy products in China's middle market. But that obstacle was removed when the firm reengaged in the fight, lowering its costs by buying a local dairy.

Likewise, Caterpillar hasn't diverted its focus away from China and the importance of the good-enough space. The company plans to triple its sales by 2010, opening more manufacturing plants and dealerships and forming more joint ventures with local companies. "Operational and sales success in China is critical for the company's long-term growth and profitability," said Rich Lavin, vice president of Caterpillar's Asia Pacific Operations Division, in November 2006. Shortly thereafter, the company moved its divisional headquarters—from Tokyo to Beijing.

Innovation in Turbulent Times

When resources are constrained, the key to growth is pairing an analytic left-brain thinker with an imaginative right-brain partner.

Darrell Rigby, Kara Gruver, and James Allen

Innovation is daunting in the best of times. In turbulent economic conditions, when innovation is frequently called upon to deliver even greater results with fewer resources, it can feel hopeless. In the last few years, however, we have seen a growing number of companies confront this challenge directly, drawing upon the BothBrain® approach outlined in this article.

Innovation, which we define as the profitable application of creativity, must do two things: 1) generate brilliant ideas and 2) successfully commercialize the best of those ideas. Although few individuals possess world-class capabilities in both of these cognitive specialties, BothBrain methodologies build complementary teams (think of Steve Jobs and Tim Cook at Apple or Bill Bowerman and Phil Knight at Nike) and collaborative processes to change the way the innovation game is played. This approach transforms strategic visioning, hiring, training, mentoring, partnering, brainstorming, incubating, and even stage-gating processes to make innovation more stimulating and far more profitable. BothBrain workshops have now become catalyzing highlights in hundreds of our most creative breakthroughs.

nnovation is a messy process—hard to measure and hard to manage. Most people recognize it only when it generates a surge in growth. When revenues and earnings decline during a recession, executives often conclude that their innovation efforts just aren't worth it. Maybe innovation isn't so important after all, they think. Maybe our teams have lost their touch. Better to focus on the tried and true than to waste money on untested ideas.

The contrary view, of course, is that innovation is both a vaccine against market slowdowns and an elixir that rejuvenates growth. Imagine how much better off General Motors might be today if the company had matched the pace of innovation set by Honda or Toyota. Imagine how much worse off Apple would

HBR June 2009

be had it not created the iPod, iTunes, and the iPhone. But when times are hard, companies grow disillusioned with their innovation efforts for a reason: Those efforts weren't very effective to begin with. Innovation isn't integral to the workings of many organizations. The creativity that leads to game-changing ideas is missing or stifled. Why would any company gamble on a process that seems risky and unpredictable even in good times?

In talking with executives about innovation, we often point to the fashion industry as a model. Every successful fashion company essentially reinvents its product line and thus its brand every season. It repeatedly brings out products that consumers didn't know they needed, often sparking such high demand that the previous year's fashions are suddenly obsolete. A fashion company that fails to innovate at this pace faces certain death. Understanding that, fashion companies have refined an organizational model that ensures a constant stream of innovation whatever the state of the economy.

At the top of virtually every fashion brand is a distinctive kind of partnership. One partner, usually called the creative director, is an imaginative, right-brain individual who spins out new ideas every day and seems able to channel the future wants and needs of the company's target customers. The other partner, the brand manager or brand CEO, is invariably left-brain and adept at business, someone comfortable with decisions based on hard-nosed analysis. In keeping with this right-brain–left-brain shorthand, we refer to such companies as "bothbrain." They successfully generate and commercialize creative new concepts year in and year out. (See the sidebar "Hemispheric Conditions.") When nonfashion executives pause and reflect, they often realize that similar partnerships were behind many innovations in their own companies or industries.

The world's most innovative companies often operate under some variation of a BothBrain partnership. In technology the creative partner might be a brilliant engineer like Bill Hewlett and the business executive a savvy manager like David Packard. In the auto industry the team might be a "car guy" like Hal Sperlich—a major creative force behind both the original Ford Mustang and the first Chrysler minivan—and a management wizard like Lee Iacocca. The former track coach Bill Bowerman developed Nike's running shoes; his partner, Phil Knight, handled manufacturing, finance, and sales. Howard Schultz conceived the iconic Starbucks coffeehouse format, and CEO Orin Smith oversaw the chain's rapid growth. Apple may have the best-known BothBrain partnership. CEO Steve Jobs has always acted as the creative director and has helped to shape everything from product design and user interfaces to the customer experience at Apple's stores. COO Tim Cook has long handled the day-to-day running of the business. (It remains to be seen, of course, how Apple will fare given Jobs's current leave of absence.)

No industry has gone further than fashion, however, to incorporate Both-Brain partnerships in its organizational model. Of course it makes no sense for other kinds of companies to copy the fashion template exactly. But Procter & Gamble, Pixar, and BMW are among those that have borrowed heavily from fashion's approach and enjoyed remarkable results.

The Fashion Model

Fashion companies understand one fundamental truth about human beings, a truth overlooked by all the organizations that try to teach their left-brain accountants and analysts to be more creative: Creativity is a distinct personality trait. Many people have very little of it, accomplished though they may be in other areas, and they won't learn it from corporate creativity programs. Other people are inordinately creative, both by nature and by long training. They are right-brain

Hemispheric Conditions

So-called left-brain or right-brain capabilities don't always reside purely in the eponymous regions of the cerebral cortex. But most of us have strongly preferred approaches for drawing on our brains to solve problems, and few of us are extraordinarily skilled at drawing on all regions of the brain.

Roger Sperry earned the Nobel Prize for Medicine in 1981 for his work with epileptic patients whose corpora callosa—the bundles of nerves connecting their left and right hemispheres—had been severed. When the two hemispheres could no longer communicate with each other, their differences became more obvious.

For most people, the left hemisphere is better at processing language, logic, numbers, sequential ordering, and linear functions. It does well in mathematics, reading, planning, scheduling, and organizing. The right brain specializes in nonverbal ideation and holistic synthesizing. It is better at handling images, music, colors, and patterns. Right-brain processing happens quickly, in nonsequential fashion.

Almost nothing in people's heads is processed solely by one hemisphere; both contribute to nearly everything. But they do so in different ways, and people's cognitive preferences exhibit significant differences. That may stem from a kind of bodily winner-take-all phenomenon. "We use the best of what we have," explains the psychologist Robert Ornstein, a professor at Stanford and the chairman of the Institute for the Study of Human Knowledge. "The left and right hands aren't completely different in writing ability, but a right-hander would never use the left if she didn't have to. So even if one hemisphere is only 20% better than the other, there will be a big difference in how it's used in normal practice." Just as there are right-handers and left-handers, most people tend to think in ways that we can reasonably characterize as right brain and left brain.

dominant. Innovation comes as naturally to them as music did to Mozart, and like Mozart, they have cultivated their skills over the years. The first lesson from fashion is this: If you don't have highly creative people in positions of real authority, you won't get innovation. Most companies in other industries ignore this lesson.

It isn't just innovation in the usual sense of products and patents that fashion companies pursue. Their creative people typically imagine a whole picture and see every innovation as a part that has to fit that whole. They are less concerned with perfecting any one component than with creating a brand statement that enhances the entire customer experience. At Gucci Group, for example, creative directors concern themselves with anything that affects the customer—the look and feel of retail stores, the typography of ads, and the quality of postsale service as well as the design of new products. Not every facet of the brand has to meet the narrow profit-and-loss test that many nonfashion companies require of their innovations. Gucci may only break even on its latest runway apparel, but those designs generate excitement among shoppers, who feel that they are sharing in the glamour of high fashion when they buy a Gucci item. Similarly, Starbucks doesn't maximize sales per square foot in its cafés (heresy to many competitors), because it allows—even encourages—customers to linger for hours over a cup or two of coffee. Yet that innovative, homelike environment is precisely what distinguishes the chain from other coffee shops in the eyes of the customer.

Conventional companies look at innovation differently, and wrongly. Without creative people in top positions, they typically focus on innovations that can be divided and conquered rather than those that must be integrated and harmonized. They break their innovations into smaller and smaller components and then pass them from function to function to be optimized in sequence. The logic is simple: Improving the most important pieces of the most important processes will create the best results. But breakthrough innovation doesn't work that way. What if a movie studio hired the best actors, scriptwriters, cinematographers, and so on, but neglected to engage a director? The manufacturers of several portable music players tout technical specifications that are apparently superior to those of Apple's iPod. Yet they continue to lose sales and profits to Apple, because the iPod offers an overall experience—including shopping, training, downloading, listening, and servicing—that the others have not yet matched. Little wonder that many companies may increase their patent portfolios yet grow disillusioned with their innovation efforts.

What is required to harness this kind of creativity and apply it to the needs of a business? Creative people can't do it alone: They're likely to fall in love with an idea and never know when to quit. But conventional businesspeople can't do it alone either; they rarely even know where to start. And a true BothBrain individual—a Leonardo da Vinci, say, who is equally adept at artistic and analytic pursuits—is exceedingly rare. So innovation requires teamwork. Fashion companies have learned to establish and maintain effective partnerships between creative people and numbers-oriented people. They structure the business so that the partners can run it effectively, and they ensure that each is clear about what decisions are his or hers to make. These companies have also learned to foster right-brain–left-brain collaboration at every level, and so continue to attract the kind of talent on which their survival depends.

People: Building Effective Partnerships

To anyone outside the fashion industry, it's astonishing how commonly designers team up with talented business executives. Until 2003 Calvin Klein's business alter ego was Barry Schwartz. The pair grew up together in the same New

Paired for Innovation

Left Brain
• Rational, logical, linear
• Sequential analytic processing
• Language, grammar, verbal
• Literal
• Objective
• Time-sensitive
• Accuracy

Right Brain
• Imaginative, intuitive, whimsical
• Holistic framing, pattern synthesis
• Visualization, pictures, gestures
• Perceptual, metaphorical
• Subjective
• Time-free
• Ambiguity, paradox

Hewlett-Packard	
David Packard	Bill Hewlett

Both trained as engineers, but Packard became the executive leader and Hewlett supplied the engineering spark.

Parfums Chanel	
Pierre Wertheimer	Coco Chanel

Perfume legend Coco Chanel teamed up with Wertheimer to provide business discipline to her fledgling enterprise.

Pixar	
John Walker	Brad Bird

Creative tension between the producer Walker and the director Bird sharpens the resulting movies.

York City neighborhood and had been partners since the beginning of the Calvin Klein label. Marc Jacobs, the creative director of Louis Vuitton and Marc Jacobs International, relies on his longtime partner, Robert Duffy, to manage the business. "Marc Jacobs is not Marc Jacobs," he told *Fortune* magazine. "Marc Jacobs is Marc Jacobs and Robert Duffy, or Robert Duffy and Marc Jacobs, whichever way you want to put it." Yves Saint Laurent partnered with Pierre Bergé, Miuccia Prada with Patrizio Bertelli, Valentino Garavani with Giancarlo Giammetti.

Most of these well-known teams date back years. But a partnership may not work out, or one of the duo may move on, so creating new partnerships is among a leader's chief tasks. Soon after the Unilever veteran Robert Polet became the chief executive of Gucci Group, in 2004, he replaced the CEO of the flagship brand and eliminated two of the three creative directorships attached to it. His new appointments were controversial. Mark Lee, who had been heading the money-losing Yves Saint Laurent brand, became the Gucci brand's CEO. Frida Giannini, in her early thirties at the time, became its sole creative director. Innovation flourished, and the Gucci brand's revenues grew by 46% during the four years of the partnership (Lee has since decided to leave Gucci).

Building a strong partnership isn't simply a matter of throwing two individuals together, of course. "It's truly like a marriage," Polet told *Time* magazine in 2006. "It has ups and downs, and you have disagreement, [but] with a common purpose and within a common framework." Polet may be understating the contentiousness that often characterizes these relationships. Some—like some marriages—don't work at all. (Think of Steve Jobs and his earlier partner at Apple, John Sculley.) Many others are punctuated by shouting matches, temporary separations, and similar signs of intense discord. Marc Jacobs sometimes infuriated Robert Duffy. The Pixar director Brad Bird and the producer John Walker are "famous for fighting openly," Bird has been quoted as saying, "because he's got to get it done and I've got to make it as good as it can be before it gets done."

Some of the tension between partners is productive. ("Our movies aren't cheap, but the money gets on the screen because we're open in our conflict," says Bird, the Oscar-winning director of *The Incredibles* and *Ratatouille*.) And some of it is destructive, dooming the relationship. The executive who oversees a brand should have finely honed matchmaking skills—but should also be ready to order a divorce when required.

You can improve the chances that a partnership will work. Here's how:

Define a partnership-friendly structure. What should the partners be in charge of? The scale and scope of an innovation unit depend on both the company and the industry. Robert Polet's arrival at Gucci Group followed the departure of the famously successful designer-executive team of Tom Ford and Domenico De Sole. Ford had served as creative director for all the group's brands, including Yves Saint Laurent and Bottega Veneta. Polet thought this centralized structure stretched Ford's creative genius too thin. "The business model—I call it one size fits all—hasn't worked for all the brands," he said in 2004. "They have the same target consumer, the same retail strategy, and a central creative direction I'm not sure has worked well for all." Polet made each brand a unit of innovation, established a creative-commercial partnership at the top of it, and asked the partners to focus on the needs of a distinct group of consumers.

Such decentralization usually deepens insights into customer opportunities and competitor vulnerabilities and allows greater creative freedom. It's vital, however, to have an organizational structure that balances the benefits of decentralization with the efficiency of centralization. Otherwise a company will go through repeated cycles of spawning lots of local innovations to keep growing revenues in good times and then reversing course to achieve efficiencies in downturns. Danone's dairy division found that balance recently by shifting more innovation responsibilities from regional offices to a centralized team made up of both creative and commercial people. The regional groups had developed several great products, including the popular "probiotic" drink Actimel. But Danone's new-product portfolio came to contain too many regional products with limited scale and poor financial returns. The centralized team conducted global research to assess opportunities and make the necessary trade-offs. It was able to invest enough marketing dollars to turn Actimel into one of the company's fastest-growing global brands.

Executives at conventional companies often hamper innovation by failing to distinguish between innovation units and capability platforms. Innovation units are profit centers—similar to business units. They may be defined by brands, product lines, customer segments, geographic regions, or other boundaries. Their work involves choosing which customers to serve, which products and services to offer, which competitors to challenge, and which capabilities to draw upon. What they have in common is that the innovation buck stops there. The units' leaders have to balance creative aspirations with commercial realities, which is why a partnership at this level is so important.

Capability platforms, on the other hand, are cost centers. They build competencies that innovation units can share. Shared platforms create economies of scale, allowing a company to make investments that individual businesses could not afford and to take risks that smaller units could not tolerate. Like innovation units, capability platforms should also be sources of competitive advantage. In a fashion house they might include distribution and logistics facilities, color and fabric libraries, and advertising-media purchasing services. A company should create capability platforms only when its innovation units will choose to "buy" from them rather than to develop the capabilities independently or acquire them from outsiders. Innovation units own their final results, so they must also own as many capability-sourcing decisions as possible. Protectionist policies that force them to use substandard corporate resources hamper innovation.

Establish roles and decision rights. Some years ago two psychologists at Cornell University wrote an article titled "Unskilled and Unaware of It: How Difficulties in Recognizing One's Own Incompetence Lead to Inflated Self-Assessments." The title alone captures a pitfall for left-brainers: Unskilled at coming up with breakthrough innovations, they may nevertheless believe they are good at evaluating them. They are usually wrong. Joseph Stalin allegedly denounced a Dmitri Shostakovich composition as "chaos instead of music," banning for almost 30 years a work by the man many music critics have called the most talented Soviet composer of his generation.

Many companies nevertheless give left-brain analytic types an opportunity to approve ideas at various stages of the innovation process. This is a cardinal error. Uncreative people have an annoying tendency to kill good ideas, encourage bad ones, and—if they don't see something they like—demand multiple rounds of "improvements." They add time, cost, and frustration to the innovation process even in a boom. In a downturn the effect is magnified. Financial analysts are sent in to prune the new-product portfolio. Charged with reducing costs, they often clumsily break up whatever partnerships exist and get rid of the creative people who were essential to them.

A better approach, in any economic environment, is what Polet has called "freedom within the framework"—a well-defined division of responsibility that plays to both partners' strengths. At Gucci the CEO and creative director of each of the group's 10 businesses work together to craft a sentence that captures the essence of the brand. Then each brand's CEO establishes the framework within which creative decisions will be made: objectives, methods for accomplishing them, budget constraints, and so on. He or she maps out a three-year plan showing the brand's strategic direction and projected financial performance. During tough times the financial resources may be limited, but the CEO and the creative director decide together how to deal with those constraints.

Product development occurs within this context. Merchandisers working under the brand's chief executive develop market grids showing customer segments, competitive products, and price ranges. If there's an opening on the grid, it becomes the target for a new product: a handbag, say, for a specific niche, with a particular price point and a particular margin. Product specialists offer options for materials and manufacturing processes. The creative director then takes over, with full freedom to create a product that meets those specifications. If trade-offs have to be made, the creative director calls the shots, so long as the specs aren't violated. The ultimate judge of the innovation is the marketplace, not a higher-ranking individual or committee within the organization.

Foster talent and nurture collaboration. The partnerships at the top of fashion companies are the most visible. But BothBrain organizations like Gucci understand the importance of replicating these partnerships at all levels of the company. They hire both right-brain and left-brain people. They make sure that both types have strong mentors and career paths that suit their aspirations. They seek to extend and capitalize on individuals' distinctive strengths rather than constantly struggling against deeply ingrained cognitive preferences. When the organizations find partnerships that work well, they create opportunities for those people to work together as frequently as possible.

The particulars, of course, will vary from one company to another. At Gucci the creative directors are responsible for hiring other creative people who, the directors believe, will live and breathe the values of a particular brand. Gucci's human resources director, Karen Lombardo, says she looks for competencies and personality traits that foster teamwork. Are job candidates comfortable with ambiguity? Can they accept the fact that they don't have control over the final product? Can they function well in an environment without detailed job descriptions? Gucci also runs a program to develop leaders on the commercial side. One of its goals is to make leaders more aware of different styles of thinking and communicating, including their own.

Chris Bangle, until 2009 the design head and de facto creative director at BMW, described his job as "balancing art and commerce"—which, he said, required that he "protect the creative team" and "safeguard the artistic process." That meant knowing his designers well enough to let them wrestle with the fuzzy front end in ways that improved ideas rather than killing them prematurely. It also meant knowing the right moment to intercede and shift the focus of product development from design to engineering, so that designers didn't "tweak and tinker forever." Bangle made a point of fighting to preserve the integrity of designers' creations, thus gaining their trust, even though he might eventually decide to kill a particular concept. (See "The Ultimate Creativity Machine: How BMW Turns Art into Profit," HBR, January 2001.)

Transferring the Model to Other Industries

Maintaining the balance in a creative-commercial partnership is always difficult. When Polet joined Gucci, he found a company with a strong design culture. What its people needed, he believed, was an equally powerful appreciation for the commercial aspects of the business.

He started the rebalancing process by setting ambitious targets for sales and earnings growth: The Gucci brand, which accounted for 60% of revenues and most of the group's operating profits, would double sales within seven years, and almost all the money-losing brands would turn profitable within three years. To reach these objectives, Polet moved the organization's focus away from personalities and toward the brands themselves. Its advertising messages abandoned heady runway fashions in favor of products that core customers actually bought. He spoke frequently about making the brand, not the talent, the star. He selected creative directors who shared his philosophy and were more passionate about the product than about potential celebrity. He stressed teamwork over one-man or one-woman shows, encouraging a "culture of interchange" among brands, geographies, and management levels. He established quarterly management committee meetings, annual leadership conferences for the top 200 managers, and a variety of experience-sharing meetings for other functional experts.

Polet also challenged the conventional wisdom that customer research was irrelevant to luxury goods; he commissioned an international focus group of 600 Gucci customers along with regular reviews of the customer feedback by Gucci executives. He encouraged his managers to learn from successful competitors—among them Zara, a Spanish apparel retailer that produces inexpensive interpretations of designer goods in cycles as short as two weeks rather than the traditional six to eight months. (The suggestion that an eight-month production cycle was unnecessarily long reportedly so angered one senior executive that he stormed out of the meeting.)

Though Polet's changes were often controversial, they worked. All but one of the brands met their three-year plans, several ahead of schedule. Results were so impressive that *Fortune* named Robert Polet Europe Businessman of the Year for 2007.

Can the rebalancing process work in the opposite direction—that is, can non-fashion companies boost their right-brain potential by learning fashion's lessons? The experience of Procter & Gamble under A.G. Lafley suggests that they can. Lafley became CEO of P&G in June 2000. From the beginning he believed that creativity was a missing ingredient in the company's innovation strategy. P&G's technical innovations lacked the design elements that create holistic, emotional experiences for consumers and build their passion for brands. Believing that design could become a game changer for the company, Lafley set out to shake up the culture by increasing the flow of creativity. He proclaimed, "P&G's ambition is to become a top design company as part of becoming the innovation leader in its industry."

In 2001 Lafley tapped Claudia Kotchka from the package design department to create P&G's first global design division. Kotchka reported directly to him, which sent a strong signal to the organization. The company hired about 150 midcareer designers over five years—another powerful signal. Lafley established a design advisory board, bringing in outside experts at least three times a year to examine and shape innovations. Kotchka and Lafley also launched Design Thinking, an initiative to teach new ways of listening, learning, visualizing, and prototyping. They redesigned corporate offices and other venues to open up work spaces and encourage collaboration. They built innovation centers around the world, replicating home and shopping environments to encourage cocreation insights with consumers and retail partners. Realizing that designers tend to "listen with their eyes," Lafley encouraged research that focused less on what customers said than on what drove their emotions, beliefs, and behaviors.

Inside a converted brewery on Cincinnati's Clay Street, P&G built an innovation design studio. Conference rooms there are filled with whiteboards, chalkboards, toys, and crayons. When a significant opportunity or challenge surfaces at P&G, team members from a variety of functions are released from their regular responsibilities for several weeks to immerse themselves in creative problem solving at Clay Street. Skilled facilitators train and guide the group. Experts from both inside and outside P&G are called in to provide opinions. The studio seeks to create "Eureka!" moments, and Lafley claims that every team that has gone to Clay Street has had one.

Under Lafley, P&G's organic growth has averaged 6%—twice the average for the categories in which it competes—and its stock reached record highs before the current downturn. Its cultural transformation has produced such positive results that *Chief Executive* magazine named Lafley CEO of the Year in 2006.

Both Polet and Lafley launched their transformation programs as new CEOs (Polet came from outside Gucci; Lafley had spent 23 years at P&G). They both set compelling and credible objectives, making it clear that the goal was to accelerate profitable growth as well as to increase creativity. Both focused on the need for greater collaboration and teamwork, increasing respect for the unique talents of all cognitive styles in the organization and emphasizing simultaneous cooperation rather than development processes that passed innovation decisions from one function to another. Both also strengthened mechanisms for listening to customers, though in somewhat different ways. And both started by building on legendary cultural strengths—Gucci's design talents and P&G's brand-management skills. The difference, of course, lay in the starting points of their organizations and, therefore, in the priorities and specific techniques each relied on. They used hiring, development, and talent management programs to rebalance their cultures—more left brain here, more right brain there.

Any executive with half a brain knows that innovation is essential to success. The problem is that it takes both halves of a brain to make it happen—the imaginative, holistic right brain and the rational, analytic left brain.

Consider the wide range of activities that might be necessary to improve innovation significantly. Management might need better visioning skills to foster a culture of curiosity and greater risk taking—primarily right-brain activities. Left-brain analytic tools might be needed to steer innovation investments toward the most promising areas. The business might need more creativity to generate ideas, but also analytics to constrain unprofitable projects. The right-brain design process might not be strong enough to transform intriguing ideas into practical products. Or the analytic left brains might need to fund the product pipeline to favor a different mix of large and small bets. Sometimes the products are fine but marketing needs to create stronger, more emotional bonds with customers, or engineers need to boost efficiency and profitability through improvements in cost or quality.

BothBrain organizations recognize that such changes won't necessarily happen all at once. They put together people with the necessary brain orientation in the right places and at the right times. Indeed, we frequently find BothBrain principles flourishing and innovation thriving in some parts of an organization even as other parts languish. Many executives have struggled to recognize and replicate the patterns of success—a decidedly right-brain task. But with BothBrain hypotheses firmly in mind, you can apply left-brain scientific testing methods. One way to get started is to pick two or three business areas in which substantial innovations feel important and achievable, despite today's sluggish economy. Build creative-commercial partnerships with exceptional leaders, even if that means moving key team members around. Give them bold challenges and freedom within a framework. Create a strong capability platform or two. Then track the results, including innovation levels, customer behaviors, financial performance, and cultural health.

We suspect you'll say what Robert Polet told us: "I could never go back to the conventional way of doing business."

The Future of Shopping

Successful companies will engage customers through "omnichannel" retailing: a mashup of digital and physical experiences.

Darrell Rigby

This article was published at the end of 2011. Way back then, many traditional retailers hoped that the future it described (which threatened to cannibalize sales from their physical stores) would prove to be a distant and exaggerated risk. But by the end of the 2012 holiday season, digital retailing had reached an undeniable tipping point. Online sales flourished while store sales disappointed. Many retailers began to wonder if their precious stores had turned into costly liabilities.

However, some companies are thriving—those developing "omnichannel" strategies to creatively and seamlessly integrate the best of both online and offline worlds. They are helping customers to shop however and whenever they want. With the rapid advances in mobile computers—more commonly called smartphones or tablets—the leaders put previously unimaginable information into the hands of shoppers and store associates. And they are revamping supply chains to enable stores to double as fulfillment centers capable of next-day or even same-day deliveries. The question today: How many companies will evolve in this omnichannel world faster than their customers do?

It's a snowy Saturday in Chicago, but Amy, age 28, needs resort wear for a Caribbean vacation. Five years ago, in 2011, she would have headed straight for the mall. Today she starts shopping from her couch by launching a videoconference with her personal concierge at Danella, the retailer where she bought two outfits the previous month. The concierge recommends several items, superimposing photos of them onto Amy's avatar. Amy rejects a couple of items immediately, toggles to another browser tab to research customer reviews and prices, finds better deals on several items at another retailer, and orders them. She buys one item from Danella online and then drives to the Danella store near her for the in-stock items she wants to try on.

HBR December 2011

As Amy enters Danella, a sales associate greets her by name and walks her to a dressing room stocked with her online selections—plus some matching shoes and a cocktail dress. She likes the shoes, so she scans the bar code into her smartphone and finds the same pair for $30 less at another store. The sales associate quickly offers to match the price, and encourages Amy to try on the dress. It is daring and expensive, so Amy sends a video to three stylish friends, asking for their opinion. The responses come quickly: three thumbs down. She collects the items she wants, scans an Internet site for coupons (saving an additional $73), and checks out with her smartphone.

As she heads for the door, a life-size screen recognizes her and shows a special offer on an irresistible summer-weight top. Amy checks her budget online, smiles, and uses her phone to scan the customized Quick Response code on the screen. The item will be shipped to her home overnight.

This scenario is fictional, but it's neither as futuristic nor as fanciful as you might think. All the technology Amy uses is already available—and within five years, much of it will be ubiquitous. But what seems like a dream come true for the shopper—an abundance of information, near-perfect price transparency, a parade of special deals—is already feeling more like a nightmare for many retailers. Companies such as Tower Records, Circuit City, Linens 'n Things, and Borders are early victims—and there will be more.

Every 50 years or so, retailing undergoes this kind of disruption. A century and a half ago, the growth of big cities and the rise of railroad networks made possible the modern department store. Mass-produced automobiles came along 50 years later, and soon shopping malls lined with specialty retailers were dotting the newly forming suburbs and challenging the city-based department stores. The 1960s and 1970s saw the spread of discount chains—Walmart, Kmart, and the like—and, soon after, big-box "category killers" such as Circuit City and Home Depot, all of them undermining or transforming the old-style mall. Each wave of change doesn't eliminate what came before it, but it reshapes the landscape and redefines consumer expectations, often beyond recognition. Retailers relying on earlier formats either adapt or die out as the new ones pull volume from their stores and make the remaining volume less profitable.

Like most disruptions, digital retail technology got off to a shaky start. A bevy of Internet-based retailers in the 1990s—Amazon.com, Pets.com, and pretty much everythingelse.com—embraced what they called online shopping or electronic commerce. These fledgling companies ran wild until a combination of ill-conceived strategies, speculative gambles, and a slowing economy burst the dot-com bubble. The ensuing collapse wiped out half of all e-commerce retailers and provoked an abrupt shift from irrational exuberance to economic reality.

Today, however, that economic reality is well established. The research firm Forrester estimates that e-commerce is now approaching $200 billion in revenue in the United States alone and accounts for 9% of total retail sales, up from 5% five years ago. The corresponding figure is about 10% in the United Kingdom, 3% in Asia-Pacific, and 2% in Latin America. Globally, digital retailing is probably headed toward 15% to 20% of total sales, though the proportion will vary significantly by sector. Moreover, much digital retailing is now highly profitable. Amazon's five-year average return on investment, for example, is 17%, whereas traditional discount and department stores average 6.5%.

What we are seeing today is only the beginning. Soon it will be hard even to define e-commerce, let alone measure it. Is it an e-commerce sale if the customer goes to a store, finds that the product is out of stock, and uses an in-store terminal to have another location ship it to her home? What if the customer is shopping in one store, uses his smartphone to find a lower price at another, and then orders it electronically for in-store pickup? How about gifts that are ordered from a website but exchanged at a local store? Experts estimate that digital information already influences about 50% of store sales, and that number is growing rapidly.

As it evolves, digital retailing is quickly morphing into something so different that it requires a new name: omnichannel retailing. The name reflects the fact that retailers will be able to interact with customers through countless channels—websites, physical stores, kiosks, direct mail and catalogs, call centers, social media, mobile devices, gaming consoles, televisions, networked appliances, home services, and more. Unless conventional merchants adopt an entirely new perspective—one that allows them to integrate disparate channels into a single seamless omnichannel experience—they are likely to be swept away.

An Industry Stuck in Analog

Why will digital retailing continue to grow so fast? Why won't it peak sometime soon, or even implode the way it did the last time around? Anyone who has shopped extensively online knows at least part of the answer. The selection is vast yet remarkably easy to search. The prices are good and easily compared. It's convenient: You can do it at home or at work, without using gasoline or fighting to park. Half of online purchases are delivered free to U.S. consumers—up 10 percentage points over the past two years. Many returns are free as well. Product reviews and recommendations are extensive. Little wonder that the average American Customer Satisfaction Index score for online retailers such as Amazon (87 points) is 11 points higher than the average for physical discount and department stores.

The advantages of digital retailing are increasing as innovations flood the market. For instance, Amazon has already earned valuable patents on keystone innovations such as 1-Click checkout and an online system that allows consumers to exchange unwanted gifts even before receiving them. Digital retailers drive innovation by spending heavily on recruiting, wages, and bonuses to attract and retain top technical talent. They were also among the first to utilize cloud computing (which dramatically lowers entry and operating costs) and to enhance marketing efficiency through social networks and online advertising.

Customers are out in front of this omnichannel revolution. By 2014 almost every mobile phone in the United States will be a smartphone connected to the Internet, and an estimated 40% of Americans will use tablets such as the iPad. If you doubt whether consumers are ready for technology-driven retail solutions, find a "dumb" video display in any public location and look for fingerprints on the screen—evidence that people expected it to be an interactive touchscreen experience.

Meanwhile, traditional retailers are lagging badly. Online sales account for less than 2% of revenue at Walmart and Target. Nor are traditional retailers pioneering digital innovations in other channels, such as mobile shopping and call centers, or seamlessly integrating these technologies in their most important channel—physical stores.

It's not surprising that these retailers are bringing up the rear. As a consultant, I often walk through stores with senior retail leaders whose knowledge of physical retailing is impressive: They know precisely where a fixture should be, exactly how lighting is likely to affect sales, and which colors work best in which departments. As a group, however, they are shockingly subpar in computer literacy. Some retail executives still rely on their assistants to print out e-mails. Some admit that they have never bought anything online. Technophobic culture permeates many great retail organizations. Their IT systems are often old and clunky, and knowledgeable young computer geeks shun them as places to work.

But it isn't just computer illiteracy that holds traditional retailers back. Four other factors are at work as well.

Retailers were burned by e-commerce hype during the dot-com bubble. Many created separate online organizations to maximize valuations. The separate organizations targeted different customer segments, inhibited collaboration, and created serious frictions and jealousies. When the predictions of dot-com domination proved wildly optimistic, overpriced acquisitions began failing, and store organizations smugly celebrated. A decade later, real collaboration between retailers' store and digital operations remains rare.

Digital retailing threatens existing store economics, measurement systems, and incentives. Traditional retailers live and die with changes in same-store sales, in-store sales per labor hour, and compensation systems based on such metrics. That was fine when online sales were 2% to 3% of revenues, but the whole system falls apart when that number reaches 15% to 20%.

Retailers tend to focus on the wrong financial metric: profit margins. If a change dilutes margins, it's bad. But Bain's research shows that retailers' stock prices are driven by return on invested capital and growth rather than by margins. Amazon's five-year operating margin is only 4%—far below the 6% average for discount and department stores. But with faster inventory turns and no physical store assets, Amazon's return on invested capital is more than double the average for conventional retailers. As a result, Amazon's market value, $100 billion, is roughly equivalent to that of Target, Best Buy, Staples, Nordstrom, Sears, J.C. Penney, Macy's, and Kohl's combined.

Conventional retailers haven't had great experiences with breakthrough innovation. They are most comfortable with incremental improvements and with following the well-known dictum "Retail is detail." Too many store reinvention programs have launched with great fanfare, only to die unceremonious deaths. Propose a more novel approach and retailers will ask why, if it's such a good idea, nobody else is doing it.

Retailers tend to believe that their customers will always be there. But as customers grow more comfortable with omnichannel shopping, they grow less tolerant of what they encounter in stores. Sales associates are hard to find. When you find one, he or she doesn't know much about the merchandise. Stockouts are frequent, checkout lines long, returns cumbersome.

An omnichannel world, in short, represents a major crisis for traditional retailers. Customers are passing them by. Online players are gaining. To keep up, existing retailers will need to create an omnichannel strategy—and pick up the pace of change.

Redesign Shopping from Scratch

The first part of any such strategy is facing reality. Retailing executives must acknowledge that the new technologies will get faster, cheaper, and more versatile. They need to forecast the likely digital density in their categories and prepare for the effects. What should I do differently today if I believe that 20% of our sales will soon come from digital retailing—and that 80% of our sales will be heavily influenced by it? Should we be opening any new stores at all? And if so, how different should they be? How should we adjust to a world of greater price transparency? What happens when traffic-building categories shift online and no longer pull customers into our stores?

Situations like these call for start-from-scratch, across-the-board innovation. In the book *Idealized Design: How to Dissolve Tomorrow's Crisis . . . Today,* co-author Russell L. Ackoff recounts a similar turning point at Bell Labs in 1951. The vice president in charge of the labs asked a group to name the organization's most important contributions to telephonic communications. The VP pointed out that each one, including the telephone dial and the coaxial cable, had been conceived and implemented before 1900. He challenged the group to assume

How Fast Is Your Industry Moving Online?

Online competition increases predictably as online prices, selection, convenience, and customer trust improve relative to physical stores. Here's how three industries scored for key drivers (1 = low; 5 = high). Try this yourself: If your total is between 30 and 35, digital capabilities are or will soon be a strategic priority for your firm. If it's below 30, you should focus on developing digital tools to build traffic, enhance in-store experience, and increase basket size before competitors do.

	Books	Apparel and accessories	Groceries
Price			
Prices often lower online (delivered)	5	3	1
Digitized products create lower costs	5	1	1
Value of price comparisons	5	3	2
Selection			
Value of broad assortments	5	4	3
Value of customization	2	3	1
Searches in stores often futile	4	3	2
Convenience			
Research and information intensity	5	3	2
Web tools trump store experience	4	2	2
Ease of delivery and returns	5	3	1
Trust			
Reliability of product descriptions	5	2	2
Frustration in stores	4	4	2
Trust in online retailers	5	3	1
Total	**54**	**34**	**20**

that the phone system was dead and had to be rebuilt from scratch. What would it look like? How would it work? Soon Bell's scientists and engineers were busy investigating completely new technologies—and came up with concepts for push-button phones, call waiting, call forwarding, voicemail, conference calls, and mobile phones. Retailers need the same start-over mentality.

The design specifications of omnichannel retailing are growing clearer by the day. Customers want everything. They want the advantages of digital, such as broad selection, rich product information, and customer reviews and tips. They want the advantages of physical stores, such as personal service, the ability to touch products, and shopping as an event and an experience. (Online merchants take note.) Different customer segments will value parts of the shopping experience differently, but all are likely to want perfect integration of the digital and the physical.

The challenge for a retailer is to create innovations that bring the vision to life, wowing those customers and generating profitable growth. Let's see what this might mean in practice.

The Threat Threshold for Physical Retailers

As e-commerce sales for U.S. retailers climb, store-based companies face treacherous landscape ahead. In books, the path above 15% digital penetration first brought consolidation; then Borders closed stores, filed for bankruptcy, and liquidated. The largest store-based retailer, Barnes & Noble, lost money in fiscal 2011 and struggled to raise additional funding. Physical retailers of music, videos, and consumer electronics face similar challenges. Even apparel and accessories, once considered too experiential to sell online, could approach tipping points in the next five years.

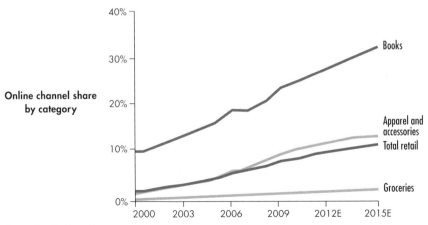

Source: Forrester Research

Pathways and pain points. Retailers traditionally defined their job with three simple imperatives: Stock products you think your target customers will want. Cultivate awareness of what's in the store. When prospective customers enter the store, make it enticing and easy for them to buy. The job in an omnichannel world is more complex. Products themselves can more easily be customized to the preferences of individuals or small groups. Shoppers' awareness depends not solely on company-generated marketing efforts but also on online expert reviews or recommendations from friends on Facebook and Twitter. The shopping experience includes not just visiting the store but searching for various vendors, comparing prices, quick and hassle-free returns, and so on.

Retailers today have a variety of precision tools that they can apply to discrete parts of these shopping pathways. Consider the job of creating awareness, which in the past relied mostly on mass-market advertising, promotions, and the like. Today marketers can send coupon codes and offers to customers' mobile devices. They can optimize search terms and location-based promotions. They can provide targeted offers to customers who check in to stores through external platforms like Foursquare. The list of possibilities is getting longer by the day.

Using such tools at each point in the pathway, retailers can identify sets of targeted customers defined by (increasingly) narrow parameters and create appealing interactions. Earlier this year, for example, the U.K. retailer Tesco studied its South Korean operation, known as Home plus, to determine how it could increase grocery sales to time-starved Korean consumers. The answer: Bring the store to the consumers at a point in the day when they had time on their hands. In a pilot program, Home plus covered the walls of Seoul subway stations with remarkably lifelike backlit images of supermarket shelves containing orange juice, fresh vegetables and meat, and hundreds of other items. Consumers wanting to do their food shopping could simply scan each product's Quick Response code into their smartphones, touch an on-screen button, and thereby assemble a virtual shopping cart. Home plus then delivered the physical goods to the shopper's home within a few hours. According to Tesco, more than 10,000 consumers took advantage of the service in the first three months, and online sales increased 130%.

Omnichannel retailers can devise different ways of wowing each target segment. Some segments can be served much the way they were in the past. Others will require more imagination and innovation. Disney, for example, is reimagining its retail stores as entertainment hubs with a variety of interactive displays that will entice all segments of the family to visit more often and stay longer. But retailers will have to devote resources to this search for innovations along the customer's pathways. The trick will be to identify each segment's unique paths

Bringing Digital and Physical Retailing Together

Omnichannel retailing is the way forward for retailers seeking to satisfy customers who increasingly want everything. They want the advantages of digital—such as nearly limitless selection, price transparency at the click of a mouse, and personalized recommendations from friends and experts. They also want the advantages of physical stores—such as face-to-face interaction with store personnel, products available for trying on or trying out, and the social experience of shopping as an event. Different customers will value parts of the shopping experience differently, but all are likely to want perfect integration of the digital and the physical.

Advantages of digital	Advantages of physical
Rich product information	Edited assortment
Customer reviews and tips	Shopping as an event and an experience
Editorial content and advice	Ability to test, try on, or experience products
Social engagement and two-way dialogue	Personal help from caring associates
Broadest selection	Convenient returns
Convenient and fast checkout	Instant access to products
Price comparison and special deals	Help with initial setup or ongoing repairs
Convenience of anything, anytime, anywhere access	Instant gratification of all senses

and pain points and create tailored solutions rather than the one-size-fits-all approach that has characterized much retailing in the past.

The experience of shopping. Traditional retailers have suffered more than they probably realize at the hands of Amazon and other online companies. As volume trickles from the stores and sales per square foot decline, the response of most retailers is almost automatic: Cut labor, reduce costs, and sacrifice service. But that only exacerbates the problem. With even less service to differentiate the stores, customers focus increasingly on price and convenience, which strengthens the advantages of online retailers.

If traditional retailers hope to survive, they have to turn the one big feature that Internet retailers lack—stores—from a liability into an asset. Stores will continue to exist in any foreseeable future—and they can be an effective competitive weapon. Research shows that physical stores boost online purchases: One European retailer, for instance, reports that it captures nearly 5% of online sales in areas near its physical stores, but only 3% outside those areas. Online and offline experiences can be complementary.

The traditional store, however, won't be sufficient. For too many people, shopping in a store is simply a chore to be endured: If they can find ways to avoid it, they will. But what if visiting a store were exciting, entertaining, emotionally engaging? What if it were as much fun as going to the movies or going out to dinner—and what if you could get the kind of experience with products that is simply unavailable online?

This is hardly beyond the realm of possibility. Jordan's Furniture, a New England chain, achieves some of the highest furniture sales productivity in the country by using themed "streets" within its stores, a Mardi Gras show, an IMAX 3-D theater, a laser light show, food courts, a city constructed of jellybeans, a motion-simulation ride, a water show, a trapeze school, and special charity events. Cabela's and Bass Pro Shops not only have some of the highest-rated websites; they also have some of the most engaging physical stores. These kinds of store experiences are expensive to create. Might digital technology improve the customer experience in stores more cost-effectively?

In fact, it is already doing so. Digital technology can replace lifeless storefront windows with vibrant interactive screens that change with the weather or time of day and are capable of generating recommendations or taking orders when the store is closed. It can allow customers to design products or assemble outfits and display their creations in high-visibility locations like Times Square. It can create engaging games that attract customers, encourage them to stay longer, and reward them for cocreating innovative ideas.

Digital technology—in the form of tablets, for example—can also give sales associates nearly infinite information about customers, describing the way they like to be treated and creating precise models of their homes or body types that enable perfect choices. It can change pricing and promotions accurately and instantaneously. It can provide customized recommendations. Virtual mirrors accelerate and enliven the dressing room experience by connecting customers with trusted friends. Technology can eliminate checkout lines, capture transaction receipts, file rebate claims, and speed returns. It can give a call center operator full access to a customer's purchase and complaint history.

My objective here is not to enumerate every possible innovation. Rather, it's to illustrate how the opportunities for digital technology in stores, mobile devices, call centers, and other channels are just as abundant and viable as they are for websites. Moreover—and this is key—retailers in many categories can link these channels and technologies to create an omnichannel experience with stores that is superior to a purely digital retail strategy.

One task is to apply these innovations early enough, frequently enough, and broadly enough to change customer perceptions and behaviors. Adopting successful innovations three years after competitors do is unlikely to generate much buzz or traffic. Of course, many digital innovations will fail, and the effects of others will be hard to quantify. So a second task is to upgrade testing and learning skills to 21st-century levels. It was hard enough to gauge the effects of pricing changes, store-format upgrades, or newspaper versus TV ads in the old world. (Remember John Wanamaker's famous lament that he knew he was wasting half his advertising budget but didn't know which half?) An omnichannel world makes those test-and-learn challenges look like child's play. Retailers must now try to assess the effects of paid search, natural search, e-circulars, digital displays, e-mail campaigns, and other new techniques and third-party innovations such as SCVNGR, a location-based social network game—and must gauge those effects on both physical and digital channels (which include mobile apps as well as the Internet).

Leading-edge companies such as PetSmart and the U.K. pharmacy chain Boots have begun applying science to this task: They are testing digital and physical innovations with clinical-trial-style methodology, using sophisticated software to create control groups and eliminate random variation and other noise. All this is costly, but it's hard to see how retailers can avoid doing more of it.

The Omnichannel Organization

How can retailing companies organize themselves around an omnichannel strategy? Historically, mobilizing an organization to develop and integrate breakthroughs that threaten the base business has been one of management's greatest challenges. Disruptive innovation requires a separate team that has autonomy, a distinctive set of talents, different knowledge bases, and a willingness to take bold risks. Integrating innovative ideas with the base business, in contrast, requires collaboration, compromise, and detailed planning. It's a bit like putting a satellite into orbit. Send it too far from the core and it will drift aimlessly into outer space, wasting money and squandering opportunity. Launch it too close to the core and gravitational forces will overwhelm it, causing it to crash and burn. So mobilizing an organization to both develop and integrate omnichannel innovations is challenging. But it can be done.

One approach is to create separate formal organizational structures but coordinate key decisions—something most retailers failed to do the first time around. Apple launched its online store in 1997, midway through the dot-com bubble. When it began opening retail stores in 2001, the company established its online and offline channels as wholly separate organizations, each challenged to maximize sales without worrying about potential conflicts. At first, collaboration between the units was limited largely to coordinating merchandise assortments, new product release dates, and pricing policies. Fortunately for Apple, its innovative products and unparalleled service trumped its lackluster channel integration. Over time, however, customers began to expect more from a preeminent technology company. Apple increased the level of collaboration, enabling cross-channel returns and using its often frenzied product releases to experiment with new systems for checking a store's inventory or reserving items online for purchase in the stores. When Apple revamped its physical stores in 2011, it replaced information cards near demo products with iPads, which provide extensive information and product comparisons in much the way the online site does. The iPads also give customers information on omnichannel support options, and they can page an in-store specialist for further assistance.

Innovative organizations also need to attract and retain innovative people—imaginative, tech-savvy, often young individuals who spin out new ideas every day. Retailers haven't appealed to many of these innovators in recent years. Now that they must compete with the likes of Amazon and Google, they will have to upgrade their recruitment efforts. They may find some of the people they need buried deep within their own organizations. Others they will find in creative centers such as New York and San Francisco, or around college campuses.

In the past, big retailers have had difficulty hiring innovative people and luring them to headquarters operations in Arkansas or Minnesota or Ohio. And they have had little success creating autonomous disruptive groups and linking those groups to their core operations. But the same technologies that are driving omnichannel strategies can help solve both problems. Desktop videoconferencing, mobile applications, social networks, collaborative groupware, shared knowledge bases, instant messaging, and crowdsourcing not only help Amy shop; they also help Sheldon and Rajesh work together—wherever they may live—and integrate their ideas with their employer's existing capabilities.

The department-store company Macy's may be showing the way here. In February 2009, when Macy's consolidated its U.S. divisions into New York, it conspicuously left a digital team in the heart of Silicon Valley. Since then Macys.com has started to add 400 people to its existing team of 300. To attract and retain talented technologists, the division launched its own recruiting microsite touting its enviable location, fashion glitz, and unique blend of entrepreneurial ingenuity and business acumen. It rapidly expanded its participation in the social media most favored by desirable recruits. It studied the characteristics of its most successful executives and then developed professional training programs in communication skills, time management, effective negotiations, and financial expertise so that recruits had opportunities for advancement. It capitalized on the local network of technology entrepreneurs, venture capitalists, and leading-edge software and hardware providers not only to identify talent but also to catalyze collaboration and new ways of thinking. These organizational strategies have helped Macy's woo and energize technology stars, increase its e-commerce revenue growth to more than 30% a year over the past two years, and attain the top spot on the 2011 L2 Digital IQ Index for specialty retailers.

For most companies, making changes like these is a tall organizational order. Move too slowly and you're in danger of sacrificing leadership and scale, just at a time when market share is shifting rapidly. Move too quickly, however, and you may not have adequate time for testing and learning. The time-honored rule of the judicial system sets the best course: with all deliberate speed. Retailers need to test and learn quickly but refrain from major moves until they know exactly what they hope to gain.

Is it all worth it? A successful omnichannel strategy should not only guarantee a retailer's survival—no small matter in today's environment. It should deliver the kind of revolution in customer expectations and experiences that comes along every 50 years or so. Retailers will find that the digital and physical arenas complement each other instead of competing, thereby increasing sales and lowering costs. Ultimately, we are likely to see more new ideas being implemented as customers and employees propose innovations of their own. In today's environment, information and ideas can flow freely. Retailers that learn to take advantage of both will be well positioned for success.

Customer Focus

Loyalty-Based Management

To build a profitable base of faithful customers, try
loyal employees.

Fred Reichheld

*In the early 1990s we noticed that some companies were dramatically outperforming
their competitors for reasons that couldn't be found in any business-school textbook.
Their secret? Loyalty. These companies treated customers right, inspiring them to
stick around, buy more, and sing the company's praises. Employees, inspired by this
dedication to customers, worked hard and came up with new ideas for ever-better
service. The major development in the two decades since has been the creation of
a practical method—the Net Promoter® system—for measuring loyalty, and for
bringing the voice of the customer directly to frontline employees and managers. Our
clients, thousands of other companies, and Bain itself use Net Promoter score(NPS®)
to gauge their performance in the eyes of customers week in and week out. They use it
to look systematically at their products and services, their operations and procedures,
and their overall customer strategy—and to continually improve on all these fronts.*

*Today, more and more companies are pursuing the goal of enriching the lives of
the people they serve and the people on their payroll. That is a higher calling for all
businesses—and on this dimension loyalty is the prime measure of success.*

Despite a flurry of activities aimed at serving customers better, only a few
companies have achieved meaningful, measurable improvements in customer loyalty. In manufacturing as well as services, business leaders intuitively
know that when customer loyalty goes up, profits do too. Yet few companies have
systematically revamped their operations with customer loyalty in mind.

Instead, most companies adopt improvement programs on an ad hoc basis.
Hearing about the success of a loyalty leader, such as MBNA's credit card business, which loses customers at half the industry rate, companies copy one or
two of MBNA's practices. They set up customer-recovery units, for instance, that

HBR March–April 1993

try to save defecting customers—who, because they are probably less homogeneous than MBNA's customer base, may or may not be profitable. Or they adopt MBNA's policy of delivering employee paychecks in envelopes labeled "Brought to You by the Customer"—while failing to base the bonuses inside those envelopes on incentives that enhance customer value and loyalty. Not surprisingly, payoffs don't materialize.

Building a highly loyal customer base cannot be done as an add-on. It must be integral to a company's basic business strategy. Loyalty leaders like MBNA are successful because they have designed their entire business systems around customer loyalty. They recognize that customer loyalty is earned by consistently delivering superior value. By understanding the economic effects of retention on revenues and costs, loyalty leaders can intelligently reinvest cash flows to acquire and retain high-quality customers and employees. Designing and managing this self-reinforcing system is the key to achieving outstanding customer loyalty.

The economic benefits of high customer loyalty are considerable and, in many industries, explain the differences in profitability among competitors. When a company consistently delivers superior value and wins customer loyalty, market share and revenues go up, and the cost of acquiring and serving customers goes down. Although the additional profits allow the company to invest in new activities that enhance value and increase the appeal to customers, strengthening loyalty generally is not a matter of simply cutting prices or adding product features. The better economics mean the company can pay workers better, which sets off a whole chain of events. Increased pay boosts employee morale and commitment; as employees stay longer, their productivity rises and training costs fall; employees' overall job satisfaction, combined with their knowledge and experience, leads to better service to customers; customers are then more inclined to stay loyal to the company; and as the best customers and employees become part of the loyalty-based system, competitors are inevitably left to survive with less desirable customers and less talented employees.

The forces in a loyalty-based system are cumulative. The longer the cycle continues, the greater the company's financial strength. At MBNA, a 5% increase in retention grows the company's profits by 60% by the fifth year. And at State Farm Insurance Companies, another champion of customer loyalty, small increases in retention create substantial benefits for the company and its policyholders.

Learning how to compete on the basis of loyalty may be complex, but it is not mysterious. It requires, first of all, understanding the relationships between customer retention and the rest of the business and being able to quantify the linkages between loyalty and profits. Only then can daily decisions reflect systematic cost-benefit trade-offs. It involves rethinking four important aspects of the business—customers, product/service offerings, employees, and measurement systems. To get the full benefit of a loyalty-based system, all these facets must be understood and attended to simultaneously because each is essential to the workings of the whole. If any area is overlooked or mis-understood, the system will underperform. When all areas are aligned, they reinforce each other, and the results are outstanding.

The "Right" Customers

Customers are obviously an essential ingredient of a loyalty-based system, and success depends on their staying with the company a long time. But not all cus-tomers are equal. Companies should target the "right" customers—not necessar-ily the easiest to attract or the most profitable in the short term but those who are likely to do business with the company over time. For various reasons, some cus-tomers don't ever stay loyal to one company, no matter what value they receive. The challenge is to avoid as many of these people as possible in favor of custom-ers whose loyalty can be developed.

Demographics and previous purchase history give some indication of a cus-tomer's inherent loyalty. People who buy because of a personal referral tend to be more loyal than those who buy because of an advertisement. Those who buy at the standard price are more loyal than those who buy on price promotion. Home owners, middle-aged people, and rural populations also tend to be loyal, while highly mobile populations are inherently disloyal because they interrupt their business relations each time they move.

But generalizing about the right customer fails to take into account the fact that a customer who is disloyal and therefore expensive for one company may be valuable for another. USAA, a loyalty leader with a remarkable 98% retention rate in its field of auto insurance, has created a steady client base among military officers, a group known for frequent moves. Military officers are not very profit-able for most insurers, but by developing a system tailored to that group's par-ticular needs, USAA has made it possible and economical to keep them.

The heart of USAA's system is a centralized database and telephone-sales force that customers can access from anywhere in the world. The system itself rather than the insurance agent provides continuity with the customer. That con-tinuity works to the customer's and company's advantage. The military officer doesn't have to find a new agent every time he or she is redeployed, and USAA doesn't have to transfer records or create new ones. More important, USAA avoids having to lure a new customer to replace the one it would have lost.

Finding loyal customers requires taking a hard look at what kinds of customers a company can deliver superior value to. If the analysis is done well, that customer segment will be fairly homogeneous, and that homogeneity improves the economics of serving the segment. MBNA, a loyalty leader in the credit card business, provides cards primarily to members of affinity groups such as the American Dental Association or the Georgetown University Alumni Association. Because members in these groups share important qualities, MBNA has been able to understand their common needs and has made adjustments to serve them well. Its data-processing systems are designed so every group can receive customized packages of services. As a result, MBNA keeps its customers once it gets them. When AT&T introduced its Universal Card, other credit card companies lost market share, but MBNA held its ground.

Historical attrition rates can also point the way to the most promising customer segments. Direct marketers such as L.L. Bean have accounting systems that track individual customers year by year. Other companies can get similar information by asking a sample of customers to reconstruct their purchase patterns from various suppliers over the past five years. This will reveal attrition rates and lifetime value for each type of customer.

With knowledge of which customers are likely to be loyal comes knowledge of which customers are not. Companies can then direct resources away from customers who are likely to defect and toward those likely to stay. Special promotions and other kinds of pricing strategies aimed at acquiring new customers often backfire. Companies typically use pricing as a blunt instrument to bring customers in indiscriminately, when instead, they should use pricing to filter out precisely the customers unlikely to be loyal. Cable television companies talk about increasing retention rates but then recruit new customers via price promotions and free sampling—techniques that draw out of the woodwork precisely those customers hardest to keep. Those recruitment efforts merely load the pipeline with people who are inherently disloyal.

Even attempts to recover customers who threaten to leave are often a waste of resources. Investments in service-quality improvements may be counterproductive when they are focused on customers the business actually should get rid of. Auto insurers discovered that certain segments of young drivers were a drag on profits. It took 10 years to break even on them, but due to high attrition, only 10% to 15% would stay that long. The industry also realized that it took at least four years before most companies could break even on the average customer, in part because of the high front-end commission paid to salespeople for signing new customers. If the customer didn't stay with the same insurer for four years, the company never recouped those costs.

Lifetime Products and Services

Once a company has identified the customers it *should* keep, it has to go about the business of keeping them. Often that means adding new products and services to meet customers' evolving needs. Companies that fail to use their knowledge of customers to develop the product or service those people will need next are leaving the door open for another company to lure them away. Although it is tempting to use new products to win whole new markets, it almost always makes better sense to stick with existing customer segments. Over time, the company develops intimate knowledge of those people, and then can make good intuitive market judgments. Also, it is easier to build sales volume with customers who already know the company than it is with newcomers. USAA, for example, having come to understand one narrow market segment inside and out, found it relatively easy to go beyond auto insurance to offer mutual funds, life insurance, health insurance, and credit cards.

When Entenmann's of New York, a loyalty leader in specialty bakery products sold through grocery stores, saw its sales leveling off, it monitored customer purchase patterns in each local market. It discovered that as its core customers aged, they were looking for more fat-free and cholesterol-free products. Through direct contact with customers via telephone surveys and focus groups, the company found that consumers would buy those products from Entenmann's if they were available.

So the company had a choice. It could create a new line of products to serve those customers, or it could search for a whole new market segment. Ultimately, the company determined that it was much more economical to develop new fat- and cholesterol-free products than to go with another group of customers. Entenmann's new product line has been highly successful. It addressed the changing needs of the company's core clientele and even attracted new customers.

In yet another industry, Honda has emerged as the loyalty leader in the midpriced U.S. auto market. Life-cycle marketing has helped propel Honda's owner repurchase rate to 65%, versus an industry average of 40%. After the success of the subcompact Civic, Honda's next car, the Accord, was designed to meet the needs of Civic owners, who continued to care about reliability, conservative design, and value as they moved from their early twenties to marriage and family. Honda added the Accord wagon when it noticed customers defecting to other brands as their families grew.

By growing through the repeat purchases of its core customer base, Honda has maintained a relatively simple product line, and its manufacturing economics have benefited from this low product complexity. Honda's dealer and distribution system also benefits from low customer complexity in equally important, if less well-understood, ways.

One of the largest multifranchise dealers in the United States described this advantage as he saw it: "My Honda dealership is my most profitable because the company makes it so simple. There are fewer models and option packages. The key is the customers, who are very similar to one another." His sales and service operations are geared to the "Honda" customer. In contrast, he described his Mitsubishi dealership as a real challenge: "Salespeople have to deal with a lawyer buying a $30,000 Diamonte one minute, a construction worker buying a pickup truck the next." How can one salesperson (or service representative) develop proficiency with such customer complexity?

Curiously, Honda has had a tougher fight in Japan, where it remains a small player. Even though Honda had the same product advantages that resulted in its strong U.S. position, Toyota remains the dominant player in Japan because of its strong dealer network. In Japan, dealers don't have a lot of showrooms but instead rely on a direct sales force. Because sales force turnover is low (less than 10% per year for Toyota), they get to know customers very well. It is this enduring bond that has outmuscled Honda. In the United States, where car salespeople turn over quickly (60% to 100% annually) and customers have virtually no relationship with the sales force, Honda's product advantage blasted right through to put it out ahead.

Loyal Employees

Many companies diminish their economic potential through human resource policies that ensure high employee turnover, in part because they can't quantify the economics of retaining employees. Executives might say they want to keep employees, but if doing so means raising salaries, their conviction soon fades. They question the wisdom of increasing pay by, say, 25% in order to decrease employee turnover by 5%. Yet the fact is that employee retention is key to customer retention, and customer retention can quickly offset higher salaries and other incentives designed to keep employees from leaving.

The longer employees stay with the company, the more familiar they become with the business, the more they learn, and the more valuable they can be. Those employees who deal directly with customers day after day have a powerful effect on customer loyalty. Long-term employees can serve customers better than newcomers can; after all, a customer's contact with a company is through employees, not the top executives. It is with employees that the customer builds a bond of trust and expectations, and when those people leave, the bond is broken.

Companies wanting to increase customer loyalty often fail because they don't grasp the importance of this point. While conducting customer focus programs, they may be terminating or rotating the people who have the most influence on the customer's experience. While they are reengineering their business processes, they are failing to reengineer career paths, job content, and compensation so that employees will stay with the company long enough to learn the new processes.

Just as it is important to select the right kinds of customers before trying to keep them, a company must find the right kinds of employees before enticing them to stay. That raises the issue of hiring. The goal is not only to fill desks but also to find and hold onto workers who will continue to learn, to become more productive, and to create trusting relationships with customers. State Farm, the loyalty leader among auto insurance companies that sell through agents, has a distinctive agent-appointment strategy. Prospective agents may spend a year or more in a recruiting and selection process. During this time, they are in competition with several other well-qualified candidates. The lengthy process enables the company's field managers to select the best qualified person. State Farm often looks for candidates with roots in the community who are already likely to have long-term relationships with prospective customers.

One way for any company to find new hires who will likely stay is to look at the patterns of their own employees who defected early. Had they found the job at your company through newspaper ads, college recruiting, or personal referrals? Equally important, how long had they stayed with employers before coming to you? In a loyalty-based system, skills and education are important, but not as important as how long a prospective worker is expected to stay and grow with the business.

Although longevity deepens familiarity, some company policies render familiarity useless. Banks, for instance, are notorious for offering branch managers career paths that rotate them through a series of branch offices. Each time managers move, they take with them the knowledge learned at the branch where they put in their time. They have to start over again in each branch, building a network with the customers and the other employees. Their incentives to acquire the right customers and employees are reduced since it is their replacements who will reap the benefits. In a major bank with several hundred branches, branch managers who had been in the system an average of 12 years stayed at a given branch for only two years. Only one branch manager had remained in place and, not surprisingly, his office had the highest customer-retention rate in the entire system. It's worth noting that most banks have 50% to 100%-a-year teller turnover, which is also costly. Because most bankers cannot quantify the systems costs of these policies, they cannot justify the investments required to fix the situation.

But not all businesses follow those practices. The highly successful Olive Garden restaurant chain goes against the industry norm of moving successful managers to open new restaurants or to run bigger ones every few years and letting assistants take over. The chain hires local managers whose major asset is that they are known and trusted in the community. These managers are then kept in place so their asset appreciates in value. Learning accumulates as people stay on the job. By becoming intelligent about the business, getting to know customers, and providing the advantages knowledge gives, long-time hires add value to the company.

Leo Burnett Company's strong position in the advertising industry is largely attributable to its slavish devotion to employee retention. Most advertising firms experience high turnover of their creative people, and they make a point of rotating people through various accounts. They also experience constant client churn accompanied by massive layoffs and severe downturns in revenues and profits. At Leo Burnett, in contrast, new staffers are assigned to their first account "for life," in the words of one executive. Layoffs are rare, and customer retention is high.

Even businesses that don't rely on direct relationships between customers and employees can benefit from boosting employee retention. USAA has an information system that lets any employee pull up a customer's records instantly, so customers don't have to speak with the same employee every time. But USAA's employee turnover of around 7%—one-third the industry average—is one of the most important reasons its productivity is the best in the business. The learning unleashed by employee retention helps in other ways. When the marketing department wants to know more about customer needs or reactions to a new product, they can hold a focus group meeting of employees whose daily customer contact provides powerful insight.

Of course, employees won't stay and apply their knowledge unless they have an incentive to do so. All other things being equal, the best people will stay with the company that pays them the most. Loyalty leaders know this, and they share their "loyalty surplus" with employees as well as stockholders. They view their best employees as they do their best customers: once they've got them, they do everything possible to keep them. And they provide incentives in the form of higher salaries or bonuses and commissions that align the employees' self-interest with the interests of the company. Bonuses can be based on aggregate customer retention rates, and commissions can be designed to be small initially but grow the longer the customer stays with the company.

There are many ways reward programs can be structured to recognize loyalty. Olive Garden found that its experienced waiters and waitresses resented the fact that new hires were receiving the same base wage as they did, so management established a slightly higher base wage for employees who had served $25,000 of meals.

If employees are expected to be long-termers, companies can justify investing more in them. It becomes worthwhile to teach employees to do the right thing for the customer, which in turn leads to happier customers and ultimately to increased profits, which can be put toward the higher salaries of long-term employees. And the commitment to creating a loyalty-based system has spillover effects. Employees take pride in delivering value to a customer time and again. Their satisfaction in contributing to a positive goal is another thing that induces their loyalty to the company.

Measures of Loyalty

Even the best designed loyalty-based system will deteriorate unless an effective measurement system is established. Competitors, customer preferences, technologies, and employee capabilities are constantly changing. Measures establish the feedback loops that are the foundation of organizational learning. Only through effective learning can an organization consistently deliver value in an ever-changing world.

Unfortunately, most accounting systems do not measure what drives customer value. They can show the benefits of the one-year magic cure but not of programs and practices that take three to five years or longer to affect profits. Managers who have a year to earn a bonus or two years to turn a business around are forced to think of the usual shortcuts to higher profits: raising prices and cutting costs. Those actions alone rarely create value for customers, and although customers don't all leave at once, if they are not getting the best value, they will eventually turn to a competitor. To make matters worse, the best customers are often the first ones to go.

The first step in developing effective measures is to understand the cause-and-effect relationships in the system. The primary mission of a loyalty-based company is to deliver superior value to customers. Success or failure in this mission can be clearly measured by customer loyalty (best quantified by retention rate or share of purchases or both). Customer loyalty has three second-order effects: (1) revenue grows as a result of repeat purchases and referrals, (2) costs decline as a result of lower acquisition expenses and from the efficiencies of serving experienced customers, and (3) employee retention increases because job pride and satisfaction increase, in turn creating a loop that reinforces customer loyalty and further reducing costs as hiring and training costs shrink and productivity rises.

As costs go down and revenues go up, profits (the third-order effect) increase. Unless managers measure and monitor all of these economic relationships, they will default to their short-term, profit-oriented accounting systems, which tend to focus on only the second- and third-order effects. Focusing on these symptoms— instead of on the primary mission of delivering superior value to customers— often leads to decisions that will eventually reduce value and loyalty.

In the life insurance business, for instance, a five-percentage-point increase in customer retention lowers costs per policy by 18%. However, very few companies have quantified this relationship, and as a result, they focus their cost-reduction efforts on process reengineering and layoffs, which appear to lower costs but in fact lower employee motivation and retention, leading to lower customer retention, which increases costs!

When life insurers want to grow, they can hire more agents, raise commissions, drop prices (to new customers only, if possible), and add new products. The result: more inexperienced salespeople (low productivity and high cost) bringing in the wrong kind of customer (disloyal price shoppers) with escalating costs of product-line complexity. The only way to avoid these mistakes in insurance, or any business, is to develop systems that allow employees to track and understand the cash-flow consequences of changing customer loyalty.

It is only the true defection of the target customer that should be of concern because that means something may have gone wrong, and if it has, it's worth a considerable amount of effort to find out what. It could mean that another company has done something innovative that gives customers a better value.

It is important to define customer retention carefully and what it means in a particular industry. In the auto business, for instance, a manufacturer should worry about a customer who switches to another brand—but not about a customer who sells his or her car and takes public transportation. In an industrial setting, customers might shift a percentage of their purchases to competitors, so changes in purchase patterns should be watched as carefully as customer defections.

Customer satisfaction is not a surrogate for customer retention. While it may seem intuitive that increasing customer satisfaction will increase retention and therefore profits, the facts are contrary. Between 65% and 85% of customers who defect say they were satisfied or very satisfied with their former supplier. In the auto industry, satisfaction scores average 85% to 95%, while repurchase rates average only 40%. Current satisfaction measurement systems are simply not designed to provide insight into how many customers stay loyal to the company and for how long.

State Farm's Loyalty-Based System

State Farm insures more than 20% of the nation's households. It has the lowest sales and distribution costs among insurance companies of its type, yet its agents' incomes are generally higher than agents working for the competition. Its focus on customer service has resulted in faster growth than most other multiple-line insurers, but rather than being consumed by growth, its capital has mushroomed (all through internally generated surplus) to more than $18 billion, representing the largest capital base of any financial services company in North America. Because of careful customer selection and retention, State Farm is able to price below the competition and still build the capital necessary to protect its policyholders in years such as 1992 when they incurred $4.7 billion in catastrophe losses.

These impressive achievements can be traced to State Farm's well-designed loyalty-based system. State Farm began by choosing the right customers. The company was founded more than 70 years ago to serve better than average drivers, first in farming communities and now throughout suburban and urban markets across the United States and in three Canadian provinces. State Farm agents work from neighborhood offices, which allows them to build long-lasting relationships with their customers and provide the personal service that is the basis of the corporate philosophy.

This kind of personal service can start at an early age. Teenagers in State Farm households are usually written while still under the umbrella of their parents' policies. Many State Farm agents routinely sit new drivers down in their offices for a "dutch uncle" speech about the responsibilities of driving and the impact an accident or ticket—particularly for drunken driving—would have on their rates. Also, in an effort to educate all teens on safe driving, agents have available company-produced safe-driving materials for high schools. All these efforts tend to make the young drivers that State Farm insures more careful, and their parents grateful for the interest and help.

When agents are rooted in the community, they often know who the best customers will be. For example, they can scan the local newspaper for the high school honor roll and be sure that their young customers' good grades are recognized with premium discounts. Agents make it their business to get to know the people they insure. The most powerful computer and the brightest underwriter at headquarters simply can't compete with that level of customer insight.

Pricing policies work as a magnet to retain good customers. At the end of three years, accident-free customers get a 5% discount, followed by another 5% decrease three years later. The discounts make customers feel they've earned special status and value, and they create a disincentive to jump to another company, where they might have to start all over again.

State Farm agents not only want to attract and keep good customers, they also have the incentive to do so. Commissions are structured to encourage long-term thinking. Agents receive the same compensation rate on new auto and fire policies as for renewals, thus rewarding agents for serving existing customers, not just for drawing in new business. Unlike organizations that say retention is important while pushing salespeople to find new customers, State Farm consistently conveys the message that both are important.

Remaining focused on its target customers, State Farm provides a full life-cycle product line. Rather than bringing in lots of new customers, the company's marketing efforts encourage existing customers to buy additional products, like home and life insurance. The homogeneity of their market means that one agent can sell and service everything. The full product line preserves the agent's relationship with the customer and allows the agent to learn more about the customer's needs. In addition to benefiting the policyholder and company, this approach serves the agent well, as multiple-line customers are less expensive for the agent to service than are single-line customers. Multiple-line customers have also proven to stay with the agent longer.

State Farm agents are also loyal. According to industry studies, more than 80% of newly appointed agents remain through their fourth year, compared with 20% to 40% for the rest of the industry. And the average agent at State Farm has 13 years of tenure, compared with 6 to 9 years for the industry. This retention advantage can be attributed both to the lengthy recruiting and selection process before appointment and to the fact that State Farm agents are independent contractors who sell and service State Farm products exclusively. Because agents have built and invested in their own businesses, they are more likely to remain with State Farm than their counterparts representing other companies. In return, State Farm is loyal to its agents and distributes its products only through them. The company has built a marketing partnership with its agents and involves them in key decisions that affect them or their customers.

Agent retention and customer retention reinforce one another. The agent who is committed to a long-term relationship with the company, and indeed, to his or her own business, is more likely to build lasting relationships with customers. In addition, loyal customers make life easier for the agents, who spend more time working with people they know and like and far less time chasing new customers. Finally, agents like being part of a system that consistently delivers superior value to customers. Agents' experience, plus the fact that they spend more time servicing and selling to proven customers, raises agents' productivity to 50% above industry norms.

State Farm's business systems support its focus on loyalty. Measures of customer retention and defections are distributed throughout the organization. Agents and employees at all levels know whether the system is working and can adjust their activities. Agents find a list of their nonrenewing customers each morning when they switch on their computers, which they can use to prompt telephone follow-ups to try to retain the account. And management can use the same kind of information as a check against policyholders' satisfaction with the service, product, and price they receive.

State Farm's success in building customer loyalty is reflected in retention rates that exceed 90%, consistently the best performance of all the national insurers that sell through agents. State Farm agents make more money by operating in a business system engineered for superior loyalty. And they are more productive, which makes it possible for them to earn superior compensation (after adjusting for the fact that State Farm agents pay their own expenses) while the company actually pays lower average commission rates. The result is a 10% cost advantage. The company also keeps its costs relatively low because it avoids excessive administrative and claims costs associated with acquiring and servicing a large percentage of new customers. State Farm's system provides outstanding value to its customers, benefits for its agents, and has created a company that is a financial powerhouse.

Managing for Loyalty

The success of State Farm and other loyalty leaders shows the direct linkages between providing value for customers and a superior financial and competitive position. Doing the right thing for customers does not conflict with generating substantial margins. On the contrary, it is the only way to ensure profitability beyond the short term.

Creating a loyalty-based system in any company requires a radical departure from traditional business thinking. It puts creating customer value—not maximizing profits and shareholder value—at the center of business strategy, and it demands significant changes in business practice—redefining target customers, revising employment policies, and redesigning incentives.

Most important, if companies are really serious about delivering value and earning customer loyalty, they must measure it. And while senior executives may be daunted by the time and investment required to engineer an entire business system for high retention, they may have no alternative. Customer loyalty appears to be the only way to achieve sustainably superior profits.

Managing for loyalty serves the best interests of customers, employees, and investors. The only losers are the competitors who get the leftovers: an increasingly poor mix of customers and employees and an increasingly less tenable financial and market position. As loyalty leaders refine their ability to deliver value by more effectively harnessing the economics of loyalty, their advantages will multiply. Competitors must respond, or they will find it increasingly difficult to survive on the leftovers of the marketplace.

———————

Closing the Customer Feedback Loop

In a resource-challenged economy, empower your frontline
employees to respond fast.

Rob Markey, Fred Reichheld, and Andreas Dullweber

*For decades, companies gave frontline employees customer feedback in the form of
statistical reports: "X% of customers were completely satisfied last month and Y% dissatisfied." If parents tried to teach manners to a child the same way, they would say,
"You only said 'thank you' 24% of the time last month. You need to improve that."
Put in those human terms, it's easier to recognize that people don't learn effectively
from statistical reports about events long in the past. Little wonder, then, that the
fundamental idea of this article—connecting employees to customers through direct,
high-velocity, closed-loop feedback—has become so powerful and popular, both in
Bain's work and in the business world at large.*

*In the years since the article was published, we have witnessed a tremendous
flowering of tools, capabilities, and mechanisms for helping customer-facing employees get direct feedback from the people they serve, act on that feedback, and learn
from it. High-velocity closed-loop feedback became the core of our book* The Ultimate
Question 2.0. *This article was the seed.*

Cheryl Pasquale, a branch manager at Charles Schwab, starts her workday
with this morning ritual: As soon as she arrives at her desk, she fires up her
laptop, logs on to Schwab's intranet, and pulls up the latest customer feedback
report for her office. Generated by a brief survey the investment firm e-mails out
daily, the report shows the most recent responses from her team's clients.

Scrolling through the results, Pasquale reviews how well the six financial
consultants she supervises handled the previous day's transactions. She sorts
through the aggregate scores from customers and reads the comments of individuals who gave high or low marks and sees if any particular kind of interaction
has elicited praise or complaints. As she clicks through the screens, Pasquale
notices that several customers have voiced frustration with how hard it is to use

the in-branch information kiosks. She decides she'll ask her team for insights about this in their weekly meeting. Some customers are confused by one of Schwab's forms; she reminds herself to raise this with other branch managers at the regional meeting later in the month. And she spots an opportunity to counsel a new account rep on how to build better rapport with clients in their next one-on-one training session.

A "manager alert"—a special notice triggered by a client who has given Schwab a poor rating for a delay in posting a transaction to his account—grabs her attention. The client has indicated that he's willing to discuss the issue in a follow-up call, so Pasquale makes a note to try to reach him that day. Surprising as it may seem, she usually looks forward to such calls. They give her a chance to find out what's on customers' minds and solve their problems—and potentially turn critics into fans.

Every day, managers at each of Schwab's 306 branch offices and five call centers conduct a similar drill. It's an integral part of a new focus on direct customer feedback that the firm's founder, Charles Schwab, credits with turning around the company. When he came out of retirement to take its helm in 2004, the business was struggling. "We had lost our connection with our clients—and that had to change," Schwab confessed to shareholders in the annual report. The new customer feedback system has helped reestablish that connection. In 2008, the firm saw its revenues increase by 11% and the scores that customers gave the company jump by 25%. And while the financial services industry was rocked by turbulence, Schwab clients entrusted $113 billion in net new assets to the firm, and the number of new brokerage accounts increased by 10%.

Getting Customer Feedback Right

Most companies devote a lot of energy to listening to the "voice of the customer," but few of them are very happy with the outcome of the effort. Managers have experimented with a wide array of techniques, all useful for some purposes—but all with drawbacks. Elaborate satisfaction surveys that involve proprietary research models can be expensive to conduct and slow to yield findings. Once delivered, their findings can be difficult to convert into practical actions. The results also may be imprecise: Our research shows that most customers who end up defecting to another business have declared themselves "satisfied" or "very satisfied" in such surveys not long before jumping ship. The practice of sending executives out to spend time in the field can generate fresh insights, but few management teams sustain such efforts—and even if they do, they often struggle to convert those insights into prescriptions that frontline employees can follow.

Bringing in "power customers"—heavy spenders who tend to be deeply committed to the company—to talk about their experiences can shine a spotlight on critical issues. But frontline employees can't easily learn about their own behaviors from those customers or develop remedies for the problems they raise.

A growing number of companies have developed effective customer feedback programs that head off those challenges right from the start. Instead of building elaborate, centralized customer research mechanisms, these firms begin their feedback loop at the front line. Employees working there receive evaluations of their performance from the people best able to render an appraisal—the customers they just served. The employees then follow up with willing customers in one-on-one conversations. The objective is to understand in detail what the customers value and what the front line can do to deliver it better. Over time, companies compile the data into a baseline of the customer experience, which they draw upon to make process and policy refinements.

The strongest feedback loops do more than just connect customers, the front line, and a few decision makers in management, however; they keep the customer front and center across the entire organization. A number of tactics, such as hiring "mystery shoppers" to test customer service or arranging periodic forums between employees and customers, help strengthen this organization-wide focus. One approach that we believe works well across a range of industries is the Net Promoter® score (NPS®), which one of the authors of this article, Fred Reichheld, created seven years ago.

NPS immediately categorizes all customers into one of three groups—promoters, passives, and detractors—allowing employees throughout a company to see right away whether a customer experience was a success or a failure—and why. NPS is generated by asking customers a single question, "How likely would you be to recommend [this company or product] to a friend or a colleague?" Respondents giving marks of 9 or 10 are promoters, the company's most devoted customers.

A Five-Point Customer Feedback Checklist

1. Have you reached a consensus on your business's five most critical "moments of truth" with customers?
2. Do employees and managers get customer feedback routinely, on a daily or weekly basis?
3. Do you let customers know the impact their feedback had on improving your processes?
4. Do you know what percentage of detractors your operations now convert into promoters through service recovery processes?
5. Can you put a dollar value on turning a detractor into a promoter?

Those scoring their experience 7 or 8 are passives, and those scoring it from 0 to 6 are detractors. NPS is the percentage of promoters minus the percentage of detractors. Customers are then asked to describe why they would be likely or unlikely to recommend the company. The insights gathered from their answers enable employees to quickly identify issues that create detractors—and the actions required to address them. (For more on NPS, see "The One Number You Need to Grow," HBR, December 2003.)

Gathering Feedback on the Front Line

Say that thousands of transactions occur daily between customers and frontline employees at your company. Each is an opportunity to create a new promoter. But which customer experiences matter the most? We have learned that the most important interactions are "moments of truth," those relatively few points of contact that hold the greatest potential to delight—or alienate—an organization's customers. As they mine the steady flow of customer feedback, companies should pay particular attention to these touchpoints.

That was the rationale of Allianz CEO Michael Diekmann when he set out to bring his global financial services enterprise closer to its customers, in 2004. Diekmann and his leadership team recognized that no group was better positioned to pinpoint the make-or-break customer experiences—and come up with effective ways of improving them—than the tens of thousands of customer-facing Allianz employees who delivered services day in and day out. The company's management began by assembling a small customer-focus team, reporting directly to the board, that would design, build, and test a feedback system and then roll it out to frontline employees in most of the 70 countries where Allianz operated. The team chose NPS as its core metric.

Here's how the Allianz system works: After every transaction, an independent polling firm immediately contacts the customer and conducts a brief survey. It e-mails the results immediately to the employee who provided the service and publishes aggregated results on local intranet "dashboards" for everyone to review. Frontline employees then follow up by calling a sample of customers who've agreed to be contacted. After listening to the issues customers raise, they correct the problems or escalate them to someone who can.

Because the frontline employees take responsibility for lifting their work unit's feedback scores, they meet frequently to devise service improvements, both large and small. In one of the firm's European health insurance claims operations, for example, NPS feedback revealed that unexplained delays in reimbursements were a big source of customer frustration. When claims representatives followed up with dissatisfied customers, they learned that customers had to call back repeatedly to inquire about the status of payments and describe medical conditions again and again. The reps' solution: On the initial call, every policyholder would be assigned a case manager who would handle all contact until the claim was resolved. To manage customer expectations, any delay in the reimbursement process would trigger a call or text message informing the policyholder of the claim's status. Soon after the new protocol was in place, the claims unit saw a double-digit increase in its NPS and a significant rise in policy renewal rates.

This kind of closed-loop process can fade away without strong leadership and cultural reinforcement. Allianz's Australian property-and-casualty unit, half a world away from headquarters, faced this challenge by having the top executives personally call customers each month and by using employee rewards and recognition. Managers in each sales office, claims facility, and call center maintain a "compliment database," where they register feedback that praises frontline employees by name. Individual employees' successes are celebrated at regular office "town hall" meetings hosted by a senior Allianz executive.

Managing Change Through Customer Feedback

For many companies, the route to the end customer is circuitous. They sell their products to distributors, retailers, and other intermediaries. Frontline sales reps typically have little incentive or ability to reach beyond their immediate customer and connect with the people who end up choosing or using the products.

That was the situation that Grohe, a European manufacturer of premium kitchen and bathroom fixtures, found itself in. Grohe sells its products in 130 countries through more than 20 divisions, to customers like home-improvement chains, hardware stores, and building supply outlets. After new owners took control of the company in 2004, its market share began dropping steadily.

CEO David Haines decided that customer strategy was the key to reviving Grohe's growth and set three priorities. First, Grohe needed accurate insights into the chain of customer relationships to determine how frontline sales reps and marketing support teams might intervene to boost sales. Second, the company needed to quickly measure whether the new approaches its sales reps tested were working. Third, it needed a feedback system that would promote continual frontline learning and would work well in all its markets.

Brief telephone surveys revealed a major disconnect between Grohe's distributors, wholesalers, and retailers and their customers—the folks who influenced or made the ultimate purchase of the company's fixtures. Grohe sales reps learned that their direct customers, most of whom also sold competitors' products,

Give Customers a Voice in Running Your Business

Many companies have discovered that closed-loop customer feedback systems can energize their frontline workers. To inspire customer-centered learning throughout an organization, however, you also need feedback loops in the executive suite and the middle ranks. There, customer input can influence decisions on everything from where the company will compete to product development, pricing, policies, and processes.

The top-level strategy loop. Direct input from customers can help make strategies coherent. Allianz, a Munich-based financial services firm, uses Net Promoter scores to benchmark the strengths and weaknesses of its major business units around the world. Annual NPS surveys measure how each operating enterprise (OE) performs against its competitors *in the eyes of customers*. The surveys identify which OEs are customer loyalty leaders, which are at parity with their rivals, and which are laggards. When Allianz compared the scores and annual growth rates for each OE, the results were striking. Best-in-class OEs (with scores higher than their competitors) increased revenues significantly faster than OEs that trailed their rivals. CEO Michael Diekmann used those findings to send an unambiguous message to the global organization: Improving the customer experience is a core mission.

The midlevel functional loop. Middle managers in operations, marketing, and finance must convert strategies into policies and processes that attract and retain high-value customers. If these managers don't have direct customer feedback, tight budgets and other constraints can lead them to shunt customers to the sideline. The sad fact is that many organizations jeopardize their goodwill with customers by pushing up profits at their expense.

Integration into the learning loop with customers can help functional managers avoid the wrong trade-offs. For instance, instead of trying to hit Six Sigma quality levels at every touchpoint—which can be prohibitively expensive—companies can learn to focus on the few that really build or destroy loyalty.

For American Express, one of those touchpoints was the replacement of lost or stolen charge cards. While combing through Net Promoter scores and customer transactions, company analysts saw that initial requests for card replacements went unresolved at about twice the rate of other call center requests. Even more alarming, the analysts discovered that the customers requesting replacements were some of the company's biggest spenders. Follow-up surveys with card members who encountered delays revealed that their NPS ratings were one-third lower than those of peers who did not need a replacement. Tools that measure customer satisfaction only in the aggregate might never have uncovered the problem.

The company's operations managers pulled process improvement teams off many other less-urgent initiatives and focused them on card replacements. The teams developed new card replacement protocols, which increased first-call resolution rates by more than 20% and raised the NPS of the customers involved to parity with other customers.

When using NPS to set strategic direction at the top; refine processes, products, or policies in the middle; or sharpen service at the front lines, customer-focused organizations are not preoccupied with simply attaining high scores. Instead, they spur organizational action, close the loop with customers, and collect subsequent customer feedback to gauge if the actions they took produced results.

required a lot more help communicating the attributes—innovative design, ease of installation, dependability—that were Grohe's competitive advantages.

Grohe quickly launched programs to address these shortcomings. Sales reps began sponsoring workshops in distributors' showrooms to teach contractors how easy the products were to install. They provided new floor and window displays to showcase the products' decorative appeal. And they recruited a select group of high-volume distributors into an elite "Grohe Club," offering incentives and extra sales support. To close the feedback loop and determine whether the techniques were boosting customer loyalty and sales, Grohe conducted regular NPS surveys with the distributors. In the year after it launched the new program, Grohe saw its NPS climb more than 20 percentage points.

The company also uses NPS in controlled experiments to field-test ideas before rolling them out systemwide. For example, in one of its markets, the company began tracking how often sales reps visited their customers and what effect the number of visits had on NPS. It found that scores spiked at three visits and began to fall off with more frequent contact. By cutting back on the unproductive extra calls in most of its sales territories, Grohe freed up an estimated 25% of its selling capacity.

At companies where strong customer feedback systems take hold, business-unit leaders and frontline employees start to own customer loyalty the same way they own their targets for revenue, profits, and market share. Indeed, increasing positive customer feedback and meeting conventional financial objectives are becoming one and the same goal. Analysts at Grohe, for instance, have calculated that a 10% improvement in NPS correlates with a six- to seven-percentage-point increase in revenue growth.

As employees at Grohe, Schwab, Allianz, and other companies we've worked with have seen, you can't fix problems you don't know you have. And unless you keep the customers you already have coming back for more and recommending your company to their friends and colleagues, it's hard to grow a business.

The New Science of Sales Force Productivity

The data, tools, and analytics that companies are increasingly using to improve their sales forces will not only help top performers shine, but they will also help drive sales force laggards to the middle of the curve.

Dianne Ledingham, Mark Kovac, and Heidi Locke Simon

The fundamentals of sales science have changed little since we wrote this article. A company needs offerings that are carefully targeted to its core customers. It needs a systematic method of deploying sales resources to its "sweet spots," automated sales tools and procedures, and careful performance management. The first of these is worth two or three times as much as the others: When a company's front line is selling the right offerings to the right segments, it is well on its way to full potential.

The practical applications of the science, however, continue to evolve. Sales analytic tools and processes are far more sophisticated now than they were when we wrote this piece. Sales resource deployment has grown more challenging, with many B2B buyers requiring multiproduct solutions and expecting insight as well as information from sales representatives. Customer relationship executives often find that they must involve industry, product, or functional specialists at key points, yet avoid relying so heavily on them that the sales process becomes uneconomical. Companies can get bogged down in all this complexity. But many of our clients have learned to adapt their sales model and keep things simple, building systematic sales methods based on a few timeless precepts of the sort described here.

Bob Brody leaned back in his chair, frowning. Corporate wanted another 8% increase in sales from his division this year, and guess whose shoulders that goal would fall on? Ah, for the good old days, when he could just announce a 10% target, spread it like peanut butter over all his territories, then count on the sales reps for each region or product line to deliver. Sure, some would fall short,

HBR September 2006

but the real rainmakers would make up the difference. Today, the purchasing departments of Bob's customers used algorithms to choose vendors for routine buys; pure economics often trumped personal relationships. For more complex sales, purchasing wanted customized end-to-end solutions. There's no way one person could close those deals, no matter how much golf he or she played. Most of the time, you needed a team of product and industry experts, not to mention rich incentives and a lot of back-office support.

The fact was—he knew he'd have to face it sooner or later—Bob was overwhelmed. Nothing about the sales process was as simple or predictable as it used to be. Eight percent growth? He wasn't even sure where to start.

If this little fable sounds familiar, it's because managers often face similar problems. Over the past few years, we have worked through these sorts of challenges with dozens of senior executives in Brody's position. Even though the world around them was changing, they were still handing down targets from higher management and religiously putting more feet on the street, hoping that some of those new reps would once again save the day. Even arbiters of best practice such as General Electric can recall the wing-and-a-prayer style that, until recently, characterized their sales efforts. The company would give each individual his or her patch and say, "Good luck, and go get 'em," observes GE's Michael Pilot, who started his career 22 years ago as a salesperson at the organization and is now president of U.S. Equipment Financing, a unit of GE Commercial Finance.

Today, the savviest sales leaders are dramatically changing the way they run their groups. They are reinventing their sales approaches to respond to new market environments. They are expanding their lists of target customers beyond what anyone had previously considered. They are boosting their sales reps' productivity not by hiring the most-gifted individuals but by helping existing reps sell more. (See the exhibit "More Reps, or More Productivity?") As a result, their companies are growing at sometimes startling rates. Pilot's division—a large group in a mature industry—added $300 million in new business (about 10% organic growth) in 2005 alone, an improvement he attributes specifically to a reinvention of the operation's sales process. Similarly, SAP Americas, under president and CEO Bill McDermott, has more than doubled its software license business in three years, increasing its market share by 17 points.

What these leaders have in common might be called a scientific approach to sales force effectiveness. It's a method that puts systems around the art of selling, relying not just on gut feel and native sales talent—the traditional qualities of the rainmaker—but also on data, analysis, processes, and tools to redraw the boundaries of markets and increase a sales force's productivity. The goal isn't to replace

More Reps, or More Productivity?

Companies that choose to take a scientific approach to sales force effectiveness may want to evaluate the two options shown here. The growth target for this fictitious global manufacturer—in this case an increase in revenues of $1.1 billion over five years—can be attained through various combinations of productivity improvements and new hires. But the cheapest and most effective route is usually to increase productivity as much as possible through use of the four levers—targeted offerings; optimized automation, tools, and procedures; performance management; and sales force deployment—and only then to put more feet on the street. The management challenge is ensuring that you have put enough science into your sales organization to drive that productivity predictably.

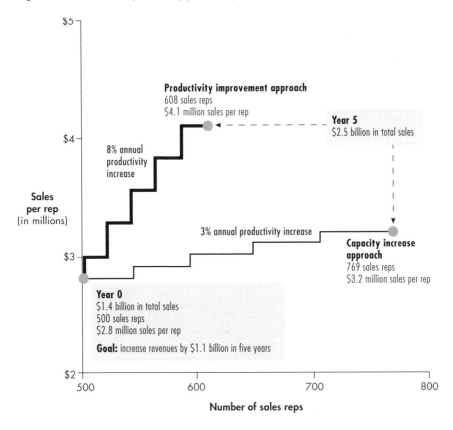

rainmakers but to narrow the gap between the top 15% or 20% and the rest of the sales force. Companies that use the tactic well have found that, while even top sellers do better, reps in the lower quartiles show dramatic improvement, with productivity jumps of 200%. Such increases enhance the performance of the sales team as a whole and enable a company to reduce the expense of hiring new reps. Some firms using the approach have seen their average sales per rep increase by as much as 50% in two or three years, though most gains cluster around the 30% mark.

No latter-day Arthur Miller is likely to write a play about the practitioners of the new method; the drama is in the results, not the details. But if "the future of business is to do things by design, not by chance," as one sales leader put it, this new science may be what's required of the men and women charged with bringing in a company's revenue.

Putting Science into Sales

GE's Pilot understands how extensive a reinvention can be. As recently as the mid-1990s, the company was still expecting sales teams to assemble and prioritize their own database of prospects for their territories. The company's field sales managers even manually classified all the names in the division's database as either high priority or low priority. "We relied on telephone books," recalls Pilot. "And newspapers. And signs on trucks as they went by or signs on buildings." By 2004, says Pilot, he knew that GE Commercial Finance had to "put some science into it."

Pilot's first step was to revise the way he segmented customers—by using data that included records of past company transactions. The new database held information such as four-digit standard industrial classification codes, the type of equipment being leased, and so on. Then Pilot asked his field managers to create a list of prospective-customer characteristics, criteria that they believed would correlate with a customer's likelihood of doing business with GE. He took the 14 features they came up with, ran regression equations against the database of transactions, and identified six criteria that had high correlations. If a prospective customer tested well on those six criteria—such as predicted capital expenditures and number of filings for new business transactions—the probability that it would do business with GE was high.

The division scored its list of prospects based on the six attributes and then worked the new list for a while. Something interesting emerged. "We found that the top 30% of prospective customers were three times more likely to do a deal with us than the bottom 70%," says Pilot. In other words, that top group was made up of the new highest-priority prospects—and yet only about half of them had previously been classified as high priority by sales managers. The company had, in effect, identified 10,000 new high-priority prospects that it would otherwise have overlooked.

But it wasn't just the increase in sales acreage that made the difference; the new information also allowed Pilot to redesign his sales force. For example, he could take on the difficult job of restructuring territories, ensuring that each one contained plenty of opportunities. In some cases, that meant narrowing assigned areas based on the caliber of leads, reevaluating territories, or creating new territories entirely. "When you look at the market with that kind of scientific approach," Pilot says, "you'll never knowingly have territories that could intrinsically underdeliver."

On the performance management front, the data allowed Pilot to get new and less-experienced reps up to speed faster. "So much of the process of ramping up salespeople is just pointing them at the right targets," he says. "If you can do that, you'll get a big boost in productivity."

Pilot also used the information to support his sales force with new tools and processes for the field, such as targeted marketing campaigns that zeroed in on high-potential segments. Now every lead and piece of business generated gets tagged to a particular campaign. "It helps you think about what worked, what didn't, and where to double down and spend dollars for greater return on the marketing side," says Pilot.

The division's $300 million in new business for 2005 reflects both an increased sales pipeline and a 19% higher rate of conversion, or closings, in a market the company once believed was maturing. That revenue, Pilot notes, "is coming from customers that we know we wouldn't have been calling on" without the new approach. "At the end of the day," he says, "it's about building our business around customers and finding ways to help them grow."

Setting Targets

Setting annual sales objectives is any company's first step in creating a sales plan. Like our fictional Bob Brody, sales leaders have traditionally set goals based on upper management's aspirations for the company. Since those ambitions typically reflect shareholder expectations, they can't be ignored. But sales leaders too often apply the targets across every region and segment, without gathering the market and competitive data that would make their goals more realistic. Since variations across regions and segments are probable, sales reps often end up with quotas that are unrealistically high or low—either of which can demoralize and demotivate a sales force.

To see how the new science of goal setting works, consider how Cisco Systems uses technology to forecast sales. The company created a site where managers could log in and see up-to-the-minute sales performance—listed by region, product line, and so on—all the way down to the level of individual account executives. The site also contains data about reps' pipelines, including the size of each opportunity, what kind of technology the customer requires, and who the competitors are. Managers hold regular pipeline calls and produce new forecasts derived from the data every week. They then roll up the numbers into weekly, monthly, and quarterly forecasts. "The forecast accuracy for our quarterly numbers tends to be within plus or minus 1% to 2%," says Inder Sidhu, Cisco's vice president for worldwide sales strategy and planning.

Like other best-practice companies, Cisco isn't sitting still. Last year it provided its reps with state-of-the-art PDAs, and it's building custom applications for the devices designed to boost productivity. One such program speeds up data entry; another lets reps check their customers' recent activity (such as whether they have ordered parts or remitted an invoice). Cisco has also jump-started its reps' motivation by developing an online personal compensation rate calculator. "People can actually go in and say, 'OK, here's where I'm at right now in the quarter,' " says Sidhu. "It tells them exactly what the deal will mean to them [financially]."

Two years ago, Aggreko North America, a division of U.K.-based equipment rental company Aggreko, adopted a scientific approach to goal setting with dramatic results: In 2005, sales rose by 29%, and sales force productivity rose by 90%. Company president George Walker says that the process begins from the top down. Executives gather regional data on critical industry-level drivers in each of the company's vertical markets—oil refining, home construction, and so on—and then they calculate the firm's share of each market to set goals for growth. Next comes the bottom-up element: Armed with the data, area sales managers develop a view of territories, accounts, and quotas for individual reps by multiplying potential market size by target shares for each market. An iterative process between the local reps and senior management ensures that the expectations for individual salespeople are in line with overall corporate objectives.

Stepping Up Productivity

Traditionally, sales managers assumed that if you wanted to see significant growth, you had to look at last year's performance and then try to gauge how many new salespeople you could add, given the potential market and the ramp-up time that each new rep would require before generating revenue.

Companies that follow a scientific approach take a much different course. They focus above all on increasing individual salesperson productivity. They can do so because the question of how to boost productivity is no longer a mystery to them. (See the sidebar "TOPSales: A Science-Driven Approach.") On the contrary, they have learned to use four levers that make productivity increases both predictable and manageable.

Targeted Offerings

Most organizations already know how to gather the data that enables them to segment their customer base. But companies pursuing a scientific approach boost productivity by taking segmentation one step further. They systematically divide their customers according to factors such as potential value of the account, share of wallet, vertical market, type of product, and type of sale. They define roles and align incentives to help sales reps position and sell the offerings that are most appropriate to each customer segment. Sales reps at these companies must have a deep understanding of the segments they serve: No one package of products and services fits all. And because many sales today can't be closed by just one individual, these companies know how to support a team approach with a careful architecture and smart management.

Targeted offerings aimed at individuals with a net worth of more than $25 million have made a big difference to Citigroup's private banking operation. That group serves business owners, real estate developers, lawyers, professional athletes, and other specialized segments, each with particular challenges and needs.

TOPSales: A Science-Driven Approach

In today's selling environment, it's not enough to rely on your star reps and hope for the best. Any sales organization that wants to boost productivity should use a scientific approach to selling based on a set of four levers (which make up the abbreviation TOPSales).

Targeted offerings. Tailor your offerings to meet the needs of each segment, and make sure reps are selling the right wares to the right prospects.

Optimized automation, tools, and procedures. Bolster your technology tools with disciplined sales management processes, such as detailed pipeline discussions, systematic account and territory plan reviews based on standard guidelines, defined lead distribution processes with tracking throughout the sales cycle for both reps and partners, and electronic dashboards for reps and territories.

Performance management. Measure and manage inputs, such as pipeline metrics and competitive installations you want to target, but reward based on outputs. Calculate the time it will take new reps to begin generating revenue, and factor that in to your sales planning. Provide training and tools to reduce that time. Incorporate metrics, incentives, and skill development into compensation systems to reward high-performing reps.

Sales force deployment. Distribute your sales resources systematically, matching sales approaches and channels to the needs and challenges of each customer segment. Create teams for complex sales, and provide reps with support to help maximize their productivity.

"The industry has changed a lot in 15 years," says Todd Thomson, chairman and CEO of Citigroup's Global Wealth Management division. "It used to be about selling stocks and bonds and then mutual funds and other things. It was mostly transaction based." Today, Citigroup focuses less on selling investment products—commodities that can be bought and sold anywhere—and instead offers wealth management services and advice on how to reach short-, mid-, and long-term goals. The products, while still important, are secondary.

To make the transition, Citigroup stayed focused on two things. First, instead of simply growing its adviser and banker base, the firm made investments in the professional development of its people and platforms, such as by providing their private bankers with finance and business training taught by leading business school professors. Second, the company segmented its clients by type and created dedicated teams focused on supporting the needs of each client group. "We have a set of products, including risk management tools, that [have been crafted] and directed toward real estate developers," says Thomson. "When our private bankers and their teams show up to talk to a developer, we're smarter about what they need and how to deliver it than the competition is." The private bankers—the team coordinators—are encouraged to increase the reach of Citigroup's management expertise, which includes dealing with equities, fixed income, trust management, and even cash management for entrepreneurial businesses. "Over the past year, we've encouraged our people to think about how to solve [customers'] problems, and we've seen a massive increase in assets from those clients," Thomson says. The result: Citigroup's U.S. private bankers generate an average of $5.5 million per rep in revenue, compared with about $4 million average sales per rep in the rest of the industry.

Optimized Automation, Tools, and Procedures

"Sales force automation" has become a buzz term in recent years, and many companies are putting IT-based tools to work to improve sales force productivity. Aggreko North America uses CRM software with a "profitability predictor" that allows its reps to tweak an offering if margins aren't where they should be. GE Commercial Finance has Monday morning sales meetings that are facilitated by a "digital cockpit" that lets managers peer into reps' pipelines. Cisco, famed for its Web-based sales tools, knows that technology is effective only if it supplements and complements disciplined sales management processes (such as routine, detailed pipeline discussions based on a well-understood characterization of various stages in the pipeline and systematic channeling of leads to sales reps).

A dramatic transformation at SAP Americas, in particular, shows how important systematic processes can be. When McDermott took over in 2002, one of his first moves was to set standards for individual sales reps that reflected the market potential: $500,000 for the first quarter of the next year, $750,000 for the second quarter, and so on. The quarterly targets alone dramatically changed many people's thinking; traditionally, SAP reps had always counted on a big fourth quarter to pull themselves through the year. Instead of allowing reps to scramble to meet annual sales goals at the end of each year, McDermott set a pipeline standard. He expected reps to have three times their annual sales quotas in their pipeline of prospects on a rolling basis, quarter by quarter. To ensure that business partners (like IBM Global Services and Accenture, which implement the systems SAP sells) would be drawn into the selling effort, McDermott decided that at least half of each individual pipeline should be assigned to a business partner that would team up with SAP to close the deals.

Merely setting such goals, however, is not enough. Supporting them with management processes, selling materials, and automated tools for measuring leading indicators and results is what makes outcomes more predictable. For example, reps are regularly informed about key industry trends and about which of SAP's comprehensive product offerings will be most relevant and valuable that year for a target segment. When reps identify clients that could make better use of key SAP products to address an industry trend, "your whole marketing muscle and your pipeline muscle are really focused on letting those clients know that they're leaving hundreds of millions of dollars of value on the table," says McDermott.

Performance Management

Most organizations have an expected level of sales attrition based on whether reps make their quotas over time. But some have added deeper levels of performance analysis that make sales productivity more predictable and thus more manageable. For instance, for each customer segment (such as global accounts, large-company accounts, and so on), SAP has analyzed how long it takes for new reps to become productive and how their productivity increases after that. They can also determine the average productivity rate for seasoned reps. This helps managers staff their segment territory plan more effectively. And it helps them know more quickly when a new hire isn't meeting the standard. "People generally reach their productivity plateau at 12 months," McDermott explains. "If they are not there, they are not going to get there. And that's about 10% of our new hires."

The key to retention is to set people up to succeed. That shouldn't be a matter of good fortune; it should be a result of data-driven planning. Every successful company we studied measures inputs—a rep's pipeline, time spent prospecting, or specific sales calls completed—as well as outputs, thereby helping the reps stay on top of the process. "If you're not looking at the in-process measures and you're simply looking at the results," says McDermott, "you're missing the most important element, which is the future."

The best companies offer development opportunities to successful reps. Thus Citigroup's Thomson, who also oversees the wealth management business of Smith Barney, a division of the company, notes that successful financial advisers at his firm not only keep a higher percentage of the revenue they generate but also are rewarded with professional development that enables them to broaden and deepen their wealth management practices.

Data-driven companies also align incentives with the behaviors that are critical to a rep's financial success. That can entail adjusting metrics and commissions so that veteran reps can't simply coast on past sales. Or it can mean tailoring compensation systems to the type of sale. For example, one of Aggreko North America's business lines, called Aggreko Process Services, provides engineering services to supplement the temperature control equipment that the company rents to oil refineries (among other customers). Reps who sell these offerings—often involving a long and complex sales cycle—don't work on straight commission. Instead, they are paid a relatively high salary plus a bonus based on achieving targets. Meanwhile, reps who sell less-complex rentals, such as those to construction companies, earn a higher proportion of their compensation in commissions.

Sales Force Deployment

How a company goes to market—how it organizes and deploys not just its reps but its sales, support, marketing, and delivery resources—is a critical part of the sales process. Any company that has watched its territory-based sales reps migrate downmarket toward easy sales rather than profitable ones is facing a deployment problem. Its resources simply aren't being put where they can generate the greatest return.

One simple way to fix a deployment issue is to create a demand map of the market using segmentation information and then to compare it with your deployment map. The point is to substitute data for gut feel to identify where the best prospects are and to synchronize that information with the companies that sales reps actually call on.

But an analytical approach to deployment goes well beyond simply matching up reps with particular prospects. Best-practice companies also typically benchmark themselves on whether approaches to sales are paired up with the right customers.

Most companies, for example, utilize a range of sales channels: enterprise or other direct sales, inside sales, the Internet, dealers or value-added resellers, and so on. Having access to detailed information about the behavior and profitability of customer segments and microsegments allows sales executives to decide how best to deploy these different resources. For instance, inquiries about Aggreko

North America's commodity rentals are directed to the Internet or closed by tele-sales; inquiries about large consultative projects are sent to specialized sales reps. The ideal salesperson for the firm's construction-related business, says company president Walker, isn't necessarily a construction expert but a rep who "knows how to make 50 sales calls a week" and can close deals quickly. "The perfect rep for Aggreko's refinery business," Walker continues, "is someone who is comfortable with long sales cycles and complex, technology-intensive solutions."

Another question that leading sales organizations ask themselves is, Are the field reps spending as much time as possible selling? When we measure sales-people's "non-customer-facing time," we find that it often amounts to more than half of their total hours. If sales executives uncover that kind of problem, they have a variety of tools at their disposal. They may be able to channel some of the reps' administrative functions to support staff. They may want to reorganize territories to minimize time spent in transit. They also may simplify the systems

A New Role for Rainmakers

High-performing salespeople have always delivered the goods for their businesses. Can they be helpful in other ways as well? While we believe there is no substitute for the right segmentation strategy, processes, leadership, tools, and incentives, we also think that companies often fail to take full advantage of their top salespeople.

But that may be changing. Today, relationship sales consultants such as Andrew Sobel (coauthor of Clients for Life) and Tim Leishman (of consulting firm Leishman Performance Strategy) are taking a page from cognitive science and showing that it's possible to teach the underlying behaviors of top salespeople. In our experience, the best companies are aiming to do this instead of first searching for new stars. They are defining a new role for their rainmakers as collegial mentors who can impart what appear to be instinctual relationship-building skills. These firms are also having their rainmakers teach new hires how to break customer-winning behaviors down into actions they can adapt to their own personalities.

One pharmaceutical services company took just such an approach: It created a three-step training initiative that paired sales stars (who brought in about half the company's revenues) with new hires. During the "first steps" phase, the stars educated the newcomers about the market and took them on sales calls so they could observe firsthand how the high-performing veterans worked. During the "walking" phase, the newcomers made the calls—but the stars joined them, watched them, and offered tips and feedback. For the remainder of the year (the "running" phase), the stars met regularly with the newcomers to discuss progress and share ideas. The approach took about a year and capitalized not only on the high performers' desire to share their skills but also on their desire to earn: They received a 1% commission on all revenue brought in by the mentee during the yearlong program.

that the reps are expected to deal with. Several years ago, sales executives at Cisco set a goal of reducing reps' nonselling time by a few hours a week and charged the IT department with making it happen. The improvement led to several hundred million dollars in additional revenue.

All four of the levers help increase sales force productivity. What's most interesting, however, is that they seem to have the greatest effect on lower-ranked performers and so narrow the gap between top performers and everyone else. When we studied the results of a systematic sales force effectiveness program launched in several branches of a large Korean financial services provider, we found that the branches experienced a 44% rise in weekly sales volume, compared with a 6% decline in other branches. The top quartile of customer-service reps increased their product sales by 6%, the second quartile by 59%, the third quartile by 77%, and the bottom quartile by an astonishing 149%. A study of a comparable program in the Korean offices of another global financial-services firm found similar, though not identical, results. Increases in assets under management ranged from 2% in the top quartile to 33% in the second quartile to 54% in the third quartile, with the lowest quartile registering a 44% increase.

Beyond Best Practice

Finding, attracting, and holding on to talented salespeople is more difficult than ever. And companies can no longer afford to depend on them the way they once did. "It's gotten incredibly expensive to hire stars from competitors," acknowledges Citigroup's Thomson. Relying on the persuasive or relationship-building powers of a small group of talented individuals is simply insufficient for predictable, sustainable growth. (See the sidebar "A New Role for Rainmakers.")

Fortunately, sales executives like Bob Brody don't need to depend exclusively on rainmakers to achieve their numbers. They can get much more out of their entire sales force by using a hard-nosed, scientific approach to sales force effectiveness. Like any science, of course, this one is evolving. The tools and processes we have described are today's best practice, but in a few years, they will almost certainly be standard operating procedure for any company that hopes to compete effectively in the global marketplace.

Operational Excellence

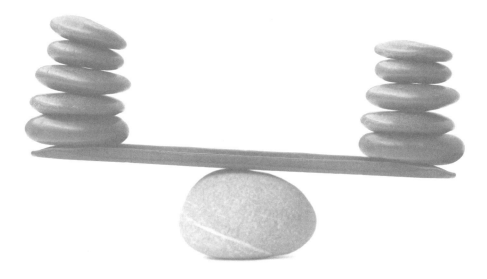

Look Before You Lay Off

Downsizing in a downturn can do more harm than good.

Darrell Rigby

For many years we were struck by the irony of hearing executives declare, "Our employees are our most valuable assets," and then watching them discard thousands of those prized assets at the first sign of difficult times—with widely disparate financial results.

This article appeared in the heart of the early-2000s recession, when massive layoffs were hitting the headlines. But though layoffs peak in a downturn, they are a continuing issue in today's turbulent global economy. Executives hope to cut costs, boost profitability, and stimulate investor interest, all in one bold move. Our analysis shows how misguided this approach can be. Layoffs by themselves do not typically generate better performance. And investors do not reward companies for layoffs unless they see other reasons for future improvement. Data of this sort changes the conversation in executive suites. Today, more of our clients are asking themselves where their company is headed and what their strategy is for getting there before determining which actions will deliver the most favorable results.

Layoffs, the conventional wisdom goes, are a necessary evil during economic downturns. The problem is, the conventional wisdom is wrong. Researchers at Bain & Company analyzed the layoffs at S&P 500 companies during the early stages of the current downturn (from August 2000 through August 2001) and found that even as layoff numbers reached record levels, most companies weren't downsizing. Rather, a small group of poorly performing companies accounted for the vast majority of firings, and their experience shows that reactive downsizing can backfire.

About a quarter of all S&P 500 companies announced layoffs during the study period, letting a total of about 500,000 workers go. That may sound like a lot, but the figure represents only 2.2% of the overall S&P 500 workforce. Just 22 downsizers cut 15% or more of their employees, accounting for 40% of the total cuts. The telecommunications industry alone was responsible for almost a third of the total layoffs, as shown in the exhibit "Who Did the Firing?"

HBR April 2002

Who Did the Firing?

Not everyone has downsized. The communications industry as a whole, including telecoms and network equipment makers, accounted for almost a third of all layoffs by S&P 500 companies between August 2000 and August 2001.

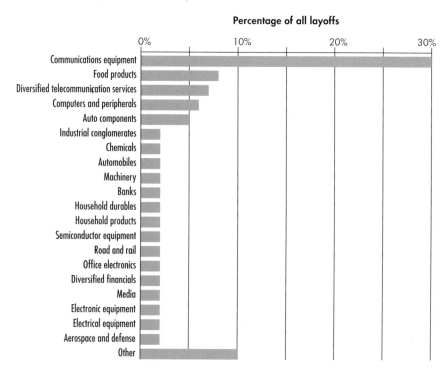

Percentage of all layoffs

The layoff numbers reported by companies, moreover, may have been exaggerated. Companies often include in their announcements not only true layoffs but also staff cuts achieved through attrition, early retirement, internal transfers, and divestitures of businesses. Because job cuts are normally carried out over many months or even years, improving economic conditions can lead companies to halt these staff reductions before they're completed.

Why would a company overstate its staff cuts? Because many managers assume that shareholders like layoffs, seeing job cuts as a signal that the company is serious about controlling costs. But the research tells a different story. More often than not, investors interpret downsizing as a symptom of mismanagement or eroding demand, and they shun the stock.

During the study period, companies with few or no layoffs performed significantly better than those with large numbers of layoffs. Businesses that laid off 3% or less of their workforces did just as well as companies with no layoffs at all: Both groups posted 9% share price increases, on average. By contrast, share prices remained flat in companies that let go 3% to 10% of their employees, such as Newell Rubbermaid, and prices plunged 38% among those, like Sapient and Qwest, that fired more than 10% of their workforce.

Part of the explanation for this is obvious: Large and repeated downsizings are symptomatic of flawed strategies that inevitably produce below-par results. But that's not the whole story. Even when we clustered the S&P 500 into groups with comparable sales growth rates, companies with no layoffs outperformed those that downsized. (See the exhibit "The High Price of Layoffs.") For example, among companies whose revenues fell at least 5%, those that implemented layoffs, such as Palm and Compaq, suffered an average stock price decline of 8%, while those that had no new layoffs, such as Waste Management, actually rose 19%. The hardest hit companies were those like Nextel whose sales grew more than 20% yet still resorted to layoffs. Shareholders had expected those companies to grow at even higher rates and were severely disappointed by the message of slower growth combined with the prospect of hefty restructuring costs.

If we categorize the layoffs by root cause, we find that shareholders are astute about which job cuts to reward and which to punish, as the exhibit "Strategy Matters" shows. Companies that invoked layoffs to cut costs, like insurer

The High Price of Layoffs

Among companies with similar growth rates, those that didn't downsize consistently outperformed those that did.

Average percent stock price change
August 16, 2000, to August 15, 2001

| Sales growth rates | < −5% | −5%–0% | 0%–5% | 5%–20% | > 20% |

no layoffs
layoffs

Strategy Matters

Shareholders punish companies that invoke layoffs solely to cut costs and reward those that downsize as part of a broader business strategy.

	Reason for layoffs		
	Cost cutting	Creating merger synergy	Repositioning
Announcements	158	19	17
Employees laid off	375,000	95,000	30,000
Change in stock price*	2%	9%	13%

*From 30 days before the announcement to 90 days after

Humana, saw their shares, on average, grow a mere 2% from 30 days before the announcement to 90 days after. But companies like Unilever that laid off workers as part of a strategy to consolidate mergers and capture business synergies watched their stocks rise, on average, by 9% in the same period. Share prices got an even bigger boost at companies that laid off more than 3% of their workforce in conjunction with announcing a strategic repositioning—changing their product lines or markets, for example. Companies in this group saw their stocks rise an average of 13%. When Office Depot, for example, announced job cuts as part of a plan to pull out of unprofitable regions, refocus on business customers, and adopt smaller store formats, its stock jumped 30%.

A final caution about making reflexive layoffs in a downturn: Clearly, companies with falling revenues and shrinking profits need to act. Layoffs, at times, are inevitable. But our calculations show that unless the eliminated jobs remain unreplaced for at least six to 12 months—and sometimes for longer than 18 months in knowledge-based businesses—a company will fail to earn a financial payback. That's because severance packages, temporary declines in productivity or quality, and rehiring and retraining costs more than offset the short-term wage savings. The average recession lasts only 11 months: If it takes a company three to six months to realize it is in a downturn and another three to six months to institute layoffs, it can find itself zigging just when it should be zagging.

Executives should carefully consider all options for coping with a downturn before letting workers go, especially if they're going to binge on rehiring as soon as the economy rebounds. The smartest companies make sure they are addressing the right issues in the right ways before they jettison jobs.

Innovation Versus Complexity: What Is Too Much of a Good Thing?

To get at the roots of profit-destroying complexity, companies need to identify their innovation fulcrum, the point at which the level of product innovation maximizes both revenues and profits.

Mark Gottfredson and Keith Aspinall

Complexity plagues the business world. Many CEOs say it's top of mind. The most visible symptom is often product-line complexity, which is the focus of this article. The "Model T" approach described here helps companies zero-base their product lines and determine exactly how much complexity they need to satisfy their core customers. With the help of such tools, our clients have simplified product platforms and designed products with more common parts. They have created packages of options and features to appeal to their most important customers, thus avoiding the bind of trying to offer every buyer a uniquely customized product.

But the reality is that complexity spreads across the enterprise, and taking steps to address it in one area by building a more focused product portfolio, for instance, is like squeezing a balloon—complexity bulges out in other parts of the business. The big opportunity is an integrated approach that tackles complexity in other forms as well—strategic complexity, organizational complexity, complexity in dealings with customers. It's a major undertaking, but the focused companies we have worked with accelerate their performance and pull away from competitors.

Walk into the In-N-Out Burger restaurant on Fisherman's Wharf in San Francisco, and one of the first things that may strike you is the number four. Four colors: red, white, yellow, and gray; four cash registers with four friendly faces behind them; and just four items on the menu. You can buy burgers, fries, shakes, and sodas. All the ingredients are delivered fresh to the store, where they're prepared in the open kitchen behind the cashiers. You'll see a few folks eating at the restaurant's tables or tucking into their food outdoors on patio

---

HBR November 2005

benches, but most customers come in with a handful of cash—no credit or debit cards, thank you—and head back out with their meals.

Four is In-N-Out Burger's innovation fulcrum—the point at which the number of products strikes the right balance between customer satisfaction and operating complexity. Four means simple purchasing, simple production, and simple service. And, it turns out, in a world where fast-food restaurants are forever adding formats and menu items, simple means profitable growth. With its chain of about 200 restaurants throughout California, Arizona, and Nevada, the family-owned company expanded its sales by 9.2%, to $308 million, in 2003, a rate just about double the fast-food standard. Analysts estimate In-N-Out's margins at 20%, again supersized for the industry.

So where's your company's innovation fulcrum? What's the number of product or service offerings that would optimize both your revenues and your profits? If you're like most managers, you're probably scratching your head right now. You don't have a clear idea of where that point lies. All you know—or at least strongly suspect—is that it's considerably lower than where you are today.

The fact is, companies have strong incentives to be overly innovative in new-product development. Introducing distinctive offerings is often the easiest way to compete for shelf space, protect market share, or repel a rival's attack. Moreover, the press abounds with dramatic stories of bold innovators that revive brands or product categories. Those tales grab managerial and investor attention, encouraging companies to focus even more insistently on product development. But the pursuit of innovation can be taken too far. As a company increases the pace of innovation, its profitability often begins to stagnate or even erode. The reason can be summed up in one word: complexity. The continual launch of new products and line extensions adds complexity throughout a company's operations, and, as the costs of managing that complexity multiply, margins shrink.

Managers aren't blind to the problem. Nearly 70% admit that excessive complexity is raising their costs and hindering their profit growth, according to a 2005 Bain survey of more than 900 global executives. What managers often miss is the true source of the problem—the way complexity begins in the product line and then spreads outward through every facet of a company's operations. As a result, the typical corporate response to complexity—launching a Six Sigma or other lean-operations program—often falls short. Such efforts may reduce complexity in one obvious area, but they don't address or root out complexity hidden elsewhere in the value chain. Profits continue to stagnate or fall.

In working with scores of companies since the 1980s, we've studied how complexity infects a company's entire value chain and identified the most common culprits for its spread: bad economic data, overoptimistic sales expectations, and entrenched managerial assumptions. Based on our research, we've developed a comprehensive approach to simplifying a business, centered on a company's innovation fulcrum. By finding the right balance between complexity and innovation—the way In-N-Out Burger has—companies can reduce costs by as much as 35% and lift revenues up to 40%. For many businesses, the innovation fulcrum becomes a turning point toward higher profits and greater sales.

Why Lean Is Not Enough

The usual antidotes to complexity miss their mark because they treat the problem on the factory floor rather than at the source: in the product line. Consider the case of a large, sophisticated high-tech manufacturer, long frustrated by its inability to reduce its inventory of parts and components. The company uses cutting-edge lean-manufacturing techniques to streamline production processes, and its labor force works at world-class productivity rates and routinely hits Six Sigma quality targets. But its inventory-turn rate, the number of times a year the company goes through its entire inventory, remains stuck at seven, a far cry from its goal of 12. Spurred by management's desire to fulfill customer needs and maximize sales, the company has steadily expanded its product line to the point that it now encompasses thousands of SKUs. To make all those products, the company must stock about 400,000 parts from hundreds of suppliers. Given the unpredictable variations in demand, particularly for less popular products, the manufacturer is forced to maintain extensive safety stocks in order to avoid having to shut down the plant while awaiting the delivery of a particular part. Because the product line's size drives inventory requirements, the turn rate lies beyond the reach of lean-manufacturing programs.

This company's problem is not unusual. It's natural for businesses to add products to keep customers happy. Smart marketers have no trouble justifying each addition as a means of adding or protecting revenues. But as more products are added, the costs of the resulting complexity begin to outweigh the revenues, and profits start falling. From that point on, every new offering—however attractive in isolation—just thins margins further. The more aggressively the company innovates in product development, the weaker its results become. (It's not just manufacturers that suffer from profit-eroding complexity. It affects service firms and knowledge companies as well. See the sidebar "The High Price of Service Complexity.")

What makes the problem particularly damaging is that it tends to be invisible to management. Look at what happened when one automaker started offering tinted windshields as an option. On the surface, the move looked like a clear winner. The company's marketers calculated that nearly 40% of customers would buy the option for $120, while the supplier would charge just $8 per unit. Moreover, installing tinted glass rather than clear glass seemed to add no labor costs on the assembly line. With new revenue far outstripping direct costs, adding the new option seemed to guarantee a quick profit boost.

But it didn't turn out that way. Offering tinted windshields, in combination with many other options, led to a whole range of higher costs that never showed up in the company's analysis. On the factory floor, the automaker had to adjust its work flows, add new quality-control tests, and even change the routes of its forklifts—all of which increased production costs. Purchasing and material-handling costs went up to accommodate the added part. Assembly-line errors crept up as proliferating options made workers' jobs less predictable. The tinted windshields added complexity to the company's operating and accounting software, which already produced millions of option codes to account for often-minor variations in assembly. Because the systems could no longer "control" for every option, orders now came to the factory floor in random patterns—for example, three cars in a row might require tinted windshields, followed by five that didn't. Workers' walk and reach time increased because they had to double-check order sheets to determine which windshield to install. The increased customization also caused unexpected peaks in demand, leading to dips in quality as workers rushed to finish tasks. Forecasting became more complex, resulting in cars with options packages no one wanted on dealers' hands. Perhaps most

The High Price of Service Complexity

The downsides of product complexity for manufacturers have been documented in many studies. But manufacturers don't suffer alone. In fact, in service and knowledge businesses, the continual introduction of new, information-rich offerings can have even more destructive consequences. It can leave virtually every employee struggling to make sense of a complex service portfolio, undermining both productivity and customer responsiveness.

One telecommunications company, for example, has used the power of information technology to slice and dice its service set into ever more finely differentiated options. The firm hoped it would boost revenues by more precisely fulfilling the needs of every imaginable buyer. But offering so many options has had the opposite effect. The company's customer-service reps are now forced to sort through more than a thousand promotion codes while they're talking to a potential customer. Most of the promotions offer distinct levels of discounts and product benefits. Making sense of them all is an overwhelming task. The result? Sales agents give slow and often inaccurate answers to inquiries—and customers grow frustrated and head toward a competitor.

pernicious, when a dealer discounted a car to move it off the lot, the forecasting system would see that sale as true marketplace demand, triggering inaccurate forecasts of orders that were likely to come. All of this led to a ratcheting up of inventories to avoid possible stockouts. The "clear winner" ended up losing the company money, though management didn't make the connection at the time.

Traditional financial systems are simply unable to take into account the link between product proliferation and complexity costs because the costs end up embedded in the very way companies do business. Systems introduced to help manufacturing and other functions cope with the added complexity are usually categorized as fixed costs and thus don't show up on variable margin analyses. That's why so many companies try to solve what really are product problems by tweaking their operations—and end up baffled by the lack of results.

What Customers Want

To meet the complexity challenge, you have to begin at the source: with the way your company views customers and their needs. In most cases, managers over-estimate the value buyers place on having many choices. Deeply entrenched in management thinking, that mistaken assumption sets the stage for product pro-liferation. But some companies have begun to challenge that belief. They have launched efforts to determine how much product or service choice customers really want and then gear their operations to efficiently provide that degree of complexity—and no more. These organizations are finding, in other words, their innovation fulcrums. (For an important caveat, see the sidebar "You Can Be Too Simple, Too.")

You Can Be Too Simple, Too

Complexity is not always bad. In many cases, maintaining some degree of complex-ity is essential to effective operations and astute risk management. The high-tech hardware manufacturing sector, for example, suffers frequent supply disruptions for a number of reasons. These include cyclical capacity shortages (notorious in memory chips), technology schedule slippages (for new CPUs, for example), and regional crises affecting suppliers (such as earthquakes). If alternatives are not available, the financial implications can be devastating. Getting too simple in your inventory may prevent you from having enough $2 capacitors on hand, which stops production of a critical video card, which, in turn, holds up production of a high-end workstation. Supply disruptions have cost high-tech OEMs hundreds of millions of dollars in profits. In situations like these, it makes sense to maintain redundant supply sources—even though doing so adds considerable complexity to the supply chain.

In 2003, the global food company H.J. Heinz decided to take on its complexity issues. The company launched a Remove the Clutter initiative aimed at "aggressively attacking complexity on many levels," as the company's annual report put it. The effort focused in particular on Heinz's product line, which, over the years, had ballooned to more than 30,000 SKUs as a result of mergers and acquisitions and a focus on creating local brands and products around the globe. As the company analyzed the portfolio, it discovered that many products actually had little appeal to customers. For example, of its three flavored ketchup variations—Hot & Spicy, Mesquite, and Zesty Garlic—only Hot & Spicy had attracted a loyal clientele and was generating meaningful sales. By the end of 2004, Heinz had discontinued its least profitable SKUs, trimming the total to about 20,000. The cuts reduced manufacturing, packaging, raw materials, and procurement costs while unclogging store shelves to make room for its profitable products. The initiative helped add a full percentage point to the company's gross margin.

Similarly, Starbucks decided a few years ago to streamline its artisan approach to making drinks by automating and standardizing certain elements of the latte manufacturing process. Today, Starbucks still has a very complex product line on the surface—customers can customize their lattes by size, type of milk, temperature, and flavor additives—but all the variations are based on a standard platform. The process change made very little difference to customers: Their desire for a "custom" product continued to be satisfied even as Starbucks' speed of service increased significantly.

Navistar International, the industrial equipment manufacturer, has also found its innovation fulcrum. In the truck industry, manufacturers typically offer customers pages of options for customizing their vehicles, leading to innumerable build permutations and hidden complexity across the value chain. Navistar challenged the widely held assumption that consumers want a custom-built product, and, in the mid-1990s, introduced a companywide strategy to focus its assembly plants and streamline product lines.

A key piece of this strategy was Navistar's Diamond Spec program, which created a simpler and quicker ordering process for one class of truck while reducing manufacturing complexity. Customers now chose from 16 preengineered modules instead of thousands of individual components. Not long after its launch, Diamond Spec accounted for 80% of dealer orders for that class of truck. The shortened ordering process from days to hours and the guaranteed improvements in quality and performance resulted in consumers placing 120% more orders during the pilot than initially forecast.

Clearly, when organizations prune their offerings to better fit the needs of customers, they do more than cut costs; they often boost sales as well. In many cases, in fact, the revenue gains are even greater than the cost savings. Consider Chrysler's California Velocity Program, launched in the late 1980s. For certain car lines, the carmaker identified the 200 top-selling configurations out of an initial list of about 5,000. The company then used detailed market analysis to suggest to each dealer which four to six of those 200 configurations would be the hottest sellers in its local area. The dealers would then focus on stocking those particular configurations on their lots. This was critical because the months-long process of special ordering a car caused 92% of all customers to buy directly off the lot. If a configuration near what the customer wanted was not on the lot, the dealer was likely to lose the sale. Chrysler tested the initiative in California, using the rest of the United States as a control. After just a year, the automaker found that average dealer sales in California were 20% higher relative to the control dealerships, and the margins of the California dealers were significantly better as well. By more tightly tailoring their offerings to customer needs, dealers sold more cars more quickly, while avoiding the discounting traditionally required to move "turkeys" off the lot. Fewer choices meant happier customers and higher sales. Chrysler then rolled out the program nationally, and over the next four years the company increased overall revenues by 40%.

The Model T Analysis

How exactly can you find your own company's innovation fulcrum? We've distilled the experiences of successful companies into a two-step process that we call a Model T analysis. First, you determine your zero-complexity baseline, the process cost of selling an absolute minimum number of standard products. What, in other words, would be your company's equivalent of Henry Ford's one-size-fits-all 1920s Model T? For Starbucks, the Model T might be a medium-size cup of brewed coffee. For a bank, it might be a basic checking account. Next, you add variety back into the business system, product by product, and carefully forecast the resulting impact on customer sales as well as the cost impact across the value chain. When the analysis shows the costs beginning to overwhelm the added revenues, you've found your innovation fulcrum. (For an overview of the process, see the exhibit "Finding Your Model T.")

Setting the Baseline

What would your company look like if it made and sold only a single product or service? Answering that question is important for two reasons. First, virtually every complexity reduction exercise we have seen that does not do this has failed to break through organizational resistance. Typically, marketing wants more

Finding Your Model T

What would be your company's equivalent of Henry Ford's one-size-fits-all Model T? To figure that out, begin by considering one of your highest volume products or SKUs. This will usually give you the clearest snapshot of the overall business systems—from marketing and manufacturing operations to relationships with suppliers and retailers—that may need to change. Make sure to choose a configuration that is average in terms of content, cost, and cycle time through the system.

In some instances, a company may have more than one Model T. This is often the case when products:

- are targeted at entirely different customer segments;
- have separate manufacturing processes;
- rely on platforms that are so different that the supply chains cannot be compared.

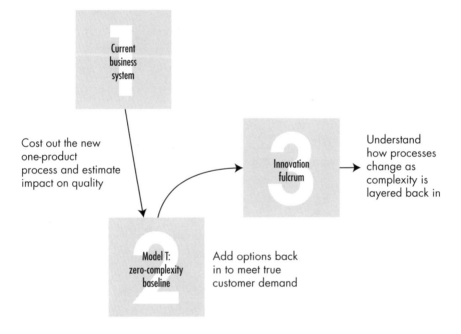

product diversity, while operations wants less. Starting from a purely theoretical baseline allows long-opposed sides to suspend their defensiveness and "not invented here" mentality. Participants—especially senior executives from marketing and operations who will lead the initiative—can begin thinking about change without asking for commitments.

Second, a baseline changes the lens through which managers view the business. It enables them to see through a company's existing complexity—a difficult challenge given the way financial reports hide process costs. Only by stripping away all the products, options, and configurations do managers get a clear sense of the extent of the complexity and its costs. In working with one company, for example, we determined that its products could be configured in 10 billion different ways. A much more profitable competitor, in contrast, offered 3,000 possible permutations. Our client's managers were unable to comprehend the operational implications of going from 10 billion to 3,000 configurations. When we asked one of them what would change under such a scenario, he shook his head and replied, "We only build 1,000 units a day, so I can't think of anything that would change." But when we asked the managers to imagine producing just one standard product, their eyes lit up. They immediately realized how they'd be able to streamline processes, strip away entire IT systems, and simplify transaction processing. One manager was particularly struck by how making only one product would change the forecasting process for parts. Each night he took an inventory of all 46,000 parts in the plant to ensure he had what he needed to manufacture any of the 10 billion permutations that customers could, theoretically, request. "If we don't have enough in stock or arriving by truck in time to meet the next day's schedule, then we have parts flown in. On average, 15 planes a day fly in to the plant from our suppliers around the country." He then pointed out, "All those costs would disappear instantaneously."

Choosing the right Model T can be tricky. Most companies should look for an average version of their basic offering, avoiding stripped-down versions on the one hand and elaborate models on the other. That way, variations in the cost of product features won't distort the analysis. Big companies operating in many markets may find it difficult to isolate a single "typical" offering. In such cases, managers should look for a proxy—a smaller competitor that's operating with a much more basic set of offerings. A national or international fast-food chain, for instance, might use In-N-Out Burger as a proxy for its own baseline. By analyzing the smaller, simpler company's operations and financials, the larger enterprise could estimate what its own costs and revenues would be if it minimized its product set.

It's also sometimes possible to look outside your immediate industry to gain insight into your baseline. For example, the Royal Bank of Canada examined the operations and results of local Money Marts, simple check-cashing operations that were thriving in low-income urban neighborhoods, as a model for its baseline set of services.

Adding Variety

Having established the cost of producing a baseline offering, you now need to add back in the options that will be valued by customers. The simplest

Gauging the Complexity of Your Business

The Roman poet Ovid surmised, "The cause is hidden; the effect is visible to all." Such is certainly the case with complexity today. It doesn't appear on balance sheets or on quarterly reports, but its impact can be conspicuous. We tend to see the most complexity in businesses that build products to stock, have a sophisticated supply chain or assembly environment, or sell products through retail stores. To determine the complexity of your business, begin by looking at your number of offerings, sales volume, modularity, and where complexity shows up in your value chain. Below, we offer a simple set of diagnostic questions for manufacturers, retailers, and service businesses. If you answer "yes" to any of these questions, your business is likely overly complex.

	Manufacturing	Retail	Services
Number of offerings	Is your total number of SKUs or possible product configurations greater than 1,000 or more than 50% greater than that of your lowest-complexity competitor?	Do your fastest-turning SKUs sell more than twice as frequently as your slowest? Are your inventory turns more than 10% slower than your lowest-complexity competitor?	Does your sales force have trouble understanding and communicating your most profitable offerings to core customers because of the complexity of the offerings?
Sales volume	Do less than 20% of SKUs, build combinations, or product configurations make up more than 80% of your sales volume?	Do less than 20% of SKUs, build combinations, or product configurations make up more than 80% of your sales volume?	Do less than 20% of SKUs, build combinations, or product configurations make up more than 80% of your sales volume?
Modularity	Have any of your competitors created modular or bundled products?	Is your approach to customer segmentation aimed at "offerings for many to attract the many" rather than "delighting the few to attract the many"?	Can you bundle offerings to meet specific segment needs?
Where complexity shows up	Does complexity show up early in the process, such as in engineering (creating change orders) or in assembly (creating unpredictability in the operation)?	Do you find that you frequently have to discount to sell slow-moving inventory?	Do you have excessive error rates, low close rates, or frequent customer abandonment due to customer confusion?

possible offering, after all, will rarely be the optimal offering. Henry Ford found that out when he continued to churn out basic Model Ts while Chevrolet was introducing new models. Ford soon saw his company's market share and profits erode. By expanding the product line, item by item, a company can forecast the costs that greater complexity will add as well as the incremental revenues that will be gained. Using detailed market research and customer analysis, managers can determine, in concrete terms, the level of choice customers demand. The company adds complexity back in only when it knows that a segment of customers will want the additional SKUs and be willing to pay more than the full systems costs the added complexity entails. (See the exhibit "Adding Variety, Carefully.")

The secret to this second step is to take a painstakingly methodical approach, adding only a single element of complexity at a time and then tracing the effect through the value chain. To return to the fast-food business, consider how Burger King recently used a combination of five measures to identify how adding a product or ingredient, in this case a premium sandwich bun, could benefit its overall business. Using consumer, operational, supply chain, financial, and strategic criteria to evaluate its bread carriers and selection of buns, Burger King saw that several of its current products were relatively complex and costly to handle, requiring special manufacturing and distribution. For instance, sourdough breads and baguettes were baked, frozen, and then shipped, refrigerated, through distribution centers. But using the same evaluation criteria, Burger King identified one attractive new product, the 5-inch corn-dusted bun, which could go through Burger King's core hamburger-bun supply chain.

Adding Variety, Carefully

When an industrial supplier saw that offering one additional option caused a huge leap in costs, it determined that its innovation fulcrum, the complexity level at which it would maximize both profits and revenues, rested at seven options.

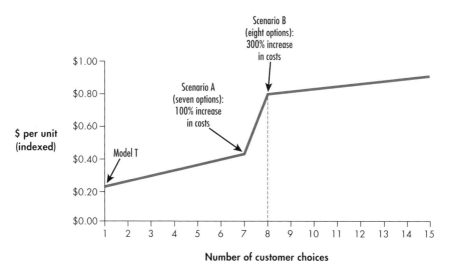

Burger King discovered that adding corn-dusted buns would benefit four critical stakeholders. First, consumers ranked the fresh-baked buns high on key dimensions of quality, including freshness, taste, and appearance. Second, the fresh-bread suppliers could deliver corn-dusted buns alongside standard buns on their current delivery routes. This would increase the drivers' average order and drop sizes, making each restaurant shipment more cost-effective. Third, corn-dusted buns would be simpler for restaurants, since suppliers would handle the inventory management, and the buns would not require costly frozen storage. Finally, the franchisees would benefit as the better products drove higher unit sales, and the simpler logistics resulted in lower unit costs. By analyzing the impact of the additional variety across all stakeholder groups, Burger King could see that the corn-dusted bun would be a winning addition.

Keeping It Simple

As we've seen, complexity is insidious. Getting rid of it is only half the challenge. The other half is keeping it out. Once a company is balanced on its innovation fulcrum, it must be vigilant in preventing the proliferation of products and in reassessing its optimal fulcrum point as, for example, customer needs and production technologies evolve. Four practices can help stem complexity creep:

Raise the hurdle rate. Requiring a higher rate of return on new products not only makes it more difficult for marketers to arbitrarily add SKUs, it also increases discipline in the innovation process. Consider one consumer apparel company that markets a diverse portfolio of iconic, global brands as well as some other national brands. While new styles from the classic brands tended to remain attractive to customers for years on end, innovative styles from the lesser known brands had short shelf lives—and were becoming a drag on profits. To solve the problem, the company started by reducing complexity, dropping thousands of SKUs and million of dollars in unprofitable sales, thereby increasing gross margins. Then, to keep a lid on complexity, the apparel maker introduced significantly higher hurdle rates for new-product introductions of its nonclassic styles, making it harder for the company to take on less profitable products. Instead of requiring a 15% return to introduce a new SKU, which had been the traditional standard, it upped the required return to 25%, a figure that more accurately reflected the added complexity costs. Finally, to ensure accountability in the innovation process, executives assigned a "product owner" to every new style. Employees in this role monitor new-product performance and quickly cull items before they become unprofitable.

Postpone complexity. The further down the value chain you introduce complexity, the less it costs you. The logic of postponement applies across a wide range of consumer durable and industrial goods sectors. Consider big-box retailing where consumers like product choices but don't want to wait for them and won't pay anything extra. Manufacturers accommodate this by designing products that are customized at the last step in the assembly or distribution process. Manufacturers can source materials and components from anywhere in the world, while assembling products just in time for customers close to the point of sale. In the kitchen department at Home Depot, for example, the retailer and manufacturers work together to provide a variety of customer options. MasterBrand Cabinets and Masco both provide entry-level cabinets that can be integrated with standard Wilsonart countertops. These manufacturers also provide higher-end custom products designed to be configured by in-store designers and then shipped directly to the job. (This approach addresses one of the biggest fears that Home Depot customers have—whether or not the company can actually deliver on its promise of an error-free custom design and installation.) In this way, Home Depot preserves economies of scale while giving customers the flexibility they want.

Institutionalize simplicity in decision making. The goal here is to manage complexity before it is hardwired into plants and costs. To do this, executives need to determine who has responsibility for making innovation decisions across the value chain. Take the example of one food company, where marketers had developed novel forms of packaging for a popular snack. From a marketing standpoint, the approach made sense. Consumer research had long supported the notion that grabbing attention in the store aisle was a prerequisite to growing sales in the impulse-driven snack market. Yet plant personnel knew that marketing's unchecked enthusiasm for innovative packaging was hurting efficiency across the supply chain.

To resolve the conflict, the company's executives entered the fray. First, they purged the excess complexity by consolidating products around a few standard kinds of packaging—an approach that reduced material costs and boosted the top line significantly. But the executives also developed a new decision-making process to ensure that complexity wouldn't sneak back in. They assigned formal roles in marketing and manufacturing that defined who would recommend, provide input, and approve new product and packaging concepts. Now brand managers no longer make decisions unilaterally but work through a series of checkpoints with manufacturing and sourcing managers.

Stay balanced. A company's innovation fulcrum can shift over time. As it becomes more experienced in production and distribution, for instance, a company can often drive down the costs of complexity, easing the penalty for adding a new product. Or, the needs of its customers may shift, either reducing or increasing the value they place on having more choices. A company needs to revisit its portfolio routinely to ensure it is optimizing profits. Here, the Japanese automakers provide an exemplary model. By the 1970s, the Big Three U.S. automakers had been competing for years on the breadth of the choices they offered consumers. The resulting complexity had driven up their costs, leaving them vulnerable to attack. Toyota and Honda made the most of this opening by striking the right balance between customer choice and operating complexity. Rather than offering customers millions of build combinations—as the U.S. automakers were doing—Honda, for instance, offered 32 build combinations with four colors.

The results were lower costs, higher-quality cars, and significant gains in market share. Even though the U.S. makers have followed their rivals' lead in becoming simpler—through reducing the number of basic platforms on which they build their various models—Toyota and Honda have been able to maintain their cost leadership by continually resetting their fulcrums. Responding to the demands of customers, for example, Honda has redesigned its engines to reduce fuel consumption and emissions. At the same time, the company has also streamlined the manufacture of its engine family, making it possible for the first time to produce different engine models on the same production line.

What's the right balance? It's a question Henry Ford should have asked before he began to see his competitors' colorful vehicles everywhere. He did, eventually, introduce the Model A, replete with multiple hues and features that won back some customer loyalty. But the lesson remains: Companies that strike the proper balance between innovation and complexity create more efficient operations and more profitable relationships with customers. They also pave the way to a competitive advantage within their industry, often by forcing onto competitors the high costs associated with customization. The need for this equilibrium may not be as obvious as it was in Ford's day, but it's just as critical.

The New Leader's Guide to Diagnosing the Business

How can an incoming leader lay the groundwork for dramatic performance improvement?

Mark Gottfredson, Steve Schaubert, and Hernan Saenz

New CEOs and general managers don't have much time to show what they can do. That was true when this article was written, as the world was heading into the financial crisis. It looms even larger for new CEOs today, as the global economy recovers and investors raise their expectations. New leaders need to conduct a quick, thorough assessment of the key factors that interfere with their company's path to full potential.

The Performance Improvement Diagnostic^{SM} *described in this article enables leaders to do exactly that. Hundreds of Bain clients and many other companies have used the diagnostic's tools to gather facts in four critical areas that shape business success. It is a valuable way to identify strengths and weaknesses and to develop plans to achieve full potential. The diagnostic can be deployed quickly. It is comprehensive— there is little risk that a company will miss a critical factor that is compromising performance. And it addresses the fundamentals of a business, showing both what can be done right away and what must be done over the long haul. It minimizes the chance that a company will take measures that enhance short-term results but compromise the longer-term journey to full potential.*

From 1999 to 2006, the average tenure of departing chief executive officers in the United States declined from about 10 years to slightly more than eight. Although some CEOs stay a long time, a lot of them find that their stint in the corner office is remarkably brief. In 2006, for instance, about 40% of CEOs who left their jobs had lasted an average of just 1.8 years, according to the outplacement firm Challenger, Gray & Christmas. Tenure for the lower half of this group was only eight months. Some of these short-timers were simply a poor fit and left of their own accord, but many others were ushered out the door because they

HBR February 2008

appeared unable to improve the business's performance. Nobody these days gets much time to show what he or she can do.

So within a few months at most, incoming CEOs and general managers must identify ways to boost profitability, increase market share, overtake competitors—whatever the key tasks may be. But they can't map out specific objectives and initiatives until they know where they are starting from. Every organization, after all, has its distinctive strengths and weaknesses and faces a unique combination of threats and opportunities. Accurately assessing all these is the only way to determine what goals are reasonable and where a management team should focus its performance improvement efforts.

Embarking on this kind of diagnosis, however, can be daunting because there are countless possible points of entry. Your company's operations may span the globe and involve many thousands of employees and customers. Should you start by talking to those employees and customers or by examining your processes? Should you focus on the effectiveness of your procurement or analyze your product lines? Managers often begin with whatever they know best—customer segments, for example, or the supply chain. But that approach is not likely to produce either the thoroughness or the accuracy that the management team and the business situation require.

What's needed instead is a systematic diagnostic template that can be tailored as necessary to an individual business's situation. Such a template has to meet at least three criteria: It must reflect an understanding of the fundamentals of business performance—the basic constraints under which any company must operate. The template must be both comprehensive and focused—covering all the critical bases of the business, but only those bases, without requiring any waste of time or resources on less important matters. And it should lend itself to easy communication and action.

This article presents a template that we think meets these criteria. It is built on four widely accepted principles that define any successful performance-improvement program. First, costs and prices almost always decline; second, your competitive position determines your options; third, customers and profit pools don't stand still; and fourth, simplicity gets results. Along with each principle, we offer question sets and analytic tools to help you determine your position and future actions.

We developed and refined this template over our combined 50-plus years of working with clients, nearly all of whom have needed to perform an accurate diagnosis quickly. We have recently used it both with large corporations and with private equity firms evaluating the potential of their portfolio companies. We tested it through a series of research studies and interviews that we conducted

Questions That Will Lead You to Breakthrough Performance

1. First Principle: Costs and prices almost always decline.

- How does your cost slope compare with your competitors'?
- What is the slope of price change in your industry right now, and how does your cost curve compare?
- What are your costs compared with competitors'?
- Who is most efficient and effective in priority areas?
- Where can you improve most, relative to others?
- Which of your products or services are making money (or not) and why?

2. Second Principle: Your competitive position determines your options.

- How do you and your competitors compare in terms of returns on assets and relative market share?
- How are the leaders making money, and what is their approach?
- What is the full potential of your business position?
- How big is your market?
- Which parts are growing fastest?
- Where are you gaining or losing share?
- What capabilities are creating a competitive advantage for you?
- Which ones need to be strengthened or acquired?

3. Third Principle: Customers and profit pools don't stand still.

- Which are the biggest, fastest-growing, and most profitable customer segments?
- How well do you meet customer needs relative to competitors and substitutes?
- What proportion of customers are you retaining?
- How does your Net Promoter® score track against competitors'?
- How much of the profit pool do you have today?
- How is the pool likely to change in the future?
- What are the opportunities and threats?

4. Fourth Principle: Simplicity gets results.

- How complex are your product or service offerings, and what is that degree of complexity costing you?
- Where is your innovation fulcrum?
- What are the few critical ways your products stand out in customers' minds?
- How complex is your decision making and organization relative to competitors'?
- What is the impact of this complexity?
- Where does complexity reside in your processes?
- What is that costing you?

in preparation for writing the book from which this article is adapted. Our experience and research convinced us that the template is a powerful tool. Its four principles cover the critical bases of virtually every business, providing managers with the minimum information required for a comprehensive diagnosis. Of course each manager will have to decide which elements of the template to emphasize (or de-emphasize) based on his or her business situation.

A word of caution: As the article makes clear, you will need to gather a lot of data quickly, ideally within the first three or four months of your tenure. Ask your senior leaders to head up teams that take on as many questions relevant to their areas of responsibility as they can handle. Ask for short, focused presentations to facilitate discussions about the main threats and opportunities. That should enable you and your teams to make quick, accurate decisions about the few areas on which to concentrate your efforts.

This process not only will show you where you are starting from (your point of departure, so to speak) but also will help you map out your performance objectives (or desired point of arrival) along with three to five critical change initiatives that will take you where you want to go. Indeed, many companies have used the template to create a set of charts showing exactly where and how the business can improve. Incoming leaders find that reaching a diagnosis within their first three to four months helps them lay a foundation for breakthrough performance—and avoid the pitfalls that other new leaders encounter all too frequently.

Analyze Costs and Prices

The first principle in our template is that costs and prices almost always decline. This may seem counterintuitive: Inflation often clouds the view, and special circumstances can sometimes drive costs and prices upward. But it is a well-established fact that inflation-adjusted costs—and therefore inflation-adjusted prices—decline over time in nearly every competitive industry. The analytic tool that best charts this principle is the *experience curve*, a graph showing the decline in a company's or an industry's costs or prices as a function of accumulated experience. For example, you might find that for every doubling of total units produced in your company, your per-unit cost in constant dollars drops by 20%. (In this case your experience curve is said to have a "slope" of 80%.) Because the same principle holds true for your competitors—and thus for your entire industry—the curve allows you to estimate where costs or prices are likely to be in the future. By comparing your company's cost curve with your industry's price curve, you can determine whether your costs are declining at the rate necessary for your company to remain competitive.

Understanding Experience Curves

Experience curves show how much industry prices and your costs have fallen each time the industry's cumulative experience (total units produced or services delivered) has doubled. They also allow you to predict how much inflation-adjusted prices and costs are likely to decline in the future.

The "slope" is the percentage of original price or cost remaining after each doubling of experience: A 70% slope, for example, means that prices have dropped by 30%.

Mapping your industry's price curve against your own cost curve can help pinpoint cost-reduction objectives. If you can reduce your costs faster than the previous CEO or general manager did, as in the graph below, you may be able to drive industry prices down faster as well, thereby putting pressure on your competitors' margins.

This chart shows the rate of price declines for every doubling of accumulated experience for a sample of both manufacturing and service industries. (The time periods here reflect a wide variety of studies conducted at different times.)

Industry	Dates	Price slope	Price decline
Microprocessors	1980–2005	60%	40%
LCDs	1997–2003	60%	40%
Brokerages	1990–2003	64%	36%
Wireless services	1991–1995	66%	34%
Butter	1970–2005	68%	32%
VCRs	1993–2004	71%	29%
Airlines	1988–2003	75%	25%
Crushed stone	1940–2004	75%	25%
Mobile phone services	1994–2000	76%	24%
Personal computers	1988–2004	77%	23%
DVD players/recorders	1997–2005	78%	22%
Cable set-top boxes	1998–2003	80%	20%
Cars*	1968–2004	81%	19%
Milk bottles	1990–2004	81%	19%
Plastics	1987–2004	81%	19%
Color TVs	1955–2005	83%	17%
DVDs	1997–2002	85%	15%

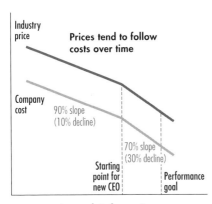

Accumulated experience

*Adjusted for changes in features and regulatory requirements

Construct Cost and Price Experience Curves

The first diagnostic questions to ask regarding this principle are "What is the slope of price change in our industry right now for the products or services we offer?" and "How does our cost curve compare with the industry's price curve and with our competitors' cost curves?" (See the exhibit "Understanding Experience Curves.")

The relationship between prices and costs in any given business area will determine some of your top priorities. If industry prices are going down while your costs are going up or holding steady, for instance, cost improvement is likely to be your single most urgent challenge. Your costs need to be decreasing over the long term regardless of what prices are doing. An upward movement in prices is frequently only temporary.

Understanding your overall cost trends, of course, is just a preliminary step. You then need to examine every segment of costs to determine where the central challenges and opportunities lie. Dig into the cost areas that are most important for your organization: manufacturing, supply chain, service operations, overhead—whatever they may be. Identify the key cost components and the trends in each one. Look specifically for instances of failure to manage to the experience curve, such as rising unit costs for labor or rising procurement costs. This kind of detailed analysis will identify opportunities for improvement at the most granular level and will provide the basis for a plan of action.

One CEO we spoke with reflected on what he called his biggest mistake in his first few months on the job. One of his company's business units was the leader in an industrial market. It had been raising prices, so it was quite profitable, and the new CEO decided to leave it alone for the time being. Then new, low-cost competitors from Asia entered the market and found that this unit had established both a price umbrella and a cost umbrella. The competitors soon undermined the unit's pricing power. The situation required urgent action to reduce costs by at least 15%, an initiative that is well under way. The lesson that CEO drew from the experience was stark: Be sure to diagnose *every* business position carefully, particularly in units that seem to be doing well.

Determine Costs Relative to Competitors'

After comparing your overall costs with industry prices and your competitors' costs, you need to take a more detailed look at your cost position in your industry. How do you compare with your key competitors in each cost area? Which company is most efficient and effective in priority areas? Where can you improve most relative to others? An analysis of cost position quantifies cost differences between your business and your competitors'; it also shows which cost elements and specific practices are different. Drill down until you understand where and how you differ, and why. That, in turn, will help you figure out where you can close cost gaps and gain or regain competitive advantage. It will also help you formulate detailed plans to do so.

Not long after he took on the top job, David Weidman, CEO of the $6.7 billion chemical company Celanese, headquartered in Dallas, asked his management team to conduct such a competitive assessment. "They came back and said, 'Holy cow, our average EBITDA to sales is seven or eight percentage points lower than the competition's,'" he told us. "And this was not in one business—this was across every organization." Weidman asked the team to identify specific areas where the company could improve relative to the competition. He wanted to find out, for instance, what one key competitor was doing in maintenance, because that company's maintenance spending was far better than Celanese's.

Understanding your cost position as well as your experience curve enables you to set proper targets. You will know, for example, that your lower-cost competitors are on their own experience curves and will have improved their own positions by the time you reach their current cost levels.

This kind of analysis presents a unique opportunity. Rather than simply comparing yourself with your top competitor, figure out which firm (including yours) is the best in each area. Maybe one is world-class in supply chain logistics practices, another in a particular manufacturing step, and so on. You can then construct a hypothetical competitor representing the best of the best, or what we call best demonstrated practices. That hypothetical company will have lower costs and better performance than any real-world company; you can use it as a benchmark for improvement, striving to leapfrog your competitors instead of just trying to catch up.

Assess the Profitability of Your Product Lines

Your next job is to determine which of your products or services are making money (or not), and why. The goal is to calculate the true margins of your products or services. First, you need to figure out direct costs for each product based on actual activities performed, rather than using standard costing. Then you must accurately allocate indirect costs—logistics, selling expenses, general and administrative expenses—to each product line and customer segment. Activity-based costing will give you a more accurate picture than you or your predecessor may have had in the past. The analysis should reveal the key cost and revenue drivers you need to address: Areas where the cost of goods sold, for instance, is out of line, or where your revenue performance is below benchmark levels.

When Warren Knowlton, until recently the CEO of the venerable British company Morgan Crucible, agreed to take the top job there, he learned that Morgan had hundreds of products, ranging from crucibles and advanced piezoceramics to body armor and state-of-the-art superconductor magnetic systems. He needed to determine which were making money and which were dragging the company down, so he drew up a list of critical questions for the heads of his business units. For example, he asked them to delineate their expectations for operating profit during the coming year and to explain expected changes from the preceding year. Then he asked for details. One question was "What percentage of your revenues represents sales to customers you would consider to have significant leverage over you?" Another was "How much of your revenue do you believe represents price-sensitive, commodity-type products?" Other questions focused on the cost side, including matters such as purchasing procedures and performance compared with that of rivals. The answers gave Knowlton a jump-start on his analysis of product-line profitability. He subsequently made major shifts in product lines to de-emphasize commodity products and unprofitable customers. Along with significant cost reductions, these moves enabled him to engineer a remarkable performance breakthrough, increasing the company's share price 10-fold in just three and a half years.

Evaluate Your Competitive Position

The second principle in our template is that your competitive position determines your options. Depending on your industry, there can be different drivers of profit leadership, including customer loyalty and "premiumness" of the product. But in most industries, one of the strongest predictors of a company's performance is its relative market share (RMS).

RMS is easy to calculate. If your company is a market leader, simply divide your share by the share held by your closest competitor (30% divided by 20%, say, equals an RMS of 1.5). If you're a follower, divide your share by that of the market leader (20% divided by 30% equals 0.67 RMS). Now plot the companies in your industry according to their RMS and their returns on assets (ROA). (See the exhibit "A Map of the Marketplace.")

You are likely to find that for many firms, higher RMS corresponds to higher ROA, and vice versa. This reflects the fact that market leaders typically outperform market followers on ROA; they have greater accumulated experience, leading to lower costs and superior customer insights, which in turn lead to higher profits. They thus have a greater ability to outinvest the competition in innovation, customer service, branding, and product support.

Compare Your Returns and Market Share with Those of Your Rivals

The ROA/RMS chart is an extraordinarily useful diagnostic tool because it helps you narrow down your options for performance improvement. There are five generic positions on the ROA/RMS chart: in-band leaders, in-band followers, distant or below-band followers, below-band leaders, and overperformers. Each has its own imperatives. Typically, for instance, in-band leaders find that they can raise the bar for competitors by investing in still-greater market share and in product or service improvements. In-band followers usually need to work hard just to keep up; only occasionally can they jump into a leadership role through heavy investment in innovation, the way Sony Computer Entertainment's

A Map of the Marketplace

One method of assessing your position in the marketplace is to plot the company's relative market share against its return on assets, and to do the same for your competitors. Companies in a well-defined industry typically line up in a fairly narrow band, reflecting the fact that market leaders usually outperform market followers on ROA. But a handful of companies ("overperformers") earn above-band returns while having a midrange or low market share, and others languish below the band with low ROA—often because they have not managed their costs down the experience curve.

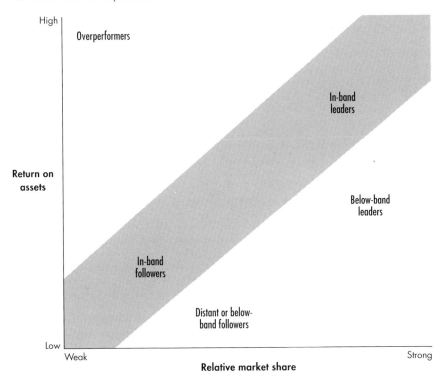

PlayStation leapfrogged Nintendo in the video game industry in the 1990s. Overperformers, which earn returns well beyond what their relative market share would suggest, typically need to maintain high levels of investment in whatever has enabled them to escape the pull of the band (assuming they aren't simply capitalizing on a temporary price umbrella). That might be a trusted or prestigious brand, an innovative or patented technology, exceptionally loyal customers, or some other asset. Below-band companies, of course, have probably not been managing their costs down the experience curve, which would be a primary reason for their underperformance.

Whatever your company's position, the band helps you understand its full potential by showing both opportunities and constraints. An in-band follower, for example, can't expect to earn the returns of a leader unless it moves up the band or escapes into the overperformer category through one of the strategies mentioned.

Band analysis can be used for two other diagnostic tasks: anticipating competitors' improvement strategies and assessing businesses in a multiunit organization.

Mapping your company against competitors is the first step toward seeing how each firm is making money or where it is failing to do so. It allows you to spot potential threats to and opportunities for your business, and to assess the strategic options available to others. For example, when we and our colleagues began compiling a band chart for credit card companies, we could find no relationship between market share and returns—a highly unusual situation. So we asked what was driving the returns of the most successful players. The analysis showed us that in this business, customer loyalty was the single most important factor in determining profitability. If every company were equally skilled at retaining customers, then market share would be the principal driver—but that wasn't the case. Because of the high cost of customer acquisition and the tendency of customers to increase their credit card use over time, sophisticated techniques for retaining customers could overcome advantages of pure scale and allow successful companies to become more profitable than their competitors. That would increase their RMS as well. Companies that had not developed such techniques were operating at a serious disadvantage.

Band analysis can also help the leader of a multiunit organization determine whether each business is achieving close to its full-potential performance. This objective was at the heart of Knowlton's decision-making process regarding Morgan Crucible's many businesses. Placing Morgan's business units on a band chart that compared their economic performance with their region-weighted relative market share, Knowlton could see at a glance that some units, such as the company's industrial rail and traction division, were in the band: They were performing as expected. Others, such as thermal ceramics, were below the band and needed to be moved upward, typically through aggressive cost control and measures designed to grow revenue. Still others were laggards in the lower left of the band and were candidates for divestiture.

Measure Your Market Size and Trends

How big is your market, exactly? Which parts are growing fastest? Where are you gaining or losing share? A simple way to map your market's size and dynamics is to draw a rectangle and then divide it into vertical segments representing your most important submarkets or products. The width of the segments should be set in proportion to the share of revenues they account for in the market. Next, divide each of these vertical segments into boxes representing the share held by each principal competitor. Create one chart for three to five years ago and one for the present. The two charts will show you the sectors and the competitors experiencing market growth. Depending on your situation, of course, you may need to customize the basic chart. A company selling telecommunications equipment in Asia might first map the Asian telecom market by country and by sector (wireline, wireless, and so on) and then break it down into competitors' market shares. Again, comparing two or more points in time will show you where, and how fast, the market is growing. Faster-growing markets attract more competitive interest, so you will need an aggressive plan to win your share.

Other tools may be useful as well. A so-called S-curve chart, for instance, which plots industry growth against time, can show the inflection points where growth accelerates and then tapers off.

Assess Your Firm's Capabilities

Your company's chances to achieve its full potential—to improve its position on the band chart—depend significantly on its capabilities. Which critical capabilities are giving you a competitive advantage? Which do you lack? Which need to be strengthened or acquired? The global technology and engineering company Emerson, for example, knows how to manage its costs so aggressively that it can acquire other businesses and then add substantial amounts of value. Companies can also succeed if they can develop capabilities they don't currently have. The iPod didn't really take off until Apple developed the capabilities to manage and sell digitized music through its iTunes store.

Every company, of course, must make decisions about which capabilities it wants to develop or maintain in house and which it wants to obtain from suppliers. The context for these decisions has changed dramatically in recent years. In many industries the primary basis of competition has shifted from ownership of assets (stores, factories, and so on) to ownership of intangibles (expertise in supply chain or brand management, for example). At the same time, a handful of vanguard companies have transformed what used to be purely internal corporate functions into entirely new industries. Thus FedEx and UPS offer world-class logistics-management services, while Wipro and IBM offer numerous business and IT services.

The result of all this is that companies can no longer afford to make sourcing decisions on a piecemeal basis—nor can they be satisfied with a "good enough" approach to selecting and working with suppliers. Today, you must assess every capability that you need in order to create or develop a product or service. You should analyze every step of your value chain, from design and engineering to product or service delivery. You should compare yourself not only with competitors in your industry at every step of the chain but also with whatever companies are the best in the world at performing each particular step. Are you the best? Or do you have some capability that creates a sustainable competitive advantage in a given step? If the answer to both questions is no, you should ask whether you can improve or acquire the relevant capability, or whether you might be better off sourcing that part of your value chain to the best supplier.

Understand Your Industry's Profit Pool

The third principle in our template is that customers and profit pools don't stand still. Markets undergo massive changes all the time, mostly because customers' desires and needs evolve. Companies repeatedly discover that the landscape they operate in has altered significantly and that the plans and strategies that worked so well yesterday no longer work today. They find that the *profit pool* from which they were drawing their earnings has dried up or attracted new competitors, and that deep new pools of profit have appeared elsewhere. (For more on profit pools, see Orit Gadiesh and James L. Gilbert, "Profit Pools: A Fresh Look at Strategy," HBR, May–June 1998.) For these reasons, you'll need to examine the profit pools you currently draw on and those that might hold potential for the future.

Study Customer Needs and Behavior by Segment

Correctly segmenting customers and developing proprietary insights into their purchasing behavior is one of the most powerful methods of building loyalty, increasing growth, gaining market share, and thus expanding your share of the profit pool. Which are the biggest, fastest-growing, and most profitable segments? How well do you meet customers' needs, compared with competitors and substitutes? As you raise these questions, you will want more-specific answers, such as how customers are segmented. On the basis of needs? Behavior? Occasion of use? Demographics? What are each segment's characteristics and spending habits? What share of wallet is each one currently giving you, and is there reason to think that you can increase that share?

You can use many tools to delve deeply into customer needs and behavior. These range from cluster analysis to sophisticated ethnographic research. It's often worthwhile to look at customers through many different lenses because you may spot something that customers themselves aren't even aware of. While we don't have space to discuss all such tools in this article, we'll mention a simple one that has been remarkably effective even in highly sophisticated industries. We call it a SNAP (segment needs and performance) chart. It can help you assess how well you are meeting the needs of the segments you are targeting.

Segment Needs and Performance

This SNAP (segment needs and performance) chart displays data for a fitness machine company we're calling FitEquipCo. The company exceeds customers' requirements on innovation and assortment, the attributes that rank fourth and sixth, respectively, in importance to customers. It is thus incurring costs that may not earn a return in the marketplace. Meanwhile, it is slightly underperforming competitors on quality, which is first in importance, and significantly underperforming on customer service, which is third. FitEquipCo needs to take action to close those gaps.

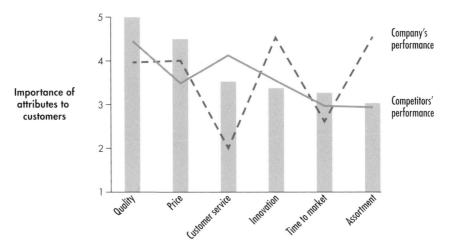

To develop a SNAP chart, start by defining the attributes of the products or services you offer that may be important to the customer segments you want to target. Then conduct research to determine how important each of these actually is to these customers. A bank, for instance, might study everything from its hours of business to its loan rates to the quality of the advice it offers and the ease of access to its ATMs. Finally, assess where you stand on each scale and where your competitors stand.

This process will show how you measure up to the competition in the eyes of your key customer segments. You can use the SNAP chart to identify which gaps are most important to close (if you're behind) or widen (if you're ahead). You can also see where you might be overshooting the mark. (See the exhibit "Segment Needs and Performance.")

Track Customer Retention and Loyalty

What proportion of customers are you retaining? Loyalty can be a critical factor in the economics of a business, particularly when the cost of acquiring a customer is high, switching costs are relatively low, or both. Accordingly, you need to know your retention rates for each segment. Doing so not only will help you determine the profitability of the segment but also will help you make plans to boost retention rates where necessary.

A good indicator of loyalty and probable retention is the Net Promoter score (NPS®), developed by our colleague Fred Reichheld. This measures customers' responses to the question "How likely is it that you would recommend this company (or product or service) to a friend or colleague?" Respondents answer on a zero-to-10 scale, where a 10 means "Extremely likely" and a zero means "Not at all likely." Those who give you a nine or a 10 are your *promoters*. Research shows they spend more with you, are likely to increase their spending in the future, and sing your praises to their friends and colleagues. Those who give you a seven or an eight are *passives,* and those who rank you zero to six are *detractors*. Promoters are an engine of growth, but detractors often cost your company more than they are worth, and they bad-mouth you to anybody who will listen.

Your Net Promoter score is simply the percentage of promoters minus the percentage of detractors. Measured relative to competitors, NPS has been shown to correlate with growth rates and with other measures of customer satisfaction. Properly implemented, NPS creates a closed learning loop among customers, the front line, and management, and thus can be used as a basis for managerial decisions, just as financial reports are. American Express and many other companies use NPS-like metrics throughout their organizations to give them quick, regular reads on customers' attitudes and potential behavior.

Segmentation and retention efforts are at the opposite ends of a six-step chain of activity that enables a company to earn more profits per customer than its competitors and then to outinvest the competitors to generate faster growth. The first steps are (1) identifying the most attractive target segments and (2) designing the best value propositions to meet their needs. The next ones are (3) acquiring more customers in the target segment and (4) delivering a superior customer experience. That enables the company (5) to grow its share of wallet and (6) to increase loyalty and retention, with more promoters and fewer detractors.

Anticipate Profit-Pool Shifts

CEOs and general managers naturally need to assess how much of their industry's profit pools their firms own today. But they must also gauge how profit pools are likely to change in the future and what opportunities or threats these shifts may create. One useful tool is a profit-pool map, which shows the channels, products, or sequential value-chain activities in the market and indicates the total profits available from them. You can then locate your business and its competitors on the map, showing how much each company takes from each part of the profit pool. It's wise to do this for all customer segments and all sets of products.

A company we'll call FitEquipCo mapped the growth (historical and projected) of its industry. Then it gathered extensive data about customers' intent to purchase or repurchase and developed profit-pool projections by product (treadmills, elliptical machines, and so on), by sales channel (mass merchants, specialty stores, and

A Map of the Profit Pool

A profit-pool map for FitEquipCo revealed some telling market developments. Although the company was shipping almost 40% of all units in the marketplace, it had only about 20% of the profits. The column widths reflect the proportion of units sold (left) and operating profits earned (right) in each channel.

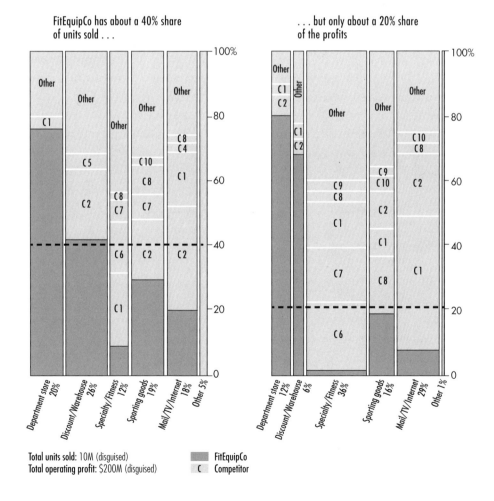

FitEquipCo has about a 40% share of units sold . . .

. . . but only about a 20% share of the profits

Total units sold: 10M (disguised)
Total operating profit: $200M (disguised)

FitEquipCo
C Competitor

so on), and by price point (entry-level, value, and premium). The map showed, for instance, that FitEquipCo needed to build up its distribution through sports specialty stores, which delivered higher margins. Through such measures, the company projected, it could increase earnings by $86 million over a three-year period, more than doubling operating profits. (See "A Map of the Profit Pool.")

As with the market map, it's wise to compare at least two points in time so that you can see how the pool is evolving. Often a significant threat to the profit pool comes from companies that don't yet compete in your industry or are still too small to be noticed. Yet these competitors can turn an industry upside down. Think, for example, of the effects minimill companies such as Nucor had on the U.S. steel industry.

Simplify, Simplify

The fourth principle in our template is that simplicity gets results. A couple of years ago, researchers from Bain & Company surveyed executives in 960 companies around the world, asking them about complexity in their organizations. Nearly 70% of the respondents told us that complexity was raising their companies' costs and hindering growth. Another team of researchers studied the impact of complexity on the growth rates of 110 companies in 17 different industries. The researchers found that the least complex companies grew 30% to 50% faster than companies with average levels of complexity, and 80% to 100% faster than the most complex companies. In one particularly dramatic example, a telecommunications company that offered consumers only about one-fifth the number of options offered by a competitor was growing almost 10 times as fast.

Gauge the Complexity of Your Products or Services

To diagnose your company's level of complexity, begin by asking how complex your product or service offerings are and what that degree of complexity may be costing you. Benchmark your line of products or services against the competition's; try to identify your "innovation fulcrum," the point at which the variety of products or services you offer maximizes your sales and profits. It will be helpful to construct what we call a Model T chart, showing the costs when you add features to the basic product or service. It's valuable to do this exercise not only with your own company's data but also with your competitors'. (For more on complexity and the Model T chart, see Mark Gottfredson and Keith Aspinall, "Innovation Versus Complexity: What Is Too Much of a Good Thing?" HBR, November 2005.) Ask yourself which of your competitors has the advantage as variety and complexity in the industry increase—and why. You can apply what you learned from your customer segmentation research to this assessment. If you know what customers want now and what they are likely to want in the future, you can better judge what level of variety is appropriate for your marketplace.

The complexity test is a necessary counterbalance to tools such as customer segmentation. The temptation, after all, is to divide your customer base into finer and finer subcategories and tailor your offerings to each segment, all in the name of giving customers exactly what they want. That was one way Charles Schwab, the financial-services firm, got itself into a difficult situation in the early 2000s. Schwab added a plethora of new offerings and divisions, including a firm specializing in institutional investments and an East Coast wealth-management company. In 2004, founder Charles Schwab returned to the firm as CEO and promptly took steps to reduce the complexity. He sold off most of the recent acquisitions, reduced the number of service offerings, and streamlined internal roles and processes. These and other moves allowed him to take out some $600 million in costs, reduce commissions, gain market share, and increase the firm's operating income by 3%.

Assess the Complexity of Your Organization

Decision-making procedures and organizations grow complex over time as well. You need to know how your company stacks up against competitors on these dimensions and what the effects of undue complexity may be. Our colleagues Paul Rogers and Marcia Blenko have developed what they call a RAPID® analysis, which allows managers to assess decision-making bottlenecks, assign clear decision roles to individuals in the organization, and hold them accountable. (RAPID is a loose acronym for the different roles people can take on: *recommend*; *agree*; give *input*; *decide*; and *perform*, or implement the decision.) Another useful tool is a spans-and-layers analysis, which shows the number of levels in an organization from the CEO to the frontline worker, and the number of people reporting up to each level. Spans that are too narrow—meaning too few people report to individual bosses—are likely to lead to excess overhead costs, slow decision making, and unnecessary managerial oversight.

When sizing up your company's decision making, turn to suppliers, distributors, and customers for feedback. They are often good judges of how quickly and effectively you can make a decision compared with others in the industry. Employees will be quick to tell you whether they feel supported and empowered by the organization's management structure or whether it just gets in their way.

Determine Where You Can Simplify Processes

Where does complexity reside in your processes? What is that costing you? St.George Bank, like others in Australia, experienced a slowdown in residential lending at one point and so was developing a growth strategy for commercial banking. But the complexity of the bank's commercial credit processes was a major constraint on growth. All loan applications, large or small, were treated in a similar way. A sizable number of applications had to be sent up the ladder to a central credit group. Then-CEO Gail Kelly and her management team determined that this level of complexity was not inevitable—for example, they could create a fast-track system for applications from existing customers that fell within certain risk boundaries. That alone led to a 30% reduction in time spent by the lending officers. The bank also increased the amounts that a local lending officer could approve, resulting in a reduction of 50% or more in deals sent to the central credit group.

How can you identify such opportunities for process improvement? As at St.George Bank, process complexity can show up in any number of areas: on the production floor, in distribution networks, in interactions with customers, in back-office procedures. The key is to figure out where complexity is unavoidable—and where, by contrast, you can put practices in place to reduce complexity while still delivering the products and services that customers want. Process mapping is a good way to get started. In a process map, diagrams show the interactions among different steps in a process and the people or departments responsible for the steps. This enables the management team to visualize and understand the whole process, spot problems and opportunities for improvement, and address them through root-cause analysis. You want to map activities, inputs, and outputs associated with each step, and the wait times between steps.

Successful streamlining of the processes produces several mutually reinforcing benefits. It increases efficiency, allowing a company to reduce head count and its costs. Streamlining also cuts down on errors and rework. It reduces cycle time, enabling the company to deliver the product or service to the customer significantly faster and enhancing customer loyalty. More-loyal customers are likely to order more, generating growth and increasing the possibilities for still greater economies in production or service delivery.

Many companies try to simplify their processes without simplifying any other aspect of the organization. This is a mistake. Process simplification tends to be undermined by unnecessary complexity in the company's product lines, organization, and decision-making procedures. So gather the data to address complexity on all three fronts and then determine the most fruitful points of attack.

A diagnostic template such as the one we've described here is powerful not because it contains any single new insight but because it covers the ground a management team needs to cover. By answering the questions we've provided, you can pull together a comprehensive set of data enabling you to understand the gap between your current performance and your full potential. You can then set specific goals and launch initiatives that will drive the company to achieve that potential during your tenure and develop the performance profile that you are shooting for. A company that has worked through such a diagnostic template might aim for objectives such as these:

- Reduce costs by $200 million to move relative cost position from 110% of best competitor to 90%.

- Increase relative market share from 0.9 to 1.2; move share of high-profit segment A from 40% to 60%, with a retention increase of six percentage points.

- Increase share of profit pool from 40% of $2 billion to 70% of $2.8 billion by expanding into a downstream service business in the most profitable product segments.

- Cut SKUs from 100,000 to 2,000; reduce organizational layers in SG&A from five to three; outsource 20% of all G&A costs.

Objectives like these can translate into marching orders for an entire organization. Because they stem from a comprehensive diagnosis, everyone can understand them and see why they are important. Both managers and employees are more likely to buy in and put their shoulders to the wheel.

Diagnosis, of course, is only one part of a performance-improvement program. You still must decide on where you want the company to go, along with the three to five critical initiatives that will get you there. But a thorough, accurate diagnosis is what makes the rest possible. It's an indispensable first step toward breakthrough performance.

High-Performance Organization

Who Has the D? How Clear Decision Roles Enhance Organizational Performance

Your organization can become more decisive—and can implement strategy more quickly—if you know where the bottlenecks are and who's empowered to break through them.

Paul Rogers and Marcia Blenko

Today's companies are complex, and decisions often get trapped in the organizational mire. This article helped to show companies how they can cut through the complexity by assigning clear decision roles. It led to a series of other articles and eventually to the book Decide & Deliver: 5 Steps to Breakthrough Performance in Your Organization, *published in 2010.*

The decision-rights tool the article describes—RAPID®, a loose acronym for Recommend, Input, Agree, Decide, and Perform—was quickly embraced by clients and many other organizations. RAPID on its own, however, produces mixed results. Assigning decision roles is a powerful managerial tool, but unless it is accompanied by other organizational changes it usually falls short of the desired effects. A company must commit to a common decision style and language. It needs accountability principles to govern who has the "D"—decision authority—in any given situation. Its leaders must learn to follow the newly assigned roles and procedures, not always an easy task. A company can determine all the right roles, but unless it takes this kind of holistic approach it will wind up with binders on shelves rather than changes in everyday behavior.

Decisions are the coin of the realm in business. Every success, every mishap, every opportunity seized or missed is the result of a decision that someone made or failed to make. At many companies, decisions routinely get stuck inside the organization like loose change. But it's more than loose change that's at stake, of course; it's the performance of the entire organization. Never mind

---

what industry you're in, how big and well known your company may be, or how clever your strategy is. If you can't make the right decisions quickly and effectively, and execute those decisions consistently, your business will lose ground.

Indeed, making good decisions and making them happen quickly are the hallmarks of high-performing organizations. When we surveyed executives at 350 global companies about their organizational effectiveness, only 15% said that they have an organization that helps the business outperform competitors. What sets those top performers apart is the quality, speed, and execution of their decision making. The most effective organizations score well on the major strategic decisions—which markets to enter or exit, which businesses to buy or sell, where to allocate capital and talent. But they truly shine when it comes to the critical operating decisions requiring consistency and speed—how to drive product innovation, the best way to position brands, how to manage channel partners.

Even in companies respected for their decisiveness, however, there can be ambiguity over who is accountable for which decisions. As a result, the entire decision-making process can stall, usually at one of four bottlenecks: global versus local, center versus business unit, function versus function, and inside versus outside partners.

The first of these bottlenecks, *global versus local* decision making, can occur in nearly every major business process and function. Decisions about brand building and product development frequently get snared here, when companies wrestle over how much authority local businesses should have to tailor products for their markets. Marketing is another classic global versus local issue—should local markets have the power to determine pricing and advertising?

The second bottleneck, *center versus business unit* decision making, tends to afflict parent companies and their subsidiaries. Business units are on the front line, close to the customer; the center sees the big picture, sets broad goals, and keeps the organization focused on winning. Where should the decision-making power lie? Should a major capital investment, for example, depend on the approval of the business unit that will own it, or should headquarters make the final call?

Function versus function decision making is perhaps the most common bottleneck. Every manufacturer, for instance, faces a balancing act between product development and marketing during the design of a new product. Who should decide what? Cross-functional decisions too often result in ineffective compromise solutions, which frequently need to be revisited because the right people were not involved at the outset.

The fourth decision-making bottleneck, *inside versus outside partners*, has become familiar with the rise of outsourcing, joint ventures, strategic alliances, and franchising. In such arrangements, companies need to be absolutely clear about which decisions can be owned by the external partner (usually those about the execution of strategy) and which must continue to be made internally (decisions about the strategy itself). In the case of outsourcing, for instance, brand-name apparel and footwear marketers once assumed that overseas suppliers could be responsible for decisions about plant employees' wages and working conditions. Big mistake.

Clearing the Bottlenecks

The most important step in unclogging decision-making bottlenecks is assigning clear roles and responsibilities. Good decision makers recognize which decisions really matter to performance. They think through who should recommend a particular path, who needs to agree, who should have input, who has ultimate responsibility for making the decision, and who is accountable for follow-through. They make the process routine. The result: better coordination and quicker response times.

Companies have devised a number of methods to clarify decision roles and assign responsibilities. We have used an approach called RAPID, which has evolved over the years, to help hundreds of companies develop clear decision-making guidelines. It is, for sure, not a panacea (an indecisive decision maker, for example, can ruin any good system), but it's an important start. The letters in RAPID stand for the primary roles in any decision-making process, although these roles are not performed exactly in this order: recommend, agree, perform, input, and decide—the "D." (See the sidebar "A Decision-Making Primer.")

The people who *recommend* a course of action are responsible for making a proposal or offering alternatives. They need data and analysis to support their recommendations, as well as common sense about what's reasonable, practical, and effective.

The people who *agree* to a recommendation are those who need to sign off on it before it can move forward. If they veto a proposal, they must either work with the recommender to come up with an alternative or elevate the issue to the person with the D. For decision making to function smoothly, only a few people should have such veto power. They may be executives responsible for legal or regulatory compliance or the heads of units whose operations will be significantly affected by the decision.

People with *input* responsibilities are consulted about the recommendation. Their role is to provide the relevant facts that are the basis of any good decision: How practical is the proposal? Can manufacturing accommodate the design change? Where there's dissent or contrasting views, it's important

A Decision-Making Primer

Good decision making depends on assigning clear and specific roles. This sounds simple enough, but many companies struggle to make decisions because lots of people feel accountable—or no one does. RAPID and other tools used to analyze decision making give senior management teams a method for assigning roles and involving the relevant people. The key is to be clear who has input, who gets to decide, and who gets it done.

The five letters in RAPID correspond to the five critical decision-making roles: recommend, agree, perform, input, and decide. As you'll see, the roles are not carried out lockstep in this order—we took some liberties for the sake of creating a useful acronym.

Recommend. People in this role are responsible for making a proposal, gathering input, and providing the right data and analysis to make a sensible decision in a timely fashion. In the course of developing a proposal, recommenders consult with the people who provide input, not just hearing and incorporating their views but also building buy in along the way. Recommenders must have analytical skills, common sense, and organizational smarts.

Agree. Individuals in this role have veto power—yes or no—over the recommendation. Exercising the veto triggers a debate between themselves and the recommenders, which should lead to a modified proposal. If that takes too long, or if the two parties simply can't agree, they can escalate the issue to the person who has the D.

Input. These people are consulted on the decision. Because the people who provide input are typically involved in implementation, recommenders have a strong interest in taking their advice seriously. No input is binding, but this shouldn't undermine its importance. If the right people are not involved and motivated, the decision is far more likely to falter during execution.

Decide. The person with the D is the formal decision maker. He or she is ultimately accountable for the decision, for better or worse, and has the authority to resolve any impasse in the decision-making process and to commit the organization to action.

Perform. Once a decision is made, a person or group of people will be responsible for executing it. In some instances, the people responsible for implementing a decision are the same people who recommended it.

Writing down the roles and assigning accountability are essential steps, but good decision making also requires the right process. Too many rules can cause the process to collapse under its own weight. The most effective process is grounded in specifics but simple enough to adapt if necessary.

When the process gets slowed down, the problem can often be traced back to one of three trouble spots. First is a lack of clarity about who has the D. If more than one person think they have it for a particular decision, that decision will get caught up in a tug-of-war. The flip side can be equally damaging: No one is accountable for crucial decisions, and the business suffers. Second, a proliferation of people who have veto power can make life tough for recommenders. If a company has too many people in the "agree" role, it usually means that decisions are not pushed down far enough in the organization. Third, if there are a lot of people giving input, it's a signal that at least some of them aren't making a meaningful contribution.

to get these people to the table at the right time. The recommender has no obligation to act on the input he or she receives but is expected to take it into account—particularly since the people who provide input are generally among those who must implement a decision. Consensus is a worthy goal, but as a decision-making standard, it can be an obstacle to action or a recipe for lowest-common-denominator compromise. A more practical objective is to get everyone involved to buy in to the decision.

Eventually, one person will *decide*. The decision maker is the single point of accountability who must bring the decision to closure and commit the organization to act on it. To be strong and effective, the person with the D needs good business judgment, a grasp of the relevant trade-offs, a bias for action, and a keen awareness of the organization that will execute the decision.

The final role in the process involves the people who will *perform* the decision. They see to it that the decision is implemented promptly and effectively. It's a crucial role. Very often, a good decision executed quickly beats a brilliant decision implemented slowly or poorly. RAPID can be used to help redesign the way an organization works or to target a single bottleneck. Some companies use the approach for the top 10 to 20 decisions, or just for the CEO and his or her direct reports. Other companies use it throughout the organization—to improve customer service by clarifying decision roles on the front line, for instance. When people see an effective process for making decisions, they spread the word. For example, after senior managers at a major U.S. retailer used RAPID to sort out a particularly thorny set of corporate decisions, they promptly built the process into their own functional organizations. To see the process in action, let's look at the way four companies have worked through their decision-making bottlenecks.

Global Versus Local

Every major company today operates in global markets, buying raw materials in one place, shipping them somewhere else, and selling finished products all over the world. Most are trying simultaneously to build local presence and expertise, and to achieve economies of scale. Decision making in this environment is far from straightforward. Frequently, decisions cut across the boundaries between global and local managers, and sometimes across a regional layer in between: What investments will streamline our supply chain? How far should we go in standardizing products or tailoring them for local markets?

The trick in decision making is to avoid becoming either mindlessly global or hopelessly local. If decision-making authority tilts too far toward global executives, local customers' preferences can easily be overlooked, undermining the efficiency and agility of local operations. But with too much local authority, a company is likely to miss out on crucial economies of scale or opportunities with global clients.

To strike the right balance, a company must recognize its most important sources of value and make sure that decision roles line up with them. This was the challenge facing Martin Broughton, the former CEO and chairman of British American Tobacco, the second-largest tobacco company in the world. In 1993, when Broughton was appointed chief executive, BAT was losing ground to its nearest competitor. Broughton knew that the company needed to take better advantage of its global scale, but decision roles and responsibilities were at odds with this goal. Four geographic operating units ran themselves autonomously, rarely collaborating and sometimes even competing. Achieving consistency across global brands proved difficult, and cost synergies across the operating units were elusive. Industry insiders joked that "there are seven major tobacco companies in the world—and four of them are British American Tobacco." Broughton vowed to change the punch line.

The chief executive envisioned an organization that could take advantage of the opportunities a global business offers—global brands that could compete with established winners such as Altria Group's Marlboro; global purchasing of important raw materials, including tobacco; and more consistency in innovation and customer management. But Broughton didn't want the company to lose its nimbleness and competitive hunger in local markets by shifting too much decision-making power to global executives.

The first step was to clarify roles for the most important decisions. Procurement became a proving ground. Previously, each operating unit had identified its own suppliers and negotiated contracts for all materials. Under Broughton, a global procurement team was set up in headquarters and given authority to choose suppliers and negotiate pricing and quality for global materials, including bulk tobacco and certain types of packaging. Regional procurement teams were now given input into global materials strategies but ultimately had to implement the team's decision. As soon as the global team signed contracts with suppliers, responsibility shifted to the regional teams, who worked out the details of delivery and service with the suppliers in their regions. For materials that did not offer global economies of scale (mentholated filters for the North American market, for example), the regional teams retained their decision-making authority.

As the effort to revamp decision making in procurement gained momentum, the company set out to clarify roles in all its major decisions. The process wasn't easy. A company the size of British American Tobacco has a huge number of moving parts, and developing a practical system for making decisions requires sweating lots of details. What's more, decision-making authority is power, and people are often reluctant to give it up.

It's crucial for the people who will live with the new system to help design it. At BAT, Broughton created working groups led by people earmarked, implicitly or explicitly, for leadership roles in the future. For example, Paul Adams, who ultimately succeeded Broughton as chief executive, was asked to lead the group charged with redesigning decision making for brand and customer management. At the time, Adams was a regional head within one of the operating units. With other senior executives, including some of his own direct reports, Broughton specified that their role was to provide input, not to veto recommendations. Broughton didn't make the common mistake of seeking consensus, which is often an obstacle to action. Instead, he made it clear that the objective was not deciding whether to change the decision-making process but achieving buy in about how to do so as effectively as possible.

The new decision roles provided the foundation the company needed to operate successfully on a global basis while retaining flexibility at the local level. The focus and efficiency of its decision making were reflected in the company's results: After the decision-making overhaul, British American Tobacco experienced nearly 10 years of growth well above the levels of its competitors in sales, profits, and market value. The company has gone on to have one of the best-performing stocks on the U.K. market and has reemerged as a major global player in the tobacco industry.

Center Versus Business Unit

The first rule for making good decisions is to involve the right people at the right level of the organization. For BAT, capturing economies of scale required its global team to appropriate some decision-making powers from regional divisions. For many companies, a similar balancing act takes place between executives at the center and managers in the business units. If too many decisions flow to the center, decision making can grind to a halt. The problem is different but no less critical if the decisions that are elevated to senior executives are the wrong ones.

Companies often grow into this type of problem. In small and midsize organizations, a single management team—sometimes a single leader—effectively handles every major decision. As a company grows and its operations become more complex, however, senior executives can no longer master the details required to make decisions in every business.

A change in management style, often triggered by the arrival of a new CEO, can create similar tensions. At a large British retailer, for example, the senior team was accustomed to the founder making all critical decisions. When his successor began seeking consensus on important issues, the team was suddenly unsure of its role, and many decisions stalled. It's a common scenario, yet most management teams and boards of directors don't specify how decision-making authority should change as the company does.

A growth opportunity highlighted that issue for Wyeth (then known as American Home Products) in late 2000. Through organic growth, acquisitions, and partnerships, Wyeth's pharmaceutical division had developed three sizable businesses: biotech, vaccines, and traditional pharmaceutical products. Even though each business had its own market dynamics, operating requirements, and research focus, most important decisions were pushed up to one group of senior executives. "We were using generalists across all issues," said Joseph M. Mahady, president of North American and global businesses for Wyeth Pharmaceuticals. "It was a signal that we weren't getting our best decision making."

The problem crystallized for Wyeth when managers in the biotech business saw a vital—but perishable—opportunity to establish a leading position with Enbrel, a promising rheumatoid arthritis drug. Competitors were working on the same class of drug, so Wyeth needed to move quickly. This meant expanding production capacity by building a new plant, which would be located at the Grange Castle Business Park in Dublin, Ireland.

The decision, by any standard, was a complex one. Once approved by regulators, the facility would be the biggest biotech plant in the world—and the largest capital investment Wyeth had ever undertaken. Yet peak demand for the drug was not easy to determine. What's more, Wyeth planned to market Enbrel in partnership with Immunex (now a part of Amgen). In its deliberations about the plant, therefore, Wyeth needed to factor in the requirements of building up its technical expertise, technology transfer issues, and an uncertain competitive environment.

Input on the decision filtered up slowly through a gauze of overlapping committees, leaving senior executives hungry for a more detailed grasp of the issues. Given the narrow window of opportunity, Wyeth acted quickly, moving from a first look at the Grange Castle project to implementation in six months. But in the midst of this process, Wyeth Pharmaceuticals' executives saw the larger issue: The company needed a system that would push more decisions down to the business units, where operational knowledge was greatest, and elevate the decisions that required the senior team's input, such as marketing strategy and manufacturing capacity.

In short order, Wyeth gave authority for many decisions to business unit managers, leaving senior executives with veto power over some of the more sensitive issues related to Grange Castle. But after that investment decision was made, the D for many subsequent decisions about the Enbrel business lay with Cavan Redmond, the executive vice president and general manager of Wyeth's biotech division, and his new management team. Redmond gathered input from managers in biotech manufacturing, marketing, forecasting, finance, and R&D, and quickly set up the complex schedules needed to collaborate with Immunex. Responsibility for execution rested firmly with the business unit, as always. But now Redmond, supported by his team, also had authority to make important decisions.

Grange Castle is paying off so far. Enbrel is among the leading brands for rheumatoid arthritis, with sales of $1.7 billion through the first half of 2005. And Wyeth's metabolism for making decisions has increased. Recently, when the U.S. Food and Drug Administration granted priority review status to another new drug, Tygacil, because of the antibiotic's efficacy against drug-resistant infections, Wyeth displayed its new reflexes. To keep Tygacil on a fast track, the company had to orchestrate a host of critical steps—refining the process technology, lining up supplies, ensuring quality control, allocating manufacturing capacity. The vital decisions were made one or two levels down in the biotech organization, where the expertise resided. "Instead of debating whether you can move your product into my shop, we had the decision systems in place to run it up and down the business units and move ahead rapidly with Tygacil," said Mahady. The drug was approved by the FDA in June 2005 and moved into volume production a mere three days later.

Function Versus Function

Decisions that cut across functions are some of the most important a company faces. Indeed, cross-functional collaboration has become an axiom of business, essential for arriving at the best answers for the company and its customers. But fluid decision making across functional teams remains a constant challenge, even for companies known for doing it well, like Toyota and Dell. For instance, a team that thinks it's more efficient to make a decision without consulting other functions may wind up missing out on relevant input or being overruled by another team that believes—rightly or wrongly—it should have been included in the process. Many of the most important cross-functional decisions are, by their very nature, the most difficult to orchestrate, and that can string out the process and lead to sparring between fiefdoms and costly indecision.

The theme here is a lack of clarity about who has the D. For example, at a global auto manufacturer that was missing its milestones for rolling out new models—and was paying the price in falling sales—it turned out that marketers and product developers were confused about which function was responsible for making decisions about standard features and color ranges for new models. When we asked the marketing team who had the D about which features should be standard, 83% said the marketers did. When we posed the same question to product developers, 64% said the responsibility rested with them. (See the exhibit "A Recipe for a Decision-Making Bottleneck.")

The practical difficulty of connecting functions through smooth decision making crops up frequently at retailers. John Lewis, the leading department store chain in the United Kingdom, might reasonably expect to overcome this sort of challenge more readily than other retailers. Spedan Lewis, who built the business in the early twentieth century, was a pioneer in employee ownership. A strong connection between managers and employees permeated every aspect of the store's operations and remained vital to the company as it grew into the largest employee-owned business in the United Kingdom, with 59,600 employees and more than £5 billion in revenues in 2004.

Even at John Lewis, however, with its heritage of cooperation and team-work, cross-functional decision making can be hard to sustain. Take salt and

A Recipe for a Decision-Making Bottleneck

At one automaker we studied, marketers and product developers were confused about who was responsible for making decisions about new models.

When we asked, "Who has the right to decide which features will be standard?"
    64% of product developers said, "We do."
    83% of marketers said, "We do."

When we asked, "Who has the right to decide which colors will be offered?"
    77% of product developers said, "We do."
    61% of marketers said, "We do."

Not surprisingly, the new models were delayed.

pepper mills, for instance. John Lewis, which prides itself on having great selection, stocked nearly 50 SKUs of salt and pepper mills, while most competitors stocked around 20. The company's buyers saw an opportunity to increase sales and reduce complexity by offering a smaller number of popular and well-chosen products in each price point and style.

When John Lewis launched the new range, sales fell. This made no sense to the buyers until they visited the stores and saw how the merchandise was displayed. The buyers had made their decision without fully involving the sales staff, who therefore did not understand the strategy behind the new selection. As a result, the sellers had cut shelf space in half to match the reduction in range, rather than devoting the same amount of shelf space to stocking more of each product.

To fix the communication problem, John Lewis needed to clarify decision roles. The buyers were given the D on how much space to allocate to each product category. If the space allocation didn't make sense to the sales staff, however, they had the authority to raise their concerns and force a new round of negotiations. They also had responsibility for implementing product layouts in the stores. When the communication was sorted out and shelf space was restored, sales of the salt and pepper mills climbed well above original levels.

Crafting a decision-making process that connected the buying and selling functions for salt and pepper mills was relatively easy; rolling it out across the entire business was more challenging. Salt and pepper mills are just one of several hundred product categories for John Lewis. This element of scale is one reason why cross-functional bottlenecks are not easy to unclog. Different functions have different incentives and goals, which are often in conflict. When it comes down to a struggle between two functions, there may be good reasons to locate the D in either place—buying or selling, marketing or product development.

Here, as elsewhere, someone needs to think objectively about where value is created and assign decision roles accordingly. Eliminating cross-functional bottlenecks actually has less to do with shifting decision-making responsibilities between departments and more to do with ensuring that the people with relevant information are allowed to share it. The decision maker is important, of course, but more important is designing a system that aligns decision making and makes it routine.

Inside Versus Outside Partners

Decision making within an organization is hard enough. Trying to make decisions between separate organizations on different continents adds layers of complexity that can scuttle the best strategy. Companies that outsource capabilities in pursuit of cost and quality advantages face this very challenge. Which decisions should be made internally? Which can be delegated to outsourcing partners?

These questions are also relevant for strategic partners—a global bank working with an IT contractor on a systems development project, for example, or a media company that acquires content from a studio—and for companies conducting part of their business through franchisees. There is no right answer to who should have the power to decide what. But the wrong approach is to assume that contractual arrangements can provide the answer.

The Decision-Driven Organization

The defining characteristic of high-performing organizations is their ability to make good decisions and to make them happen quickly. The companies that succeed tend to follow a few clear principles.

Some decisions matter more than others. The decisions that are crucial to building value in the business are the ones that matter most. Some of them will be the big strategic decisions, but just as important are the critical operating decisions that drive the business day to day and are vital to effective execution.

Action is the goal. Good decision making doesn't end with a decision; it ends with implementation. The objective shouldn't be consensus, which often becomes an obstacle to action, but buy in.

Ambiguity is the enemy. Clear accountability is essential: Who contributes input, who makes the decision, and who carries it out? Without clarity, gridlock and delay are the most likely outcomes. Clarity doesn't necessarily mean concentrating authority in a few people; it means defining who has responsibility to make decisions, who has input, and who is charged with putting them into action.

Speed and adaptability are crucial. A company that makes good decisions quickly has a higher metabolism, which allows it to act on opportunities and overcome obstacles. The best decision makers create an environment where people can come together quickly and efficiently to make the most important decisions.

Decision roles trump the organizational chart. No decision-making structure will be perfect for every decision. The key is to involve the right people at the right level in the right part of the organization at the right time.

A well-aligned organization reinforces roles. Clear decision roles are critical, but they are not enough. If an organization does not reinforce the right approach to decision making through its measures and incentives, information flows, and culture, the behavior won't become routine.

Practicing beats preaching. Involve the people who will live with the new decision roles in designing them. The very process of thinking about new decision behaviors motivates people to adopt them.

An outdoor-equipment company based in the United States discovered this recently when it decided to scale up production of gas patio heaters for the lower end of the market. The company had some success manufacturing high-end products in China. But with the advent of superdiscounters like Walmart, Target, and Home Depot, the company realized it needed to move more of its production overseas to feed these retailers with lower-cost offerings. The timetable left little margin for error: The company started tooling up factories in April and June of 2004, hoping to be ready for the Christmas season.

Right away, there were problems. Although the Chinese manufacturing partners understood costs, they had little idea what American consumers wanted. When expensive designs arrived from the head office in the United States, Chinese plant managers made compromises to meet contracted cost targets. They used a lower grade material, which discolored. They placed the power switch in a spot that was inconvenient for the user but easier to build. Instead of making certain parts from a single casting, they welded materials together, which looked terrible.

To fix these problems, the U.S. executives had to draw clear lines around which decisions should be made on which side of the ocean. The company broke down the design and manufacturing process into five steps and analyzed how decisions were made at each step. The company was also much more explicit about what the manufacturing specs would include and what the manufacturer

A Decision Diagnostic

Consider the last three meaningful decisions you've been involved in and ask yourself the following questions.

1. Were the decisions right?
2. Were they made with appropriate speed?
3. Were they executed well?
4. Were the right people involved, in the right way?
5. Was it clear for each decision
   - who would recommend a solution?
   - who would provide input?
   - who had the final say?
   - who would be responsible for following through?
6. Were the decision roles, process, and time frame respected?
7. Were the decisions based on appropriate facts?
8. To the extent that there were divergent facts or opinions, was it clear who had the D?
9. Were the decision makers at the appropriate level in the company?
10. Did the organization's measures and incentives encourage the people involved to make the right decisions?

was expected to do with them. The objective was not simply to clarify decision roles but to make sure those roles corresponded directly to the sources of value in the business. If a decision would affect the look and feel of the finished product, headquarters would have to sign off on it. But if a decision would not affect the customer's experience, it could be made in China. If, for example, Chinese engineers found a less expensive material that didn't compromise the product's look, feel, and functionality, they could make that change on their own.

To help with the transition to this system, the company put a team of engineers on-site in China to ensure a smooth handoff of the specs and to make decisions on issues that would become complex and time-consuming if elevated to the home office. Marketing executives in the home office insisted that it should take a customer 10 minutes and no more than six steps to assemble the product at home. The company's engineers in China, along with the Chinese manufacturing team, had input into this assembly requirement and were responsible for execution. But the D resided with headquarters, and the requirement became a major design factor. Decisions about logistics, however, became the province of the engineering team in China: It would figure out how to package the heaters so that one-third more boxes would fit into a container, which reduced shipping costs substantially.

If managers suddenly realize that they're spending less time sitting through meetings wondering why they are there, that's an early signal that companies have become better at making decisions. When meetings start with a common understanding about who is responsible for providing valuable input and who has the D, an organization's decision-making metabolism will get a boost.

No single lever turns a decision-challenged organization into a decision-driven one, of course, and no blueprint can provide for all the contingencies and business shifts a company is bound to encounter. The most successful companies use simple tools that help them recognize potential bottlenecks and think through decision roles and responsibilities with each change in the business environment. That's difficult to do—and even more difficult for competitors to copy. But by taking some very practical steps, any company can become more effective, beginning with its next decision.

The Decision-Driven Organization

Forget the org chart—the secret is to focus on decisions,
not structure.

Marcia Blenko, Michael Mankins, and Paul Rogers

In the 1980s the business world offered a kind of laboratory experiment: How could government-owned companies, many of which were then being privatized, adapt themselves to compete in the commercial world? Bain consultants working with these enterprises found one key to successful adaptation: focusing on their ability to make and execute their most important decisions well. That key turned out to open a series of organizational locks: It helped clarify and simplify accountabilities, structure, and many other facets of the organization.

Since that time, business organizations everywhere have grown larger and more complex. Many management teams grasp at restructuring as the panacea for organizational challenges, where often an existing structure could work well with clearer roles, aligned incentives, adjustments in talent, and changes in behavior. An effective approach is to bring a decision lens to organizational design, identifying your critical decisions and understanding how each element of the organization is helping or hindering those decisions. This approach ensures that companies not only focus on the "hardware"—the boxes and lines of the org chart—but also the "software" that operationalizes the model—accountabilities, talent, and culture.

Many CEOs assume that organizational structure—the boxes and lines on a company's org chart—is a key determinant of financial performance. Like generals, they see their job as putting the right collection of troops in the right places. If the battle is about innovation, for example, then the CEO's duty is to create the best possible structure for channeling resources toward innovation.

This belief helps explain why reorganizations are so popular with chief executives. In fact, nearly half of all CEOs launch a reorg during their first two years on the job. Some preside over repeated restructurings. The immediate motives vary. Some are about cutting costs; others are about promoting growth. Some are about shaking up a culture; others are about shifting strategic focus. Whatever the specifics, though, reorgs almost always involve making major structural changes in pursuit of better performance.

Despite the fanfare that usually greets them, however, most reorganizations fall flat. A recent Bain & Company study of 57 reorgs between 2000 and 2006 found that fewer than one-third produced any meaningful improvement in performance. Most had no effect, and some actually destroyed value. Chrysler, for instance, reorganized its operations three times in the three years preceding its bankruptcy and eventual combination with Fiat. Each time, executives proclaimed that the company was on a new path to profitability. Each time, performance didn't improve.

We believe that this failure is rooted in a profound misunderstanding about the link between structure and performance. Contrary to popular belief, performance is not determined solely by the nature, scale, and disposition of resources, important though they may be. An army's success depends at least as much on the quality of the decisions its officers and soldiers make and execute on the ground as it does on actual fighting power. A corporation's structure, similarly, will produce better performance if and only if it improves the organization's ability to make and execute key decisions better and faster than competitors. It may be that the strategic priority for your company is to become more innovative. In that case, the reorganization challenge is to structure the company so that its leaders can make decisions that produce more and better innovation over time.

For most companies, this requires a fundamental rethinking of their approach to reorganization. Instead of beginning with an analysis of strengths, weaknesses, opportunities, and threats, structural changes need to start with what we call a decision audit. The goals of the audit are to understand the set of decisions that are critical to the success of your company's strategy and to determine the organizational level at which those decisions should be made and executed to create the most value. If you can align your organization's structure with its decisions, then the structure will work better, and your company's performance will improve.

In this article we set out the basic principles for reorganizing around decisions. Let's begin by taking a closer look at the link between decisions and performance.

What Drives Your Performance?

Organizational structure is not the only determinant of performance. In some cases, it is not even particularly important. That's why changing a company's structure to meet a particular strategic goal can actually exacerbate problems rather than help solve them. For example, an organization struggling to innovate may try to gather more and more creative input—and end up getting too many people involved, thereby slowing the pace of decision making and stifling innovation.

Take the case of Yahoo. In December 2006, then-CEO Terry Semel announced a sweeping reorganization of the company, replacing Yahoo's product-aligned structure with one focused on users and advertiser customers. Seven product units were merged into a group called Audience and another seven moved into a group called Advertisers and Publishers. A unit dubbed Technology would provide infrastructure for the two new operating groups. The idea was to accelerate growth by exploiting economies of scope across Yahoo's rich collection of audience and advertiser products. Semel's team had thought they'd carefully defined roles and responsibilities under the new structure, but decision making and execution quickly became bogged down. Audience demanded tailored solutions that Technology could not provide at a reasonable cost. Advertisers and Publishers needed its own set of unique products and so was constantly competing with Audience for scarce developer time. In response, Yahoo executives created new roles and management levels to coordinate the units. The organization ballooned to 12 layers, product development slowed as decisions stalled, and overhead costs increased.

Yahoo's experience shows how a lack of attention to the decision-making process can thwart the best-intentioned reorganization and undermine performance. Ultimately, a company's value is no more (and no less) than the sum of the decisions it makes and executes. Its assets, capabilities, and structure are useless unless executives and managers throughout the organization make the essential decisions and get those decisions right more often than not.

Our research and experience confirm the tight link between performance and decisions. In 2008, we and our colleagues at Bain & Company surveyed executives worldwide from 760 companies, most with revenues exceeding $1 billion, to understand how effective those companies were at making and executing their critical decisions. We used the responses to assess decision quality (whether decisions proved to be right more often than not), speed (whether decisions were made faster or slower than competitors), yield (how well decisions were translated into action), and effort (the time, trouble, and expense required for each key decision). Then we calculated a composite score for each company and compared that score with each firm's financial performance. (See the exhibit "Rate Your Decision Effectiveness" to learn how your company compares with our sample.)

We found that decision effectiveness and financial results correlated at a 95% confidence level or higher for every country, industry, and company size in our sample. Indeed, the companies in our sample that were most effective at decision making and execution generated average total shareholder returns nearly six percentage points higher than those of other firms. We also found that many companies have enormous scope to improve their performance. Top-quintile companies

Quick Test: Rate Your Decision Effectiveness

How do your organization's decision abilities stack up against the competition? While hardly a full-scale survey, this short test can give you a quick-and-dirty assessment of decision strengths and weaknesses.

Quality

When looking back on critical decisions, we find that we chose the right course of action

4 Most of the time
3 Some of the time
2 Infrequently
1 Never

Q Score ___

Speed

We make critical decisions

4 Much faster than competitors
3 Somewhat faster than competitors
2 Somewhat slower than competitors
1 Much slower than competitors

S Score ___

Yield

We execute critical decisions as intended

4 Most of the time
3 Some of the time
2 Infrequently
1 Never

Y Score ___

Effort

In making and executing critical decisions

4 We put in exactly the right amount of effort
3 We put in somewhat too much/too little effort
2 We put in way too much/nowhere near enough effort
1 We're off the charts

E Score ___

To tally your overall score, multiply your scores for quality (Q), speed (S), and yield (Y) to get your QSY. Next, divide your effort (E) score by 4, and multiply the result by the QSY. If you're putting in exactly the right amount of effort, your QSY wouldn't change. But if you scored effort as a 3, then your score would be 3/4, or 75%, of the QSY.

Using our database, you can compare your decision score with the performance ranges for each benchmark quartile. If you score over 25, for example, you are performing at the level of the top-quartile companies in our survey. Relative to our sample, your organization would appear to decide and deliver.

Total Score [Q x S x Y x (E/4)] ___
More than 25 = You're doing great; keep it up.
21–25 = Pretty good, but could be great.
16–20 = Worse than 50% of companies. Time to act.
15 or less = Major decision reboot required.

score an average of 71 out of 100 in decision effectiveness, while companies in the other four quintiles score, on average, 30 and below. This means that the typical organization has the potential to more than double its decision effectiveness.

What's more, the research revealed no strong statistical relationship between structure and performance. Survey respondents' views about the structure of their company were not an accurate predictor of either decision effectiveness or financial results.

The conclusion we draw is simple: In a reorganization, decisions rather than structure should be the primary focus. Let's see what that involves.

Conducting a Decision Audit

Many reorganizations begin with a SWOT analysis: What are our organization's strengths, weaknesses, opportunities, and threats? What are our resources and capabilities? What risks do we face? The idea is to determine if the company has everything it needs to support its strategy. All this sounds sensible, and in many ways it is. But the risk is that you'll end up with an organization that's misaligned with your strategy, all because you have ignored decisions. The proper place for this type of SWOT analysis is not, in fact, as a prelude to organizational change but earlier, when you are determining your company's strategy.

A better way to begin a reorganization is with a decision audit. The first step in conducting one is to identify the key decisions you need to make and execute, given your strategy to create maximum value for your shareholders. The set of key decisions for a growth strategy, for instance, will be different from the set for a return-focused strategy. Of course, this exercise does not presuppose a change in strategy. It may be that the reorganization is an attempt to improve an existing strategy, in which case you'll end up with a comparison between the decisions you ought to be concentrating on and the ones you are actually making. The bigger the difference—and the greater the obstacle presented by your organizational structure—the more aggressive your reorg will need to be.

The ongoing turnaround at Ford illustrates the power of explicitly delineating a company's critical decisions. When Alan Mulally became CEO at the automaker in 2006, the company was in dire need of change. Ford had been losing a point or more of market share every year since 2000 and was on the verge of collapse. But rather than change the company's structure first and then worry about decisions, Mulally took the opposite approach. He and his team outlined the decisions that were critical to a turnaround. Only then did they begin to build the new organization around those decisions.

Fixing the company's operations and restoring profitability centered on a schematic depicting Ford's critical decisions. It spelled out the key decisions that needed to be made at each stage in Ford's value chain, along with the infrastructure required to execute them effectively. Every week, Mulally and his team tracked their progress in making and executing these decisions. They divested noncore brands such as Aston Martin, Jaguar, Land Rover, and Volvo; reduced the number of production platforms; began consolidating both suppliers and dealers; and so on. They also reorganized the company, moving from a structure based on regional business units to a global matrix of functions and geographies. This new structure enabled Mulally's team to make its most important decisions better and faster—creating global car platforms, for instance, which had been painfully difficult under the old structure. Set in this context, the reorg made perfect sense and helped restore the company to profitability in early 2010.

As you conduct your own decision audit, you need to consider two types of critical decisions:

- Big, one-off decisions that individually have a significant impact. Petro-chemical companies, for example, must make periodic multibillion-dollar investment decisions, such as if, when, or where to build a new ethylene cracker, which is critical to production. If a company builds at the wrong time, in the wrong place, or with the wrong technology, it will have to live with the consequences for many decades.

- Small, routine decisions that cumulatively have a significant impact. Amazon's continuing success can be attributed partly to a host of savvy merchandising decisions, including those related to special prices and shipping discounts, suggestions for complementary purchases, and targeted e-mail notices about new offerings. None of these decisions carries much value in any one instance. Cumulatively, however, they can mean the difference between success and failure.

Once you have identified which decisions are critical and categorized them, you can figure out where in the organization those decisions should be made. This requires an unbiased assessment of the benefits of scale and coordination versus the benefits of tailoring to local needs and staying close to the customer. In which decisions is scale a critical factor? Which decisions are better made by business units or functions? Which need coordination across many businesses?

Some decisions are fairly easy to place. Big capital-allocation decisions, for instance, are typically best made by the corporate center so that senior leaders can design and execute a coordinated portfolio strategy across the company. IT investments can usually be left to functions or business units. Decision placement is more of a challenge for product, customer, and channel decisions, which typically involve complex trade-offs. Pricing decisions, for example, need to be coordinated across customer segments and channels. Product decisions must be considered from both an internal and an external perspective. In companies with many different products or services, both the critical decisions themselves and where they should be made may vary widely across the organization.

The Xerox turnaround launched in 2001 under Anne Mulcahy offers a powerful contrast to the Yahoo story. Unlike Semel at Yahoo, Mulcahy's leadership team took a decision-driven approach to the company's reorganization. Team members went through every set of critical decisions Xerox needed to make and execute to fend off bankruptcy, and they made explicit choices about where to locate those decisions. Clarity and simplicity were the guiding principles. In the sales organization, for example, Xerox moved from a global customer structure, in which sales and pricing decisions were made by global teams organized around industry verticals, to a simpler country structure, where those decisions rested with local sales teams. The new structure enabled Xerox to eliminate several layers of middle management, increase local accountability, and take nearly $1 billion out of the company's cost structure in just two years. The simpler structure also concentrated decisions related to the shift from analog to digital technology—critical to Xerox's success in office products at the time—within the senior leadership of the Product organization, which helped accelerate the pace of new-product introductions in this vital segment. The explicit focus on where decisions should be made was critical to the successful turnaround at Xerox.

At the end of your audit, you may find that making and executing decisions better and faster than competitors doesn't require reorganization and that you can avoid the costly business of structural change altogether. If you find that you are already focused on the right set of critical decisions and you find that they are placed where they should be within the organization, then the source of performance problems is unlikely to be structural. Problems may stem instead from other organizational issues. Perhaps there is an incentive problem with the sales force. Maybe leaders place too much value on building consensus, at the expense of decisive action. Whatever the issues, they can probably be fixed without a wholesale structural redesign, which will take people's minds off the competition and may actually add to your problems. (See the exhibit "Do You Really Need to Reorganize?")

But for now, we'll assume that your audit does reveal that your structure needs to change. Let's look at how to go about doing that.

Building the Decision-Driven Structure

All complex organizations must be broken down into manageable pieces to ensure that roles and responsibilities for making and executing critical decisions are clear. A good way to determine what the important decisions are in your company is to look at the sources of value in your business and then organize the macrostructure around them.

Take the case of British Gas, a division of the multinational energy and utility company Centrica. In 2006, faced with a serious performance crisis, the

Quick Test: Do You Really Need to Reorganize?

A comprehensive survey of your organization can help you understand what's undermining or supporting effective decisions—and whether structure or something else is likely to be the most important issue. But this quick test can serve as an early warning device.

Structure
Our structure helps—rather than hinders—the decisions most critical to our success.
1 Strongly disagree
2 Disagree more than agree
3 Agree more than disagree
4 Strongly agree

Roles
Individuals understand their roles and accountability in our most critical decisions.
1 2 3 4

Processes
Our processes are designed to produce effective, timely decisions and action.
1 2 3 4

Information
The people in critical decision roles have the information they need when and how they need it.
1 2 3 4

Measures & Incentives
Our measures and incentives focus people on making and executing effective decisions.
1 2 3 4

Priorities
People understand their priorities clearly enough to be able to make and execute the decisions they face.
1 2 3 4

Decision Style
We make decisions in a style that is effective (for example, that appropriately balances inclusiveness with momentum).
1 2 3 4

People
We put our best people in the jobs where they can have the biggest decision impact.
1 2 3 4

Behaviors
Our leaders at all levels consistently demonstrate effective decision behaviors.
1 2 3 4

Culture
Our culture reinforces prompt, effective decisions and action throughout the organization.
1 2 3 4

To get your total score, add up your individual scores.

More than 35 = You're doing great; keep it up.
31–35 = Good, but room for improvement.
26–30 = Org is serious barrier to decisions.
10–25 = Major org transformation required.

Compared with companies in our database, a score above 35 puts you in the top quartile—meaning that your organization is pretty healthy. A score of 31 to 35 indicates room for improvement, but no immediate signs of organizational breakdown. A score of 30 or below indicates that you definitely have some organizational challenges to address. If you perform at 2 or less on any one issue, that particular ailment likely needs attention.

company's new leadership team started looking at the sources of value in its business. Managers began by examining differences in profitability by service, by geographic area, and by customer segment. They discovered that profitability and growth varied much more by customer segment than by any other variable.

One segment used large amounts of gas or electricity and paid regularly through guaranteed direct debits. Decisions that helped the company retain these customers, such as how to handle home moves and how best to offer additional services, were most important for this segment. A second customer segment used less energy and paid regularly through a system of prepayment cards. Here the key decisions related to controlling costs, particularly those associated with processing additional payments and with meter reading. A third segment wasn't as consistent in keeping up payments. For that group, the critical decisions related to managing receivables.

Recognizing those different sources of value, managing director Phil Bentley decided that the best way to structure the company was by customer segment. He established three separate businesses: Premier Energy, Energy First, and Pay-As-You-Go Energy. This new structure allowed him to place accountability for decisions that directly affected customers, such as service levels, positioning, and product bundling, in the business units. Corporate headquarters could focus on noncustomer-facing matters such as IT and finance. The alignment of structure and decisions helped British Gas improve its performance significantly. It reduced customer attrition from about 20% to less than 10%. Its bad debt fell, and the business began growing for the first time in years.

If decision-driven reorganization were just about an audit and, if necessary, aligning the macrostructure with the sources of value, it would be relatively easy to get your next reorg right. But the messy reality of business is that big changes need to be followed up with a whole host of smaller changes.

In most reorgs, this stage of the process usually concentrates on assigning turf and setting out a hierarchy with defined reporting lines. Once again, this approach

The Six Steps to Decision-Driven Reorganization

1. Identify your organization's key decisions.
2. Determine where in the organization those decisions should happen.
3. Organize the macrostructure around sources of value.
4. Figure out what level of authority decision makers need.
5. Align other elements of the organizational system, such as incentives, information flow, and processes, with those related to decision making.
6. Help managers develop the skills and behaviors necessary to make and execute decisions quickly and well.

is misguided, because it does not use decisions as the unit of analysis. Indeed, a focus on turf often devolves into horse trading: Powerful managers grab decision rights they shouldn't really own while weak ones surrender rights they really should own. People end up with responsibilities that are defined either too broadly or too narrowly, given the decisions they need to make. Responsibilities that are too broad result in insufficient supervision and limited accountability. Those that are too narrow can create needless hierarchy—too many watchers and too few doers—and can encourage micromanagement. Without a focus on decisions, these power struggles too often lead to creeping complexity in an organization's infrastructure.

The energy giant BP provides an excellent example of the consequences of an overly complex microstructure. Back in 1994, BP had just a handful of geographic and customer units, which were supported by a few central functions. After a period of significant merger and acquisition activity, however, the company added new geographic areas and created new functions. Spans of control narrowed, and the number of management layers increased. All of these changes increased the number of "decision nodes"—the interfaces between regions, functions, and layers required to make and execute important decisions—from about 500 in 1994 to roughly 10,000 in 2007.

Each decision node at the company introduced a different set of hurdles for new products, business development deals, and even options for reducing costs. The effects were predictable: Decision making and execution slowed, and costs mounted.

In a decision-driven reorganization, the challenge is to determine exactly what authority decision makers need, regardless of their organizational status, if they are to make good decisions and execute them effectively. BP saw that the people who were best equipped to make decisions had to get too many approvals from higher-ups or from regional heads, which delayed execution. So its new chief executive, Tony Hayward, launched a comprehensive simplification program designed to return decision rights to the appropriate people. The initiative eliminated layers of middle management, centralized some operations, and reduced overhead expenses by one-third. It moved the number of decision nodes back toward a target of 5,000. Both the company's decision effectiveness and its performance improved. By late 2009, BP had eliminated $3 billion in costs and was turning in a profit that beat analysts' expectations by 50%.

Any change in structure may necessitate changes in decision roles, incentives, information flow, performance metrics, and processes. At UD Trucks—formerly Nissan Diesel—a new strategy designed to expand UD's penetration of national accounts required a reorganization of the company. Local branch offices were combined into regions, and national account teams were established. To get the most out of the new structure, the team at UD Trucks clarified decision roles between the national account teams and the company's Truck and Service units.

Measures and incentives were reset to encourage collaboration across units and focus the sales force on key accounts. The reorganization at UD Trucks was critical, of course—the new strategy could not have been implemented without it. But goals, processes, information, measures, and incentives also needed to be aligned to make the new structure work.

Finally, you need to help managers develop the skills they need to make decisions quickly and translate them into action consistently. Smart companies mesh individuals' capabilities with the organization's decision-making demands. They invest as needed to ensure that people have the skills required to be better decision makers over time.

A good example of this took place at Hospira, the $3.9 billion pharmaceutical company spun out from Abbott Laboratories in 2004.

In 2008, Hospira embarked on a major change program. The program included an effort to build new decision capabilities across the company. The top 80 executives attended innovative training workshops that showed them how to identify an organization's critical decisions and outlined Hospira's new approach to effective, efficient decision making and execution. Executives learned to use tools that would help them get the who, what, when, where, and how of each decision right. The workshops also helped leaders learn and adopt the specific behaviors that would be required to make the changes stick.

Hospira's senior leaders began to track the company's changes in decision effectiveness at their bimonthly team meetings. They also began to gather survey data that could help them assess progress in building and sustaining decision capabilities. Since 2008, CEO Chris Begley and his team have seen significant improvements in Hospira's financial and stock price performance, which they attribute largely to improved decision making.

Adjusting to New Structures

A new strategy—or new execution of an existing strategy—can require both macrochanges and microchanges to a company's structure. But any new structure will create new boundaries that people may find hard to cope with and that may make effective decision making more difficult. To get around this problem, it may be necessary to overlay your new structure with some connections that help people reach beyond those boundaries.

In 2001, faced with the bursting of the dot-com bubble, Cisco reorganized. It moved away from the structure that had been in place for much of the company's rise to prominence—a line-of-business structure based on customer segments—and put in place a global functional organization. The logic was simple: Reorganizing around central functions would dramatically reduce the company's costs. While the pros of this move outweighed the cons, the company's leaders acknowledged that organizing around centralized functions could cause Cisco to lose customer focus and intimacy.

To prevent that, the leadership team has created over the past several years a series of corporate councils and boards directly under the company's operating committee, Cisco's most senior decision-making body. These cross-functional groups formulate and evaluate alternatives for each of the company's major strategic initiatives and then make recommendations to senior management. We find that the process accelerates decision making without sacrificing decision quality. The structural overlay of councils and boards also seems to help functional leaders collaborate and make effective decisions about budgets and resources.

Today, those teams are operating at full steam. Five "segment councils," for instance, support decision making and execution for the company's enterprise, commercial, service provider, small business, and consumer segments. Boards organized around specific market opportunities, such as collaboration and virtualization within the enterprise segment, develop tailored strategies and oversee execution. Finally, four cross-segment councils focus on the arcane but critical topics of emerging solutions, connected architecture, emerging countries, and connected business operations. These interlocking councils and boards have enabled Cisco to maintain its leadership position in the complex, fast-moving telecommunications space and build on the strength of its global functional structure.

Creating parallel decision-making authorities may appear to be in conflict with our general principles of simplicity and clear accountability, but we believe this approach leads to a more streamlined process. Organization overlays such as Cisco's councils and boards introduce valuable expertise that formal structures cannot easily accommodate. They allow fewer people to be involved in making and executing critical decisions—in effect, reducing the number of decision nodes.

It's easy to see why so many CEOs are enticed by the temptation of reorganization. Today's corporate structures can be inordinately complex. Some date from a day when the demands of the business world were quite different than they are today. Simplification, alignment, modernization, a new vision of what the organization should look like—and all of it accomplished with the stroke of a pen. But to focus exclusively on structure is to confuse means with ends and to assume a connection that may not exist. The reorgs that work best, such as those at Ford, Xerox, and Cisco, focus first on the organization's critical decisions. Then they build an organization that can make and execute those decisions better and faster than the competition. The result is what executives always seek from reorgs yet so seldom accomplish: improved performance.

Motivating Through Metrics

Fred Reichheld and Paul Rogers

To create value, companies need to make and execute their critical decisions effectively and at the appropriate level. Thus employees who are closest to the customer should be responsible for decisions about how best to serve those customers. These employees need the skills to make good decisions, and they must have the will to pull together as a team. Where does that motivation come from?

This article was one of the first to explore the power of direct customer feedback in creating this kind of motivation. Employees at the companies it describes take responsibility for making decisions about customer service. They align behind those decisions and execute them once they are made. They know when they are on the right track because customer feedback tells them so. This is a specific example of a more general point, which our clients have learned over the years: Measures alone don't mean much. But when measures are an integral part of creating value in the business—when, for instance, they are related directly to building customer loyalty— they are tremendously powerful motivators. People from the checkout clerk to the chief marketing officer can see every day how they are doing and how they can improve.

Getting the right people on board—and then all enthusiastically pulling in the right direction—has bedeviled organizations since the time of wooden ships, when the most popular form of motivation left lash marks. Today's corporate helmsmen may be more enlightened, but they still face the same challenge. How can a company transform its frontline crew into a meritocracy that pulls together?

Recently, a handful of firms have addressed this problem by tying rewards to team performance and putting customers and employees, rather than bosses, in charge of performance rankings. Some of these trendsetters are well-known global players, such as Enterprise Rent-A-Car; others are less well-known, such as Applebee's restaurants, located largely in the United States, and Ireland's Superquinn grocery stores. But all link frontline performance rankings to customer

HBR September 2005

and peer feedback, not just to productivity. And they use simple metrics that can be applied to compensation, promotions, and career transitions.

Reward Exceptional Hiring

Enterprise, one of the world's largest car-rental concerns, rewards managers for how well their reports serve customers. For managers to get promoted, their branches must deliver customer service at or above the average for all comparable branches. Success is judged by a metric called the Enterprise Service Quality index (ESQi), which shows the percentage of customers who rate a branch five out of five when asked if they were completely satisfied. If a branch doesn't achieve or exceed the company's average feedback score, the entire team is ineligible for promotion. In many branches, teams have also introduced a voluntary weekly metric called The Vote, in which team members hold an open discussion and rank one another on how well each has helped to create outstanding customer service. This personal accountability for team success has led to higher ESQi scores.

Tap That Extra 10%

Inspiring even the best employees to give their all requires setting clear goals that are more personal and immediate than a mandate to maximize overall profit. At Superquinn supermarkets, perks are determined by employees' influence on customers' spending. Recently the staff (called "colleagues" at Superquinn) in the bakery at one store was given a challenge: Increase the number of "households" (based on the Superquinn loyalty card) that purchase from the bakery. The reward was a helicopter trip around a local bay. The team set up a doughnut cooker inside the main entrance, offered every shopper a taste, and guaranteed the doughnuts' freshness. As a result, the number of households that purchased from the bakery increased from 75% to 90%—and all 20 bakery colleagues won helicopter rides.

Keep the Best

Metrics can help companies identify who isn't rowing with the team. The trick is to objectively identify and transfer cultural misfits without demotivating other employees.

At Applebee's, general managers' bonuses are based on metrics that combine measurements of financial results, "guest results" (how well patrons rate their overall dining experience), and "people results" (turnover rates on the manager's team). In the casual dining segment of the restaurant business, where Applebee's competes, an entire staff can turn over twice in one year. But

Applebee's looks beyond total turnover; recently it began measuring turnover of the top 20% of performers, the middle 60%, and the bottom 20%. Managers are rewarded for their success in retaining the top 80% and not penalized when a bottom-20 performer leaves the company. In fact, managers are encouraged to help poor performers either improve or seek other opportunities. As a result, since 2000, turnover among hourly associates has decreased from 146% to an industry-leading 84%, evidence not only that managers are more motivated to hold onto their teams but also that the teams themselves, minus poor performers, are more stable. Last year, Applebee's same-store sales growth rose 4.8 percentage points.

Making Star Teams Out of Star Players

Here's how smart companies deploy their best people to get great results.

Michael Mankins, Alan Bird, and James Root

Some companies get far more from their people than others do—more output, better and quicker decisions, greater customer loyalty, whatever. To put it in the dry terms of managerial economics, their human-capital productivity is far higher. The causes seem to fall into three baskets. A company might be better than its peers at recruiting and selecting high performers. It might have a more productive organization—a more efficient structure, a culture of productivity, and so forth—so that its people encounter fewer barriers as they go about their work. Or it might be better at creating and managing teams, which is the subject of this article.

Most companies that struggle with human-capital productivity have problems in all three areas, and we have long worked with clients to improve their hiring and their organizational efficiency. Recently we have found that team-related issues are coming to the fore, in part because executives fail to examine some long-held myths about what makes a productive team. One such myth: No team should consist exclusively of top performers, or A players. As we see in the article, companies embarked on the journey to full potential are putting that one to rest right now.

When it comes to an organization's scarcest resource—talent—the difference between the best and the rest is enormous. In fields that involve repetitive, transactional tasks, top performers are typically two or three times as productive as others. Justo Thomas, the best fish butcher at Le Bernardin restaurant in New York, can portion as much fish in an hour as the average prep cook can manage in three hours. In highly specialized or creative work, the differential is likely to be a factor of six or more. Before becoming chief justice of the U.S. Supreme Court, John Roberts prevailed in 25 of the 39 cases he argued before the Court. That record is almost nine times better than the average record of other winning attorneys (excluding solicitors general) who have argued before

HBR January–February 2013

the Court since 1950. (For other examples of star productivity, see "What 'A' Players Bring to the Table.") Across all job types, we estimate, the best performers are roughly four times as productive as average performers. That holds in every industry, geographical region, and type of organization we've examined.

Why, then, do companies so rarely bring together a team of star players to tackle a big challenge? The easy answer—indeed, the conventional wisdom—is that all-star teams just don't work. Egos will take over. The stars won't work well with one another. They'll drive the team leader crazy.

We think it's time to reconsider that assumption. To be sure, managing a team of stars is not for the faint of heart. (The conventional wisdom is there for a reason.) But when the stakes are high—when a business model needs to be reinvented, say, or a key new product designed, or a strategic problem solved—doesn't it seem foolish not to put your best people on the job, provided you can find a way to manage them effectively?

We have seen all-star teams do extraordinary work. For example, it took just 600 Apple engineers less than two years to develop, debug, and deploy OS X, a revolutionary change in the company's operating system. By contrast, it took as many as 10,000 engineers more than five years to develop, debug, deploy, and eventually retract Microsoft's Windows Vista.

Common sense suggests that all-star teams would have two big advantages:

Sheer firepower. If you have world-class talent of all kinds on a team, you multiply the productivity and performance advantages that stand-alone stars deliver. Consider auto-racing pit crews. Kyle Busch's six-man crew is widely considered the finest on the NASCAR circuit. And each member is the best for his

What "A" Players Bring to the Table

Some people argue that talent is overrated. But our estimates, based on evidence from a variety of industries, suggest that star employees outperform others by a country mile:

The best developer at Apple is at least nine times as productive as the average software engineer at other technology companies.

The best blackjack dealer at Caesar's Palace in Las Vegas keeps his table playing at least five times as long as the average dealer on the Strip.

The best sales associate at Nordstrom sells at least eight times as much as the average sales associate at other department stores.

The best transplant surgeon at a top-notch medical clinic has a success rate at least six times that of the average transplant surgeon.

position—gas man, jackman, tire carriers, and tire changers. Crew members train together year-round with one clear goal in mind: to get Busch's #18 racer in and out of the pit in the shortest possible time. The crew can execute a standard pit stop—73 maneuvers, including refueling and a change of all four tires—in 12.12 seconds. Add just one average player to Busch's crew—say, an ordinary tire changer—and that time nearly doubles, to 23.09 seconds. Add two average team members to the mix, and it climbs to well over half a minute.

Synergy. Putting the best thinkers together can spur creativity and ideas that no one member of the team would have developed alone. The blockbuster movie *Toy Story*—the top-grossing film of 1995—wasn't the product of one visionary film-maker. Rather, it was the result of an often prickly but ultimately productive collaboration among Pixar's top artists and animators, Disney's veteran executives (including Jeffrey Katzenberg, then head of the film division), and Steve Jobs. The Pixar team originally presented Disney with what Katzenberg deemed an uninspiring tale. A major revision—far more edgy, at Katzenberg's insistence—lacked the cheeriness essential to a family movie. Finally the all-star group came up with something that satisfied everyone on the team—and that would later be dubbed by *Time* magazine "the year's most inventive comedy."

To do their best, alpha teams need leaders and support staff who are all-stars too. Extremely talented people have often never worked for someone they can learn a lot from; in our experience, most relish the opportunity and pull out all the stops. And high-caliber subordinates allow team members to accomplish more. A gifted administrative assistant, for example, requires less direction and competently shoulders many routine tasks, so the other team members can focus on what they do best.

Let's look at what else you need to have in place before you even think about putting together a star team. We'll also examine what kinds of work these teams are best suited for and how to manage the very real difficulties they may present.

The Table Stakes
Good Talent Management

A surprising number of companies don't follow basic best practices for talent management. Without these in place, there's no hope of making all-star teams effective.

Understand Where Your Strengths Are

Companies that are good at managing "A" players keep comprehensive, granular data on where their people are currently deployed, what those people do, how good they are in their current roles, and how transferable their skills may be. The companies use that information to continually improve their staffing resources and deploy them more effectively. Take AllianceBernstein (AB), a $3 billion asset management company based in Manhattan and a leading equity research firm. The firm carefully rates each of its 3,700 employees every year along two dimensions: performance and potential. The senior team at AB spends several days together each year cross-calibrating both sets of ratings across the entire company.

It's also critical to understand employees' ability to fill roles outside their current one. When Caesars Entertainment, the gaming company, reorganized operations in 2011, the senior team not only developed a database on the performance and potential of the company's top 2,000 managers but also analyzed the ability of the top 150 to take on new and different jobs.

Finally, watch out for talent hoarding. In too many organizations, star players are confined to a division, hidden from the leaders of other divisions. But no company can deploy talent effectively if it doesn't treat its best people like a shared asset rather than the property of a particular unit.

Don't Create Disincentives for Teamwork

Some companies' performance assessment methods get in the way of team success. Microsoft is an example. For many years the software giant used a "stack ranking" system as part of its performance evaluation model. At regular intervals, a certain percentage of any team's members would be rated "top performers," "good," "average," "below average," and "poor," regardless of the team's overall performance. In some situations this kind of forced ranking is effective, but in Microsoft's case it had unintended consequences. Over time, according to insiders' reports, the stack ranking created a culture in which employees competed with one another rather than against other companies. "A" players rarely liked to join groups with other "A" players, because they feared they might be seen as the weakest members of the team.

Own the Pipeline

When big strategic goals are involved, a company often finds that it needs capabilities it doesn't have. The wise leader anticipates this problem by actively and continually looking for talent. The individuals responsible for executing strategy must have an ownership stake in this recruiting process, because talent is always a key component of strategy. Yet many companies continue to subcontract recruiting wholesale to the HR department and professional search firms.

Play Your Best Hand
Choose Mission-Critical Projects

We don't recommend putting together an alpha team for small projects. They're not worth the trouble or the opportunity costs. Save such teams for initiatives that have clearly defined objectives and are critical to the company's strategy. Product development efforts often fit this category, and others may as well.

Boeing's 777 airliner provides a good example of what a star team can achieve in product development. Back in 1990, Boeing recognized that it had an important gap in its offerings: It had no airplane positioned between its jumbo 747 jetliner and its midsize 767 model. To address this gap, Boeing assembled a team of its best engineers.

The design effort was different from anything the company had previously done. To be sure, there were other important factors in its success—direct input from customers, new use of technology—but it took these alpha players to master the project's extreme complexity and bring it together. The basic design was completed in less than four months. The plane entered service in less than five years. By assembling its engineering stars and having them work side by side with customers, the company was able to launch what many industry analysts view as the most successful airplane program in commercial aviation history, with nearly 950 aircraft in service today. Moreover, Boeing got the 777 to market faster than any other major plane before.

Product development projects aren't the only promising opportunities for all-star teams. Sometimes a functional overhaul rises to the level of strategic importance, as it did for Caesars Entertainment, which operates casino properties throughout the world, mainly under the Caesars, Harrah's, and Horseshoe brands. Prior to 2011, Caesars' marketing budget was managed jointly by the company's 42 U.S. properties, with each casino's marketing organization determining what promotions to offer, when to offer them, which customers to target, and so on. The trouble was that marketing performance varied greatly: The success rate for the best properties was nearly four times that of the average property. Starting in 2011, the company assembled a team of six "pod leaders" to direct marketing spending for its properties in the United States. The team, drawn from the company's most experienced marketers and comprising individuals with a wide range of exceptional skills, completely revamped Caesars' promotions. It eliminated overlapping promotions. It tested new promotions at one property before rolling them out systemwide. It focused investments on promotions that had a demonstrated track record of generating profitable revenue. Transforming the company's whole marketing effort in this manner was a difficult, complicated task that might easily have overwhelmed a less skilled team.

Yet the results were dramatic: The number of unprofitable promotions across Caesars declined by more than 20%, and the incremental profit generated by the average promotion increased by more than 10%.

Manage the Odds
Anticipate What Could Go Wrong

Even if you have excellent talent management practices in place and you've loosed your all-star team on a well-defined, strategically relevant problem, you may still face challenges. Here's what to watch out for, along with some tips for avoiding problems.

Big Egos, Little Progress

Egos can get in the way of team performance. But they don't have to. In 1992, America's first "Dream Team"—made up of the very best basketball players in the NBA—swept the Olympic Games in Barcelona, defeating its opponents by an average of 44 points. This team succeeded because the goal of representing the United States with honor at the Olympics was bigger than any one player. It also helped that team performance was the basis for members' rewards: Nobody was going to get an individual medal. These are two points that organizations creating all-star teams should keep in mind. They should also prune anyone who isn't a team player from the group, regardless of how good that person may be.

Overshadowing the Rest of the Cast

The use of "A" teams can lead to a system in which only the best feel valued, thereby demoralizing average performers. One antidote is to ensure that everyone shares in the "A" team's achievements. George Clooney and the rest of his all-star cast on *Ocean's Eleven* created an environment where cast and crew reveled in their mutual success. Reportedly, most crew members were so pleased with the experience that they sought to sign on for *Ocean's Twelve* and *Ocean's Thirteen*. Other ways to keep "B" players engaged include recognizing performance, whether it's mission-critical or not; using a common performance evaluation system for stars and nonstars; and establishing common rewards shared by all involved.

Great Team Members, Mediocre Leaders

All-star teams headed by poor leaders can produce mediocre results. Imagine a chamber orchestra made up of virtuosos—think Itzhak Perlman, Gil Shaham, Yuri Bashmet, Yo-Yo Ma, and their peers—but conducted by an amateur.

The 12-instrument arrangement of Stravinsky's Concertino might never recover. To avoid this scenario, an organization should invest as much time in picking team leaders as in picking members, ask members for feedback on the leader early (and often), and not be afraid to switch generals or even to promote a team member to leader.

Ask any group of senior executives about which resources they don't have enough of, and they are likely to acknowledge that star talent is one of the scarcest. Then ask them how confident they are that their companies deploy and manage their best players to have the greatest impact on the bottom line, and they will probably express reservations. Is it possible that executives are overlooking one powerful tool that could help them achieve that goal?

_____

Maximum Enterprise Value

Value Acceleration: Lessons from Private-Equity Masters

Private-equity firms routinely achieve eye-popping returns on the businesses they operate. Their secret? A relentless focus on four management disciplines.

Paul Rogers, Tom Holland, and Dan Haas

In 2002, business fascination with private equity was building. PE deals were growing larger, along with the returns of the top-quartile firms, and people wondered what their magic ingredient was. This article argued that there was nothing unique about private equity ownership; the "magic" was that PE firms applied rigorous business disciplines to their acquisitions—defining an investment thesis, measuring what matters, working the balance sheet, and making the corporate center active shareholders in the businesses they hold. It laid the foundation for Bain's book Lessons from Private Equity Any Company Can Use, *by Orit Gadiesh and Hugh MacArthur.*

We've worked with many of the leading PE firms, particularly in the area of post-acquisition performance improvement, to help them navigate the new economic terrain. Corporate clients now often ask for PE-style, top-to-bottom reviews of underperforming or ailing divisions. Though some observers were skeptical, private equity as a whole outperformed public equity through the financial crisis with better returns and a lower overall bankruptcy rate, adding more credibility to the formula these firms follow.

Going private was the making of auto parts manufacturer Accuride. For years, the enterprise had struggled as a unit within the giant Firestone Tire and Rubber Company (now Bridgestone/Firestone). Because Accuride's business—making truck wheels and rims—was peripheral to Firestone's core business, it found itself starved for resources and managerial attention.

Then, in 1986, Accuride was bought by a private-equity (PE) firm, Bain Capital. Freed from Firestone's bureaucratic and budgetary constraints,

HBR June 2002

Accuride took fast action. It saw that if it could become the dominant supplier to a few major customers, it would capture the lion's share of the profits in its market. Because of the customized nature of its products, gaining a large share of a major buyer's business would enable Accuride to spread its selling and tooling costs over greater volumes, producing much wider margins. And so Accuride quickly invested in a new, highly automated plant to increase its capacity and reduce production costs; the low-cost capacity enabled it to undercut competitors on the prices and terms offered to target customers. The competitors—big corporations like Goodyear and Budd—were caught flat-footed. As public companies directed toward quarterly earnings, they were unwilling to match Accuride's investments, especially since the wheel-making business also lay outside their core operations.

With its focused strategy, Accuride flourished. In less than two years, sales shot up, market share doubled, and profits leapt 66%. When Bain Capital sold the company to Phelps Dodge just 18 months after buying the business, it earned nearly 25 times its initial investment. Since then, Accuride has continued to thrive, growing at a rate of 5% a year in a mature market throughout the late 1990s.

Accuride's story is not unique. The most successful PE firms spearhead such business transformations all the time. In the process, they create exceptional returns for their investors. How exceptional? U.S. private-equity groups like Texas Pacific Group (TPG), Berkshire Partners, and Bain Capital and European groups like Permira and EQT deliver annual returns greater than 50% year after year, fund after fund.

In studying more than 2,000 PE transactions over the last 10 years, we've discovered that the secret to the top performers' success does not lie in any fundamental structural advantages they hold over public companies. Rather, it lies in the rigor of the managerial discipline they exert on their businesses. Despite the widespread assumption that the stock market forces managers to concentrate on increasing the value of their companies, many executives of public companies lack a clear focus on maximizing economic returns. Their attention is divided between immediate quarterly financial targets and vaguely defined long-term missions and strategies, and they are forced to juggle a variety of goals and measurements while coping with contending stakeholders and other bureaucratic distractions. In stark contrast, the top private-equity firms focus all their energies on accelerating the growth of the value of their businesses through the relentless pursuit of just one or two key strategic initiatives. They narrow their sights to widen their profits.

In this article, we'll look at four critical management disciplines we believe explain the successes of the leading private-equity firms. By adopting these disciplines, executives at public companies should be able to reap significantly greater returns from their own business units.

Define an Investment Thesis

The first thing PE firms do when they acquire a business is define what we call an investment thesis—a clear statement of how they will make the business more valuable within about three to five years. The best investment theses are extraordinarily simple; they lay out in a few words the fundamental changes needed to transform a company. The thesis is then used to guide every action the company takes. A good thesis provides a much clearer basis for action than the typical financial target of "last year's earnings plus $x\%$" that most public companies use. (For a discussion of the time frame of PE firms, see the sidebar "The Advantages of Medium-Term Thinking.")

Look at the simple investment thesis that Berkshire Partners developed when it invested in Crown Castle International Corporation in 1994. The

The Advantages of Medium-Term Thinking

Most public companies manage their business units by focusing simultaneously on two time lines: the very short-term and the very long-term. In the short term, they strive to hit their financial targets for the next quarter, even if it means making decisions that run counter to the overall interests of their companies. In the long term, they assume their businesses will be owned "forever," making it difficult to create any sense of urgency among managers unless a business is obviously underperforming. In contrast, PE firms manage their businesses to the intermediate term—three to five years—about the time they typically hold an investment before selling. This time frame removes the often counterproductive focus on quarterly numbers yet still creates urgency to transform the business quickly.

Consider what happened when, in 1996, Texas Pacific Group acquired Paradyne, a struggling, unprofitable telecommunications equipment arm of Lucent Technologies. Paradyne had endured for years as a relatively neglected division of a very large conglomerate. TPG quickly set expectations of a turnaround and exit within five years. Its plan entailed splitting the business in two: a cable modem business that occupied a leadership position in its mature market and that was managed for solid, profitable growth, and a speculative semiconductor business (now called GlobespanVirata) focused on DSL technology, which had been buried in Lucent's R&D basement. Both of the new companies have flourished under purposeful new ownership and management and fresh, urgent direction. TPG's initial public offerings of both businesses in 1999 created a return more than 25 times its original investment.

founders of Crown Castle had hit upon a lucrative business model: They would purchase a cellular telephone transmission tower from one telecommunications company and then lease space on it to other service providers in the area. Lacking the cash for expansion, however, the founders were stuck in a single metropolitan market, Houston. Berkshire saw that a straightforward investment thesis—replicating the business model in other major markets—could significantly increase the value of the business, so it immediately supplied Crown Castle with an initial $65 million investment to buy towers in other major metropolitan markets. To date, Crown Castle has successfully rolled out this model across the United States, the United Kingdom, and Australia, generating a 10-fold return on investment for Berkshire.

Another example is Bain Capital's investment thesis for contact lens maker Wesley-Jessen, a company it bought from Schering-Plough in 1995. Over the years, Wesley-Jessen had ascended to a leadership position in specialty contact lenses (primarily colored lenses and toric lenses used to correct astigmatism), but in the early 1990s, it lost its way. Looking to expand into bigger markets, it began to neglect its key customer base, the optometrists who wrote lens prescriptions. It let overhead grow to dangerous levels. And it overexpanded into unprofitable segments, particularly standard contact lenses. Standard lenses represented a much larger market than specialty lenses, but entering that arena meant that the company had to compete head-to-head against the industry's two 800-pound gorillas, Johnson & Johnson and Bausch & Lomb. Wesley-Jessen simply lacked the scale to turn a profit in that market. By 1995, those missteps had reduced the company to an operating loss and a perilous cash position.

When Bain Capital acquired Wesley-Jessen, it brought in a new management team to pursue a back-to-basics investment thesis: Return the company to its core business. This required drastic action. A new $100 million factory built to produce standard lenses was quickly retooled to make specialty lenses. The company stopped serving unprofitable customers such as high-volume retail optometry chains. It cut spending on advertising, promotion, and other outside services and eliminated many positions, including several levels of management in manufacturing. At the same time, it expanded its product range within the specialty segment and made selective acquisitions to bolster its leadership position in the core market.

The investment thesis proved a resounding success. Operating profit jumped to 15% of sales in 1997. On the strength of its turnaround, Wesley-Jessen completed a successful initial public offering in 1997, creating a 45-fold return on equity in less than two years.

These two examples, it's important to note, reveal an important and often overlooked truth about the top PE firms: Their investment theses tend to focus not on cost reduction but on growth. Yes, imposing a stronger strategic focus usually entails aggressive pruning of the existing business, but creating a path to strong growth is what produces the big returns on investment. Far from stripping assets to boost short-term returns, PE firms actually tend to overinvest in businesses during the first six months of their ownership. Whether a firm's planned exit is a sale or an IPO, netting top dollar demands a compelling growth story.

Don't Measure Too Much

In 1992, Robert Kaplan and David Norton introduced in these pages the balanced scorecard, a business measurement philosophy relying on a mix of financial and operational indicators. In the wake of the article, enthusiasm for expanded business metrics burgeoned, with many large companies dramatically increasing the number of measures they tracked. The top PE firms, however, have steadfastly resisted measurement mania. Believing that broad arrays of measures complicate rather than clarify management discussions and impede rather than spur action, these organizations zero in on just a few financial indicators: those that most clearly reveal a company's progress in increasing its value. When, for example, Berkshire Partners merged two acquisitions that produced industrial machines, it focused on only two simple measures of merger success: cash flow (to assess the immediate impact of the merger and the company's continuing ability to meet financial obligations) and synergy effects (to ensure the realization of projected revenue gains and cost reductions). Everything else was secondary.

PE firms have some general preferences about the measures they track. They watch cash more closely than earnings, knowing that cash remains a true barometer of financial performance, while earnings can be manipulated. And they prefer to calculate return on invested capital, which indicates actual returns on the money put into a business, rather than fuzzier measures like return on accounting capital employed or return on sales. However, managers in PE firms are careful to avoid imposing one set of measures across their entire portfolios, preferring to tailor measures to each business they hold. "We use their metrics, not our metrics," says James Coulter, founding partner of Texas Pacific Group, in explaining how his firm develops measures for its businesses. "You have to use performance measures that make sense for the business unit itself rather than some preconceived notion from the corporate center."

When Nestlé put Beringer Wine Estates on the block in 1996 as part of a general divestment of nonstrategic businesses, an investor group led by TPG snapped it up. One of TPG's first moves as owner was to revamp the winery's performance measures. Nestlé's corporate bias was to focus on return on assets and economic value added—measures that it applied to all its businesses. But while those measures may have made sense for most of Nestlé's units, they weren't the right ones for Beringer. Wine making is very asset intensive, requiring large inventories of cellared wine, not to mention extensive vineyards, so ROA and EVA would necessarily appear very low. That's because these measures pull asset depreciation and amortization out of earnings, even though they're not really cash expenses. It's essential to cellar wine to achieve the quality that commands a premium price, but ROA calculations penalize a company for holding on to inventory. The right yardsticks of financial performance for Beringer were those focused on the company's cash flows and its cash-conversion cycle (the returns it made on its cash outflows). By those measures, the company was actually doing quite well.

Once the reality of the company's strong cash position and high-quality assets was revealed, banks became more willing to lend it money. TPG was then able to finance the high level of assets (which had distorted the ROA and EVA measures downward) largely with debt. This limited the amount of equity that TPG had to put into the company and maximized the return on invested capital and return on equity. In the wake of the changes, Beringer thrived, achieving a nine-fold return on the initial investment within five years.

In addition, PE firms put teeth in their measures by directly tying the equity portion of their managers' compensation to the results of the managers' units, effectively making these executives owners. Often, the management teams own up to 10% of the total equity in their businesses, through either direct investment or borrowings from the PE firm. Public company executives may believe they're doing the same thing when they grant shares or options to their line managers, but they're usually not. Those types of arrangements typically give managers a stake in the parent company, not the individual unit. The problem is, the stock of the parent company is not usually heavily influenced by the performance of any individual unit, so equity grants don't really create ownership in the unit. But there are ways for public companies to structure compensation as PE firms do. For instance, management bonuses tied directly to the performance of the individual unit, not the entire company, can be increased as a proportion of overall compensation, with an offsetting decrease in cash compensation.

Work the Balance Sheet

PE firms rely heavily on debt financing. On average, about 60% of their assets are financed with debt, far more than the 40% that's typical for publicly traded companies. The high debt-to-equity ratio helps strengthen managers' focus, ensuring they view cash as a scarce resource and allocate capital accordingly. But PE firms also make equity work harder; they look at their balance sheets not as static indicators of performance but as dynamic tools for growth. The most sophisticated firms have, for example, created new ways to convert traditionally fixed assets into sources of financing.

Consider the story of Punch Taverns Group. TPG acquired the chain of 1,470 U.K. pubs from BT Capital Partners and other investors in 1999 for £869 million. A few months later, TPG and Punch made a bold move to acquire Allied Domecq's 3,500 pubs, squaring off against a much larger suitor, Whitbread, in

The Four Disciplines of Top Private-Equity Firms

Define an Investment Thesis

- Have a three- to five-year plan
- Stress two or three key success levers
- Focus on growth, not just cost reductions

Don't Measure Too Much

- Prune to essential metrics
- Focus on cash and value, not earnings
- Use the right performance measures for each business
- Link incentives to unit performance

Work the Balance Sheet

- Redeploy or eliminate unproductive capital—both fixed assets and working capital
- Treat equity capital as scarce
- Use debt to gain leverage and focus, but match risk with return

Make the Center the Shareholder

- Focus on optimizing each business
- Don't hesitate to sell when the price is right
- Act as unsentimental owners
- Get involved in the hiring and firing decisions in portfolio companies
- Appoint a senior person to be the contact between the corporate center and a business

what became the most hotly contested bid in the European PE market. TPG and Punch outmaneuvered Whitbread and won the deal, in part by working Punch's balance sheet to lower the cost of financing the acquisition.

TPG's financing consisted of a £1.6 billion bridge loan, which it later refinanced by securitizing its newly acquired pub assets. Thanks to the stable and predictable nature of pub revenues, Punch was able to isolate the rents it earned on real estate (an important source of cash flow to the company) and package them as real-estate investment securities that could be sold to investors. As a result, it achieved a more efficient capital structure, saving approximately £30 million in annual interest costs. In combination with a focused investment thesis—tailoring pub products and prices to local markets—the innovative use of the balance sheet enabled TPG to restore growth to a business that for years had posted flat to declining sales. Punch's pub revenues have been increasing at more than 7% annually, despite the maturity of the overall industry.

PE firms also work the balance sheet by aggressively managing the physical capital in a business. Consider how the U.S. firm GTCR Golder Rauner turned around SecurityLink (a company that installs and monitors security systems), which it bought in 2001 from telecommunications giant SBC Communications and merged with Cambridge Protection Industries (another security business it had invested in). SBC had viewed SecurityLink as a loss-making, noncore business, but GTCR's managers saw trapped value in the unit. They realized that the key to making profits lay in selling directly to customers and focusing only on regional markets where they could achieve market share leadership. Dominant market share in a locale provided scale economies for local call centers and pools of alarm technicians and installers. Selling through independent contractors or promotional marketing channels, by contrast, drained profits. When outside contractors installed alarms, they were so focused on the volume of installations that they tended to do slipshod work. That led to high rates of costly false alarms and customer attrition. In the promotional marketing channels, which used telephone sales and direct mail to sell to home owners with relatively low incomes, the focus was also on signing up as many new accounts as possible, often by providing free installations without any long-term contracts. These practices resulted in high selling costs and frequent cancellations.

So GTCR quickly established a single-minded investment thesis for SecurityLink: Pursue rapid growth in carefully targeted regional markets. This strategy created immediate opportunities to rework the balance sheet of the company. First, GTCR released capital by selling a third of SecurityLink's offices—those lying outside the target markets. Then it refocused capital previously tied up in serving the dealer and mass-market channels on building direct sales capabilities in the target regions. By homing in on fewer markets, the company was also able to dramatically reduce costs, cutting more than 1,000 sales and service jobs. The result? SecurityLink rapidly transformed itself from a loss maker into a highly profitable company, generating close to $100 million of pro forma pretax earnings in less than a year. The company was subsequently sold to alarm giant ADT, a division of Tyco. For GTCR investors, an initial $135 million equity investment grew to $586 million in just 13 months.

Make the Center the Shareholder

As public companies grow, the role of their corporate headquarters tends to shift toward administration; they become, in essence, mere employers. That's not the case at successful PE firms. Their corporate staffs view themselves as active shareholders in the businesses they hold, obligated to make investment decisions with a complete lack of sentimentality. They maintain a willingness to swiftly sell or shut down a company if its performance falls too far behind plan or if the right opportunity knocks. "Every day you don't sell a portfolio company, you've made an implicit buy decision," says TPG's Coulter.

GTCR's decision to sell its security-monitoring business to ADT just 13 months after buying it is a good case in point. The firm typically holds its acquisitions for five years, but ADT's offer—$1 billion in cash, more than four times GTCR's original investment—was simply too good to refuse. At the time, William Kessinger, a principal at GTCR, acknowledged that his firm would have liked to stay in the business. "We don't see ourselves as people who would typically buy and sell over a short period of time," he said. "This was just an unusual opportunity for us, given the size of the deal and the fact there was an interested buyer who was able to write a check for the whole thing."

PE firms are equally unsentimental in their approach to their headquarters staffs, seeing them as part of their transaction costs. Although their portfolios may represent several billions in revenue, they keep their corporate centers extremely lean. According to an analysis by Bain & Company, the average PE firm has just five head office employees per billion dollars of capital managed (the combined value of debt and equity), one-fourth the number of staffers at the typical corporate headquarters. Most corporate staffers at PE firms are deal makers and financiers, people who play core roles across an entire portfolio. If other expertise is required, outsiders are brought in on a contract basis.

More interesting than the number of corporate staffers is the way the best PE firms interact with their portfolio companies. It used to be that the firms' partners limited themselves to buying and selling companies, leaving day-to-day

The management disciplines imposed by private-equity firms require a certain type of executive, one predisposed to act as an owner, not an administrator. PE firms hire for this specific profile, and they motivate their hires by giving them equity in the companies they are running—so they truly become owners. Then the firms establish nonexecutive board governance for each portfolio company and give the board members equity, too, thus aligning all interests around the disciplines.

To find the right talent, PE firms reach wide, looking well beyond the scope of their personal contacts. In one-half to three-quarters of cases, they appoint key executives from outside the company. They rigorously screen for attitude, which is as important as a strong skill set and track record. They seek managers who, however experienced, are hungry for success and relish the challenge of transforming a company. PE firms also find ways to hold on to talent: They retain great CEOs by bringing them back into the fund or appointing them to newly acquired portfolio companies.

PE firms in the United States seldom consider the incumbent CEO of an acquired company the right person to continue to lead it. They know that weak performance is often the result of insufficient management drive. Even in Europe, firms are breaking away from the old management buyout model, in which executives come with the purchase of a company. Now these firms frequently replace senior managers. Two leading European PE firms we studied have replaced more than half the CEOs in their portfolios.

When Scandinavia's EQT recently acquired Duni AB (a global, $700 million, Swedish-based supplier of food presentation products and services), EQT appointed highly qualified, but nonindustry, executives. The former head of Whirlpool Europe was named the COO, and the former head of Shell Sweden became the CEO. The same reasoning applied to board appointments: EQT specifically went outside the industry to stack the Duni board with top experts in turnarounds, branding, and the management of highly leveraged companies. The chairman named by EQT, for example, was a former executive vice president of Asea Brown Boveri who specialized in corporate restructuring. In addition, EQT appointed to the board the CEO of Absolut Vodka, one of the world's most successful brands, and Swedish Match's former CEO, who had led two buyouts and understood the change of culture required to succeed.

Naming a nonexecutive board for a portfolio company is one way in which private-equity owners establish a performance culture. Often, such appointments mark the first time that business unit managers have been exposed to such exacting governance. But the creation of a well-functioning board not only keeps executives on track for a business transformation; it also prepares management to act as a public company in case an initial public offering is made.

management to each business's existing management team. Today, most headquarters take a more hands-on approach, providing support and advice and getting involved directly in hiring and firing managers. "We are focused on performance," says the head of one private equity firm who has replaced half the CEOs of his portfolio companies. "When we replace them, we cast the net broadly. We don't just look inside the company. We want to install a management team with the skill and the will to succeed." (For more on the people PE firms hire to fill key slots, see the sidebar "Wanted: Hungry Managers.")

Typically, a PE firm appoints a senior partner to work day-to-day with the CEO of each business. Having one high-level contact streamlines the relationship and avoids distractions. The businesses don't have to contend with a number of staffers making information requests. When this relationship works well, the portfolio company benefits greatly from the headquarters' independent and unsentimental view of the business and its markets.

A Simple Agenda

A few publicly traded companies, like General Electric and Montreal-based Power Corporation of Canada, have long managed their businesses with the rigor of private equity firms—with great success. And recently, a number of other companies have begun to adopt this highly disciplined approach. One example is GUS (previously known as Great Universal Stores), a diversified U.K. corporation with such businesses as Argos Retail Group, information services provider Experian, and luxury brand Burberry. GUS saw its share price slide in the late 1990s. In January 2000, new management took stock, led by Sir Victor Blank as chairman and John Peace, who had joined as group chief executive the previous year. "Investors were concerned that GUS was failing to manage major changes in the business—and they were right," remembers Peace. "We sat down and asked ourselves, is GUS really an unwieldy conglomerate? Should it be broken up? Instead, we realized that there were a number of real jewels in GUS, genuine growth businesses that could provide a new focus for the group. Our role was to make sure that those businesses [delivered] to shareholders."

The new team rapidly reviewed its major businesses to identify the two or three actions that would maximize the value of each one. It realigned the capital base of the company, closing down peripheral businesses so as to release funds for investment in the core. It simplified measurement and added a focus on the cost of capital to traditional, earnings-based measures. Most important, it defined more clearly the role of the corporate center, restructured incentives to provide management teams with greater ownership stakes in their businesses, reorganized top management positions to support the new core business divisions, and clarified accountabilities and decision making in order to give division managers more authority. The team also brought in new managers from outside when necessary.

Although GUS's transformation is still in its early days, the results are impressive. The company's share price has increased 50% in a down market, and, in terms of market capitalization, the company shot up on the U.K. stock market from number 85 in January 2000 to number 37 in April 2002.

Life today is tougher for companies than it was a few years back. Managerial missteps take a higher toll and are more difficult to recover from. In this environment, tough-minded, highly disciplined management becomes essential to success—and that's exactly the kind of management characterizing the top private-equity firms. By using those firms as models—and by remembering, above all, that a simple agenda is better than a complex one—executives at public companies can lead their businesses to stronger financial results even in the most challenging of markets.

Building Deals on Bedrock

A merger or acquisition will fail if you burden it with the wrong
expectations. Don't use deals to change your company's
foundation. Use them to do what you do better.

David Harding and Sam Rovit

*The research underlying this article looked back at a 15-year period (1986 to 2001)
and asked a simple question: What approach to M&A worked best? The answers
contradicted much conventional wisdom. Deals aimed solely at increasing market
share weren't necessarily productive. "Megadeals" faced daunting odds against
success. What did work, we found, was a disciplined, repeatable approach, one that
enabled companies to do what they already did better. For instance, some companies
compete on brand power, others on low cost, still others on customer loyalty. Deals
that reinforced and strengthened those competitive advantages usually generated
superior returns.*

*Deal making fell out of favor during much of the 2000s, particularly during
and after the financial crisis. But the lessons reported in this article held up, and our
clients have capitalized on them. Frequent, disciplined acquirers—companies that
developed a repeatable model for their acquisitions—continued to produce outsize
returns. As a group, their performance was significantly better than that of occa-
sional acquirers and of companies that stayed on the deal-making sidelines.*

Whether they like it or not, most CEOs recognize that their companies
can't succeed without making acquisitions. It has become virtually impossible, in fact, to create a world-class company through organic growth alone.
Most industries grow at a relatively slow pace, but investors expect companies to
grow quickly. Not everyone can steal market share, particularly in mature industries. Sooner or later, companies must turn to acquisitions to help fill the gap.

Yet acquisitions can be a treacherous way to grow. In their bids for new
opportunities, many companies lose sight of the fundamental rules for making
money in their industries. Look at what happened to manufacturing giant Newell.

HBR September 2004

When Newell's top managers approached their counterparts at Rubbermaid in 1999 about the possibility of a merger, it looked like a deal from heaven. Newell had a 30-year track record of building shareholder value through successful acquisitions of companies like Levolor, Calphalon, and Sanford, maker of Sharpie pens. Rubbermaid had recently topped *Fortune*'s list of the most admired U.S. companies and was a true blue-chip firm. With its long record of innovation, it was very profitable and growing quickly.

Because Newell and Rubbermaid both sold household products through essentially the same sales channels, the cost synergies from the combination loomed large. Newell expected to reap the benefits of Rubbermaid's high-margin branded products—a range of low-tech plastic items, from laundry baskets to Little Tikes toys—while fixing a number of weak links in its supply chain.

Rubbermaid's executives were encouraging: As long as the deal could be done quickly, they said, they'd give Newell an exclusive right to acquire their company. Eager to seize the opportunity, Newell rushed to close the $5.8 billion megamerger—a deal 10 times larger than any it had done before.

But the deal from heaven turned out, to use *BusinessWeek*'s phrase, to be the "merger from hell." Instead of lifting Newell to a new level of growth, the acquisition dragged the company down. In 2002, Newell wrote off $500 million in goodwill, leading its former CEO and chairman, Daniel Ferguson, to admit, "We paid too much." By that time, Newell shareholders had lost 50% of the value of their investment; Rubbermaid shareholders had lost 35%.

What went wrong? It's tempting to brush off the failure as a lack of due diligence or an error in execution. Admittedly, when Newell looked beneath Rubbermaid's well-polished exterior after the deal closed, it discovered a raft of problems, from extensive price discounting for wholesalers to poor customer service to weak management. And Newell's management team, accustomed to integrating small "tuck in" deals, greatly underestimated the challenge of choreographing a merger of equals.

Yet even without those problems, Newell would have run into difficulties. That's because the deal was flawed from the start. Although Rubbermaid and Newell both sold household basics to the same pool of customers, the two companies had fundamentally different bases of competition. Levolor blinds and Calphalon pots notwithstanding, Newell competed primarily by efficiently churning out prosaic goods that could be sold at cut-rate prices. Rubbermaid was a classic brand company. Even though its products were low-tech, they sold at premium prices because they were distinctive and innovative. Rubbermaid could afford to pay less attention to operating efficiency. The two companies had different production processes and cost structures; they used different value propositions to appeal to customers. If Newell's executives had remained focused on the company's own basis of competition—being a low-cost producer—they would have seen from the outset that Rubbermaid was incompatible.

How can acquirers avoid the Rubbermaid trap? We've been studying the question for years. In fact, we've analyzed 15 years' worth of data (from 1986 through 2001) from more than 1,700 companies in the United States, Europe, and Japan; interviewed 250 CEOs in depth; and worked with dozens of big companies in planning and implementing mergers and acquisitions. Our research has confirmed our experience, leading us to conclude that major deals make sense in only two circumstances: when they buttress a company's current basis of competition or when they enable a company to lead or keep up with its industry as it shifts to a different basis of competition. In other words, the primary purpose of mergers and acquisitions is not to grow big fast, although that may be the result, but for companies to do what they do better.

That means some companies should never do major deals. Firms that have a truly unique competitive edge—the Nikes, Southwests, Enterprise Rent-A-Cars, and Dells of the world—should avoid big deals altogether. For such companies, large-scale acquisitions are usually counterproductive, diluting their unique advantages and hampering future growth.

It also follows that the odds are overwhelmingly against the success of a single headline-grabbing megadeal. If you already do what you do better than anyone else, a big merger or acquisition can only siphon money, resources, time, and management attention away from the core business. And even if you don't, rarely will a single deal be the solution to all your company's problems and bring no issues of its own.

Perhaps this sounds self-evident. But few companies are so strategic in their approach to mergers and acquisitions. When we surveyed 250 senior executives who had done major deals, more than 40% said they had no investment thesis—meaning they had no theory of how the deal would boost profits and stock price. And half of those who did have an investment thesis discovered within three years of closing the deal that their approach was wrong. That means fewer than one in three executives went into deals with a sound reason that actually stood the test of time for buying a company. All too many of them made the same mistake Newell did with Rubbermaid: pursuing an acquisition that conflicted fundamentally with their company's existing or desired basis of competition.

In this article, we'll examine how successful acquirers in both stable and changing industries use the basis of competition to guide their deal-making decisions. We'll also explore how a company's rigorous understanding of its basis of competition can change the way it approaches the deal-making process. But first, let's take a closer look at what we mean by basis of competition.

The Basis of Competition

Much of the allure in the notion that acquisitions enable companies to get big fast must lie in its connection with a related idea: that industry leadership equals market share leadership. That is, the leading companies in an industry are those with the most customers and the highest sales. But if this were true, American Airlines would be far more successful than Southwest, IBM would still be the industry leader in computer hardware, and Hertz would be more profitable than Enterprise.

If size is no necessary virtue in a particular industry, then virtue must lie elsewhere. In our experience, what determines industry leadership varies significantly from field to field. We propose that, broadly speaking, companies can achieve industry leadership in five ways: through superior cost position, brand power, consumer loyalty, real-asset advantage, and government protection. (See the exhibit "The Finer Points of Competitive Advantage.") Getting bigger may bolster one or more of these bases of competition, but it doesn't guarantee leadership. And recognizing which basis matters the most in a given industry can be tricky.

For instance, what's the basis of competition for the venerable British department store Harrods? While the company's name is certainly well known, its brand is not the main reason the trendy shop can sustain its high margins. And even though its upscale British service is important, customer loyalty is not the primary basis of competition either. Rather, it's the shop's premier address in London's tony Knightsbridge neighborhood—an asset advantage—that allows Harrods to charge the high prices it does.

On what basis does independent credit card issuer MBNA compete? It's not just that its size confers economies of scale. In the financial services industry, cost-to-income ratios determine the winners. The cost of acquiring new customers is so substantial that the highest returns go to the companies that capture the largest share of wallet from their best customers. In short, MBNA and companies like it compete on customer loyalty. Accordingly, MBNA's strategy focuses on bolstering customer retention by getting the right customers, not just getting the most customers. That approach guided its acquisition in 2004 of Sky Financial Solutions, a company that provides financing for dental professionals. With nearly three-quarters of all dentists in the United States already carrying an MBNA credit card, the Sky deal offered a way for MBNA to cement loyalty and expand its share of wallet.

And what about Comcast? It excels at managing blue-collar contractors and negotiating with content providers, but it does not compete primarily through asset advantage. Its monthly billing system is highly efficient, but it does not compete primarily on cost either. Competing in a regulated industry, its primary

The Finer Points of Competitive Advantage

The basis for competition differs by industry, and wise acquirers know their basis before they launch a deal.

Basis	Companies
Superior cost position	Newell, Walmart
Brand power	Procter & Gamble, Kellogg
Customer loyalty	Enterprise Rent-A-Car, MBNA
Real-asset advantage	Harrods, IMC Global
Government protection	GlaxoSmithKline, Comcast

advantage lies in being a master of red tape: obtaining rights of way and negotiating with local municipalities to assure rates. So it competes primarily on the basis of government protection.

One of the things that makes recognizing a company's basis of competition less than straightforward is that few organizations are pure play. Low-cost producer Newell, you may recall, also had some strong brands. Yet as a manufacturer, its cost position is what tends to seal its fate. Conversely, while Rubbermaid was a manufacturer, as with most consumer products companies, its earnings capacity was primarily tied to its brand power.

When firms do deals that strengthen their basis of competition, as MBNA did, they increase their earning power; when they don't, they weaken their earning power. Clearly, then, every merger or acquisition your company proposes to do—whether big or small, strategic or tactical—should start with a clear statement of how money is made in your business (what the company's basis of competition is) and how adding this particular acquisition to your portfolio will further your strategy for capitalizing on that basis and thereby make the firm more valuable. If this were easy, far more acquisitions would succeed. Let's take a look at how one company used those principles to guide its acquisitions and grow profitability in an industry whose basis of competition was stable—although at first glance it may not have seemed that way.

Building on Success

Every multinational food company with sales greater than $5 billion grew through extensive acquisitions. It's not hard to see why. New products are essential for growth, and it's cheaper to buy a new sandwich spread or snack food than to develop one. Merger and acquisition activity in this industry has been especially intense during the past 10 years, which have seen a host of acquisitions by the large food companies: Philip Morris's Kraft buying Nabisco, General Mills purchasing Pillsbury, Sara Lee gobbling up Earthgrains, to name only a few. One of the most successful acquisitions was Kellogg's takeover of Keebler, a good example of a company that knew what it was buying and why and that reaped the returns to prove it.

Kellogg's basis of competition is unquestionably its brand strength. For decades, a shelf full of household-name products like Corn Flakes, Rice Krispies, and Special K steadily delivered top-tier operating margins of 17.5% and a leading share of the ready-to-eat cereal market. The company's strong brand meant it could raise prices just enough each year to generate the upside profit surprises that shareholders love.

But by the mid-1990s, Kellogg's once-crisp universe was growing soggy. Post, the number three competitor, had initiated a fierce price war. General Mills, the traditional number two, began vying for market share lead. Retailers stepped up offerings of store brands, with companies like Ralston Foods happily supplying these goods at lower prices. Worse still, to more and more consumers, that bowl of Corn Flakes, once considered the obligatory way to start the day, was becoming a hassle in a time-constrained world. Between 1996 and 2000, Kellogg's share price dropped nearly 20% in a booming stock market.

This was the situation Carlos Gutierrez inherited when he became the company's CEO in 1999. Despite the cost pressures from Post, Gutierrez and his team recognized that Kellogg's brand strength, not its cost position, remained its strongest competitive weapon. Even if people were skipping breakfast, they still liked to snack on cereal-based products during the day. Between 1996 and 2001, the market for handheld breakfast bars grew 8% annually even as demand for ready-to-eat cereals declined 5% year after year. Kellogg had strong brands that lent themselves well to snacking, notably its Nutri-Grain bars and Rice Krispies Treats.

Firmly committed to *what* the company did—compete on brand—Gutierrez and his team focused on *how* they could do it better, paying particular attention to the capabilities Kellogg would need to sustain its brand strength in a rapidly consolidating marketplace. They concluded that the company had to excel in three areas: new-product development, broader distribution, and the creation of a culture skilled at executing business plans more quickly.

Revamping Kellogg's culture and creating new products could be addressed internally by training people differently and by redirecting spending on capital and R&D projects. Distribution, however, was another matter. The best way to deliver snacks was through a direct distribution channel. But building one from scratch would be inordinately expensive. Kellogg needed to buy one.

Gutierrez and his team set their sights on Illinois-based Keebler. Keebler was the number two cookie and cracker maker in the United States, behind Nabisco. But it wasn't Keebler's cookie-making prowess that excited Kellogg; it was where Keebler sold its cookies and how it got them there. Keebler had an outstanding direct store-delivery system. Rather than ship products to a retailer's warehouse and expect the retailer to put them on the shelves, Keebler sent out a fleet of panel trucks every day to deliver fresh snacks directly from its bakeries to store aisles, greatly speeding inventory turns.

Kellogg calculated that acquiring Keebler would add one to two points to the top line by moving Kellogg into a high-growth distribution channel and by filling that channel with an expanded line of snacks. The Keebler acquisition became pivotal in Kellogg's turnaround, as revenue rose 43% between 1999 and 2003 and operating income nearly doubled. The key to the deal's success was that it allowed the company to extend its existing brand strength into new products and additional channels.

Kellogg's decision to build its brand even as the very concept of breakfast was changing might appear risky. In our experience, however, company leaders consistently underestimate the potential left in their core businesses. High-performing companies drive their businesses to achieve full market share and profit potential before taking on something new.

That's a lesson IMC Global learned—eventually. For many years, IMC was the leading North American producer of phosphates and the number two producer of potash, two key ingredients in crop fertilizer. During the late 1990s, IMC tried to extend its traditional basis of competition—asset advantage—by bolstering its phosphate and potash mines and processing plants with a move into specialty chemicals. But what looked like a push into a related business was not. The specialty chemicals business had different supply chains and customers from those of the phosphate- and potash-mining business. What's more, the phosphate industry was still highly fragmented, and IMC overlooked the opportunity to roll up companies in its core business. The businesses IMC bought did not enhance its asset advantage, either by growing its share of potash and phosphate assets, or by adding new technology to lower its costs, or by bringing in new points of distribution. Instead, the acquisitions added leverage to the balance sheet and diverted management time and cash from maintaining IMC's leadership position in its core fertilizer business.

A new management team brought in to turn around the business recognized that future growth and profitability hinged on restoring the focus on phosphates and widening distribution in what had become a global market. The new team divested all the businesses unrelated to fertilizers that had been added during the late 1990s. In early 2004, IMC agreed to merge with $2 billion Cargill Crop Nutrition, a move that increased its phosphate mining and processing capacity. And in a market where all the growth is coming from less-developed countries, Cargill Crop Nutrition's global distribution system provides a source of competitive advantage for Mosaic, the new company. Though the deal is still in its early stages, preliminary results are good, and we expect it to be successful in the long run because the deal is squarely in line with the way IMC makes its money.

Using Deals to Power Change

At the other end of the spectrum from the IMC and Cargill scenario are the glamorous, high-profile deals aimed at transforming companies or entire industries. The idea of using acquisitions as strategic masterstrokes gained momentum throughout the 1990s, and a host of high-flying companies, including Vivendi Universal, AOL Time Warner (which changed its name back to Time Warner in October 2003), Enron, and natural gas provider Williams employed the technique.

That list alone may be enough to turn readers off to the concept. But the approach shouldn't be discarded entirely, because when the basis of competition in an industry changes, transformational deals can make sense. Advances in technology, shifts in regulations, and the emergence of new competitors can change an industry's competitive base so abruptly that even the fastest organizations can't alter their core businesses rapidly enough to adapt organically to the new market, leaving acquisitions as the best way to recast the business. Much, however, hangs in the balance. Speed is critical, the investments required are enormous, and taking half measures can be worse than doing nothing at all.

Getting it right requires companies to have a clear understanding of the new basis of competition, and one big deal seldom offers the best way to get there. Clear Channel Communications is one company that successfully used a series of deals to segue to stronger growth, after the foundation for competition in its industry shifted dramatically in the 1990s. Let's see how.

Lowry Mays was an accidental radio entrepreneur. The former investment banker found himself in the radio business when a friend backed out of a radio station deal in 1972, and Mays was left holding the property. During the next 23 years, Mays and his two sons became accomplished deal makers in broadcasting, acquiring two dozen radio stations one by one, most for less than $40 million. Government regulation formed the basis of competition in radio broadcasting during the 1970s and 1980s, and success lay in securing exclusive licenses granted by the Federal Communications Commission in particular local markets.

Knowing what their business was about, the Mayses were clever in how they built it. They were savvy financiers, bolstering cash flow from radio operations with debt financing to fund expansion. They became expert at anticipating when local radio stations were about to come up for sale. When those stations hit the market, the Mayses were prepared with strong bids.

Using this approach, the Mayses' company, Clear Channel, vaulted to number six in radio broadcast revenues, close behind Infinity Broadcasting, Evergreen Media, Disney, Chancellor Broadcasting, and Cox Broadcasting. By 1995, however, the Mayses had hit a ceiling. Federal law limited broadcasters to two stations per market and 40 nationwide, and Clear Channel was bumping up against those barriers. Then the game changed. In 1996, Congress deregulated the industry, allowing companies to own as many as eight stations in a large market and eliminating nationwide limits entirely. Overnight, the basis of competition in radio shifted. Cost leadership would determine the industry's winners rather than skill in trading up to the most lucrative local licenses. The Mayses understood that this new basis of competition favored operating on a national and possibly a global scale, which would enable broadcasters to spread their costs.

Players in the radio broadcasting industry divided into two camps: the buyers and the bought. The Mayses intended to be buyers. As the industry redefined itself, Clear Channel applied a savvy strategy to this new basis of competition. It combined aggressive acquisitions to gain scale with innovative new operating practices—such as providing packaged playlists, centrally distributing formats to stations around the country, and using the same "local" weatherman to report on cities as distant from each other as Tampa and San Diego—to capitalize on its size.

Clear Channel's coherent strategy quickly moved it to the top of the industry. At the beginning of 2004, the company owned about 1,200 radio stations in the United States and had equity interests in more than 240 stations internationally. Its next nearest competitor, Viacom, owned about one-fifth as many stations.

Clear Channel's steady focus on cost led the company to look beyond broadcasting as well. In 1997, it spotted cross selling and bundling opportunities for local advertising and diversified into the billboard business by acquiring a succession of small companies. Then, in 2000, it became the leading live-concert promoter through the acquisition of SFX Entertainment.

The financial results of Clear Channel's acquisition-driven growth strategy have been exceptional, as each deal has reinforced the company's shift to cost-based competition. From 1995 through 2003, company revenues and income grew at an astounding rate of 55% annually. Clear Channel generated a 28% average annual shareholder return during the same period.

While Clear Channel was able to adjust to the realities of a changing industry through a series of acquisitions, most firms moving to a new basis of competition will almost certainly need to consider divestitures as well. Otherwise, they will find themselves trying to compete in two different ways—a sure recipe for failure. An example of an effective acquirer-divestor is the Thomson Corporation. From 1997 to 2002, Thomson transformed itself from a traditional conglomerate that included newspapers, travel services, and professional publications into a focused provider of integrated electronic information to specialty markets. This made sense, as the growth of the Internet had changed the basis of competition in its industry from customer loyalty (newspaper subscriptions and renewals) into real-asset advantage (ownership of proprietary databases).

Starting in 1997, Thomson zeroed in on a small number of businesses in its portfolio that were especially well positioned to capitalize on the industry's shift. As Thomson's executives saw it, the new basis of competition centered on achieving scale by developing proprietary technologies that transformed the way information was delivered and integrated into the workplace. Exploiting this technological potential became the core of the Thomson investment thesis. Thomson realized that continuing to use its newspapers as a way to distribute information that originated with wire services owned by others would become an indefensible position, as the Internet made alternate modes of publication much cheaper and easier. Instead, it needed to own the information, so it divested newspapers and bought databases. Thomson sold more than 60 companies and 130 newspapers, raising $6 billion. With the proceeds, it invested heavily in its core markets by acquiring more than 200 businesses in educational, legal, tax, accounting, scientific, health care, and financial information publishing. Over the course of this transformation, the company improved its operating margin by 6%. Today, Thomson is a leader in electronic information databases; owning the information allows the company to earn superior returns.

Disciplining the Deal

Adopting such a strategic approach to M&A argues for an equally deliberate approach to managing the M&A process within your company. Yet the most common approach could hardly be called deliberate, much less strategic. Here's what usually happens.

An investment banker calls up the CEO with a target for sale and a deal book that provides background material. "This is your chance to be the industry leader," he declares. Or maybe he says, "Your core business is stagnant; you need to look elsewhere for growth."

In response, the corporate development staffers run off and do a quick screen, based on a cursory review of the book and a superficial industry overview. If they discover that the banker is bending the truth or that the company in question is in a lot of trouble, they balk. But if the deal still looks "interesting"—however that may be defined—they construct a valuation model and conduct financial and legal due diligence.

In a few weeks, the team builds a case for the deal. Then they dive into hundreds of hours of negotiations, presentations, and board discussions—all aimed more or less consciously at naming a price that will fly and getting a green light from the board.

We hope none of this sounds familiar to you, because the odds are stacked high against picking a deal successfully this way. If the acquisition team is reacting rather than acting, it's likely to pursue plain vanilla deals with prices below the valuation model, deals with limited upside and almost unlimited downside. Meanwhile, the team will turn down deals that appear to be too expensive but actually aren't in terms of their long-term strategic benefits. And it will fail to uncover opportunities it might turn up on its own if it followed a strategic road map.

The best acquirers follow a process we call "planning for opportunity." Long before any opportunity arises, these people have their basis of competition firmly in mind, and the strategy they need to capitalize on it is carefully considered. They think long and hard about what kinds of deals they should be pursuing. Then a corporate M&A team works with individuals who are closer to the ground in the line organizations to create a pipeline of priority targets, each with a customized investment thesis, and together, they look for opportunities to win over interesting prospects. They systematically cultivate a relationship with each target so that they are positioned to get to the table as soon as (or, even better, before) the target goes on sale. By this stage, canny acquirers are likely to have months or even years invested in the prospective deal. As a result, they're often willing to pay a premium or act more quickly than rivals because they know precisely what they can expect to achieve through the acquisition.

Thus, seasoned acquirer Cintas, a leading manufacturer of uniforms in the United States and Canada, assigns someone to keep in touch with each potential target, often for years. This individual, who comes from the line organization, reports to the corporate M&A team, which ensures that she stays in touch with the target and watches for favorable conditions to pull the trigger on talks. Indeed, the deal team sometimes even "puts a bullet in the gun" by giving senior executives a compelling reason to contact the target if changes

Slow and Steady

Our research shows that continual acquirers that make small deals consistently earn higher returns than those that do fewer and larger deals.

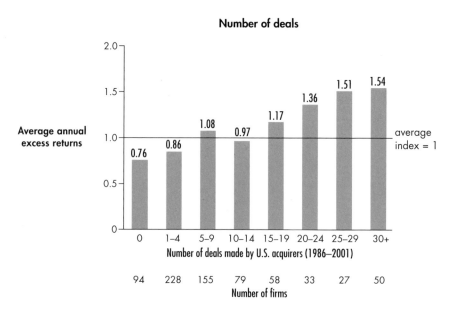

Number of deals

Average annual excess returns

average index = 1

0	1–4	5–9	10–14	15–19	20–24	25–29	30+
0.76	0.86	1.08	0.97	1.17	1.36	1.51	1.54

Number of deals made by U.S. acquirers (1986–2001)

| 94 | 228 | 155 | 79 | 58 | 33 | 27 | 50 |

Number of firms

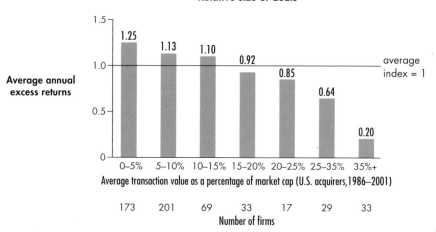

Relative size of deals

Average annual excess returns

average index = 1

0–5%	5–10%	10–15%	15–20%	20–25%	25–35%	35%+
1.25	1.13	1.10	0.92	0.85	0.64	0.20

Average transaction value as a percentage of market cap (U.S. acquirers, 1986–2001)

| 173 | 201 | 69 | 33 | 17 | 29 | 33 |

Number of firms

Source: Bain & Company Global Learning Curve study (2002–2003)

in that company, or in the marketplace, warrant it. Through this sophisticated system, the $2.7 billion Cincinnati-based company has sustained its sales growth for 34 years at a compound annual rate of 23%. Profits have grown at an even more impressive 30% annually.

By now it should be clear that strategic deal making generally argues against the big-bang approach of transforming a business through a massive acquisition. Our analysis of the deals made by 1,700 acquirers between 1986 and 2001 underscores the fact that the most successful acquirers do a lot of deals, that they do deals more or less continually, and that the average deal size is small. In our database, U.S. companies that did 20 deals or more during the 15-year period generated shareholder returns almost twice as high as the returns from companies that did no deals at all. Frequent acquirers outperformed those that did fewer than five deals by a factor of 1.7. And companies that acquired firms for 15% or less of the value of their own market capitalization on average earned returns six times higher than those that bought companies 35% of their size or larger. (See the exhibit "Slow and Steady.") The conclusion is clear: Go to the table frequently, and take small bites.

Can deal making solve your growth problem? In many cases, yes, as long as those deals are built on a sound competitive foundation and anchored in the fundamental way your company makes money. Understand that, and you've taken the first step toward M&A success. Fail to take that step, and no amount of integration planning will keep you and your shareholders from bearing the high cost of your mistakes.

Human Due Diligence

The success of most acquisitions hinges not on dollars but on people. Here's how to analyze potential people problems before a deal is completed.

David Harding and Ted Rouse

Executives who lead mergers and acquisitions have come to understand that the success of every deal hinges on people. That's partly a matter of matching the right individuals to the right jobs. But it also involves answering the question posed here: Who is the cultural acquirer? In evaluating deals, it helps to understand four essential elements of a target's culture. One, what is its style of governance—how is it run, and to what extent are decisions delegated? Two, how does it define and allocate decision rights? Three, what is the overall operating model—how is the work actually done? Four, what is the organization's approach to compensation? Acquisition teams can determine where the common elements are, which are likely to cause problems, and which approach will be dominant, the acquirer's or the target company's.

One of our clients led the acquisition team when his company merged with a large competitor. A few years later he reflected, "You told us how important it is to deal with culture. I remember thinking, 'What the heck are they talking about?'" He has since become chief operating officer of the combined company. "Now," he adds, "I get it. We are two years in and still living with harmonizing how we behave and work."

The strategic logic of Bank One's 1998 acquisition of First Chicago NBD was clear. According to the *Cincinnati Post,* the deal would make the Columbus, Ohio–based acquirer, then the United States' eighth-largest bank, "the dominant bank in the Midwest," ensuring its survival in a rapidly consolidating industry. But three years after the deal, none of the 16 top executives picked to run the merged company remained on the job. One M&A firm included the deal in its list of the top 10 M&A bloopers for 1999.

Bank One eventually recovered its momentum, but the acquisition reflects a common business problem. Too often, deal makers simply ignore, defer, or

HBR April 2007

underestimate the significance of people issues in mergers and acquisitions. They gather reams of financial, commercial, and operational data, but their attention to what we call *human due diligence*—understanding the culture of an organization and the roles, capabilities, and attitudes of its people—is at best cursory and at worst nonexistent.

The most obvious consequence of making a deal without conducting human due diligence is a significant loss of talent right after the deal's announcement. Less obvious is the problem of long-term attrition: Research shows that companies continue to lose disproportionate numbers of executives years after their merger deals have closed. (See Jeffrey Krug's Forethought article "Why Do They Keep Leaving?" HBR, February 2003.) For those who remain, confusion over differences in decision-making styles leads to infighting. Managers postpone decisions or are blocked from making them. Integration stalls and productivity declines. Nearly two-thirds of companies lose market share in the first quarter after a merger. By the third quarter, the figure is 90%.

That's the bad news. The good news is that human due diligence can help acquirers avoid these problems. When they have done their homework, acquirers can uncover capability gaps, points of friction, and differences in decision making. Most important, they can make the critical people decisions—who stays, who goes, who runs the combined business, what to do with the rank and file—when a deal is announced, or shortly thereafter.

The value of addressing these issues early is highlighted in detailed interviews Bain & Company conducted with managers involved in 40 recent mergers and acquisitions. The research compared people-related practices in successful and unsuccessful deals. In the 15 deals classified as successful, nearly 90% of the acquirers had identified key employees and targeted them for retention during due diligence or within the first 30 days after the announcement. By comparison, this task was carried out in only one-third of the unsuccessful deals.

Human due diligence lays the groundwork for smooth integration. Done early enough, it also helps acquirers decide whether to embrace or kill a deal and determine the price they are willing to pay. In hostile situations, it's obviously more difficult to conduct due diligence. But there is still a certain amount of human due diligence that companies can and must do to reduce the inevitable fallout from the acquisition process and smooth the integration. (See the sidebar "In Hostile Territory.")

So what does good human due diligence actually involve? In our experience, an acquiring company must start with the fundamental question that all deals should be built on: What is the purpose of the deal? The answer to that question leads to two more: Whose culture will the new organization adopt, and what

In Hostile Territory

The rhetoric of hostile negotiations as it plays out in public seems designed to amplify cultural differences between two companies. From the target pours the language of resistance, decrying the poor fit and often questioning the motives and track record of the acquirer, sometimes in highly personal terms. For its part, the acquirer blasts away at the performance of the target's management team, usually casting it in the worst possible light. Hostile acquirers that win the day often end up alienating at least part of the organization they are taking over, creating cultural terrorists in the process who do everything in their power to resist integration.

In this environment, it's clearly impossible to employ most of the analytic tools we describe in this article ahead of time. Executive teams can't spend time together, except in highly charged circumstances with lawyers on hand. Acquirers can't expect to see inside data on questions of employee satisfaction, compensation and promotion processes, or decision-making norms. But companies cannot afford to ignore human due diligence just because the target won't cooperate. Although hostile bids are rare, they also tend to be large. Hostile deals accounted for about 1% of all deals announced in 2006, for instance, but they accounted for 17% of deal value during the same period. Last year, the 374 uninvited bids made by corporate and private-equity buyers added up to offers worth $700 billion. What's more, such deals often turn out to be game-changing for the companies involved and their industries.

Fortunately, there is a certain amount you can do in a hostile situation in advance. You can analyze published reports and news stories about your target. Senior executives who have moved on from the target company can sometimes provide useful views of their former employer's culture. Customers and suppliers often have valuable insight into the decision-making processes and capabilities of the organization and may know how these compare with those of the acquirer. Any progress you make with this kind of human due diligence will help to test your investment thesis, determine boundaries for pricing, and identify some of the hot-button issues for the target's employees. It will also help keep you focused on life after the deal and the critical next steps you will need to take to improve it. Don't rest on your laurels once the deal is completed. On your first day as boss, launch an aggressive "get to know you" program. As you become acquainted with the people, focus especially on the next generation of leaders, usually two levels below the CEO. These managers have not fought the pitched defensive battles a hostile takeover generates and thus often see the opportunities that a business combination can provide. They will be your key allies as you move to overcome resistance and build support, because they are highly influential down the ranks of the organization. Decisions they make to stay or leave will have a significant ripple effect. You should follow up this program with employee surveys, interviews, and visits, all of which should be framed to protect your investment—the people you acquired.

Properly presented, human due diligence can be more than a learning exercise. It can be an important part of the healing process that needs to happen before your hostile acquisition can deliver the value you were so desperate to obtain.

organizational structure should be adopted? Once those questions are answered, human due diligence can focus on determining how well the target's current structure and culture will mesh with those of the proposed new company, which top executives should be retained and by what means, and how to manage the reaction of the rank and file.

Let us turn first to the question of culture. The answer is not as obvious as one would think.

Who Is the Cultural Acquirer?

In public, deal-making executives routinely speak of acquisitions as "mergers of equals." That's diplomatic, but it's usually not true. In many, if not most, deals, there is not only a financial acquirer; there is also a cultural acquirer, who will set the tone for the new organization after the deal is done. Often they are one and the same, but they don't have to be.

Consider the 2006 merger of the New York Stock Exchange with the all-electronic exchange Archipelago. In making that deal, the world's largest bourse acquired more than just technology. Archipelago's management team and governance structure will allow the NYSE to pull itself into the twenty-first century, transforming the closed-circle organization of powerful Exchange seat-holders into a company that sells shares to the public. The NYSE is the financial acquirer, but Archipelago is setting the cultural tone of the new company.

The big problem with saying that an acquisition is a merger of equals is that it allows management to postpone acknowledging which firm is the cultural acquirer, which makes pre-deal human due diligence all but impossible. Before you can evaluate potential people problems, you have to know which culture you want to end up with. Who the cultural acquirer is depends on the fundamental goal of the acquisition. If the objective is to strengthen the existing business by gaining customers and achieving economies of scale, then the financial acquirer normally assumes the role of cultural acquirer. In such cases, the acquirer will be less interested in the target's people than in its physical assets and customers, though that shouldn't discourage the acquirer from cherrypicking the best talent the target has to offer. The main focus of human due diligence, therefore, will be to verify that the target's culture is compatible enough with the acquirer's to allow for the building of necessary bridges between the two organizations.

But if the deal is intended to transform the financial acquirer's business, then the target firm is likely to be the cultural acquirer. In Disney's acquisition of Pixar Animation Studios, the integration goal was to protect Pixar's talent and begin injecting that new culture into Disney's existing organization. In cases like this, the question of organizational structure takes a backseat because the acquirer will not fold the target into its own structure; it may even do the reverse.

When deals are very large, the identity of the cultural acquirer may vary across business units. When Boeing acquired McDonnell Douglas in 1997, for instance, Boeing's objective was to tap into McDonnell Douglas's strong position with military customers. Boeing therefore viewed McDonnell as the cultural acquirer for the military aircraft and missile business. It created a separate unit to house both McDonnell's operations and its own military aircraft and missile business. It gave McDonnell executives most of the key posts in that business and took other measures to protect the McDonnell culture. On the commercial side, it was another story. Boeing was more successful in serving commercial airlines, and it acted swiftly to subsume McDonnell's commercial operation.

What Kind of Organization Do We Want?

It's rare that two firms can be combined without making hard decisions about whose structure to adopt (should business units be based on our products or their geographies?), who should report to whom, how decisions will be made, and so on. In most cases, executives looking at a deal will have ideas about which structure they prefer, but they need to know whether the proposed structure makes sense given the organizational realities of the target.

The first issue to diagnose is whether the target has a coherent, functioning organizational structure that allows it to make and execute decisions effectively. How and where are the business units deployed? What is the reporting structure? How many levels of authority stand between the top of the organization and the front line? How is authority distributed between layers? Think of this as the "hardware" of the organization.

The second issue to address is the internal dynamics of the target, or its "software." What process do the target's executives use to make strategic and operating decisions? How effective are the checks and balances on the key decision makers? Where will the most significant points of friction emerge in combining the target's functions or divisions with those of the acquirer?

To address these questions, the acquirer's human due diligence team should begin by looking at the hard data: organization charts, head counts, and job descriptions. From this research, the team should be able to create a profile of the target's basic organization, identify the reporting lines, lay out flowcharts that track how decisions are made and implemented, and describe the various official mechanisms for controlling the quality of decision making (board reviews, steering committees, and the like).

This data-based exercise, however, can take the team only so far. As any manager worth his or her salt knows, the organization chart reveals little about how effective a company's structure is. In friendly deals, therefore, the human due diligence team should approach decision makers and their reports to compare practice to theory and uncover the strengths and weaknesses of the organization: Are decisions really made through the official channels? Which departments and functions are best at making decisions? The output could consist of an additional set of flowcharts diagramming the decision-making process. Clearly, this assessment is only feasible in a friendly deal—and usually only after the intention to make the deal has been announced.

The final task for the acquirer's human due diligence team in addressing organizational issues is to take stock of the target's assets and capabilities and determine which departments and functions possess those capabilities. This, obviously, is especially important for deals where the point is to acquire assets and capabilities. The unit of analysis at this stage is not individuals, but entire business units, functions, or technical departments. The team will begin by reviewing the roles, goals, and job descriptions of key areas of the company. What is the scope of the units' responsibilities, and how well have they delivered? How does the quality of the output of the target compare with that of the acquirer? Team members should supplement these observations with a careful reading of the various units' management accounts (an exercise that will overlap with financial due diligence). It may also help to approach managers at key customers directly to ascertain their perspective on where the target excels or falls down.

When Cargill Crop Nutrition acquired IMC Global to form the Mosaic Company, a global leader in the fertilizer business, the acquisition team quickly saw that the two companies' organizations had similar structures that seemed to function well. They decided that the structure of the new company would mirror the operations and functional organization of both. With the design principles for the new organization in place, the combined company's new CEO, who came from Cargill, set out to fill the top boxes. He conducted one-on-one meetings with the top 20 executives from both companies and solicited input from the heads of HR and the CEO of IMC Global. These interviews revealed differences between Cargill's consensus-driven decision-making process and IMC's more streamlined approach, which emphasized speed. Because Cargill was the cultural acquirer as well as the financial acquirer, the more consensual approach to decisions prevailed. But armed with an early understanding of the differences in approach, the CEO was able to select leaders who would reinforce this position. Cargill managers also took time to explain the benefits of their decision-making system to their new colleagues rather than simply mandating it.

How Will the Cultures Mesh?

As we've seen, in many deals it isn't always obvious which firm is the cultural acquirer. Even when it is obvious, changing cultures is not simple. So it's critical that the acquirer get a sense of the similarities and differences between two organizations' cultures and just what the cultural transition will involve. This is so, even if the investment thesis downplays the importance of the culture.

Human due diligence efforts focused on culture have to begin with a clear understanding of what the target company's culture actually is. The acquirer should start by looking at the business press to see what the target's key stakeholders have to say about the matter and supplement that research with interviews with representatives from each group of stakeholders, if possible. The target's executives can explain how they view their mission, their values, and their own cultural style. The decision-making diagnosis we talked about above is another tool the acquirer can use to identify differences in the two organizations' processes that actually reflect fundamental cultural differences. For example, is decision making centralized or decentralized at the target company? Customers can shed light on how the target goes to market and responds to change. Competitors and suppliers can provide information on how the target is perceived in its industry. With this information, the acquirer can begin making decisions about the desired culture and put ground rules in place even before the deal is announced.

But the really useful cultural work of human due diligence starts after the deal is officially on the table. Then it becomes easier for the companies to work together openly. There's a lot a human due diligence team can learn simply by spending time at the target. Team members can see firsthand what the company's norms are about space, communication, meeting management, and dress—all important cultural symbols. They can talk to the company's "heroes" and decipher what they stand for. And they can review compensation, performance management, and other systems to get an idea of the values and behavior the company promotes.

After an announcement, a company can also start applying a useful cultural assessment tool: the employee survey. In this kind of survey, employees from both companies are asked to rate their own company's culture along a host of dimensions. They are also asked what they would like the combined company to look like in each of those categories. Along with face-to-face interviews, these survey data can reveal where friction and clashes are likely to spring up.

One leading American consumer products company we know (we'll call it U.S. Goods) used surveys effectively for cultural due diligence. The company was considering the acquisition of a European company (Eurogoods) with a similar product line and clientele. Because the acquisition's goal was to expand the geographic scope of the core business and achieve greater economies of scale in shared functions, U.S. Goods was both the financial and the cultural acquirer. It knew that the success of the merger would hinge on its ability to integrate Eurogoods into its own organization rapidly, which would, in turn, hinge on the cultural compatibility of the two organizations.

Working closely with their counterparts at Eurogoods, the U.S. Goods management team undertook a "cultural audit" of the two organizations. The team surveyed 28 key managers from Eurogoods, as well as 31 from its own organization, asking them a wide range of questions related to their personalities (for instance, their "desire to win" and their "external focus"), their management styles (such as their decision-making process and communications preferences), and their perceptions of organizational norms in such areas as compensation and career development. By comparing the answers, U.S. Goods was able to pinpoint cultural differences between the two organizations that might lead to leadership conflicts, talent flight, and integration breakdowns. The survey revealed, for instance, that Eurogoods had a more laid-back management culture than U.S. Goods, relying more on informal conversations and less on performance measures and organizational agility. With those results in mind, U.S. Goods formulated a plan aimed at addressing the cultural gaps and educating Eurogoods managers on the numbers-driven management ethic at U.S. Goods. It even had the Eurogoods team sign off on the plan before the deal closed.

While it's helpful for the acquirer to take stock of data from employee culture surveys, it's even more useful to get the managers from both companies to examine the data together in workshops. Indeed, the process of a joint review is as valuable as the data it produces. Executives participating in such workshops immerse themselves at first in the distinctions between the two cultures highlighted by the data. Then the floodgates open, and they often find they agree on many elements of the culture for the new organization, which becomes a rallying point.

Defining the values of the new culture, translating those values into specific expectations for behavior, and coming up with a plan to move both organizations to the new culture goes a long way toward understanding how each side works and what each assumes to be normal. The process also knits together the leadership team, turning its members into role models for the new culture.

Whom Do We Want to Retain?

If the financial acquirer is also the cultural acquirer, the company is likely to want to retain its own people in the top jobs. But keeping great talent from an acquired organization not only can upgrade the effectiveness of your company, it can also send a powerful message to those in the target firm about how they will be treated in the merger. What the acquirer really needs to do is get to know the management team of the target, so that it can judge who are the most talented leaders and then put the best people in each position.

In some situations, the target's people are precisely what the deal is all about. The Chinese company Lenovo's acquisition of IBM's PC business, completed in May 2005, is a case in point. In fact, the board of Lenovo's controlling shareholder allowed the company to pursue the deal if, and only if, it could recruit IBM's senior executives to manage the merged enterprise. Lenovo's interest wasn't just in the top people. The company offered a job to every IBM employee with no obligation to relocate or accept reduced compensation. That meant the company could continue seamlessly on its way, with minimal disruption of engineering projects or customer relationships.

Human Due Diligence: A Checklist

Human due diligence—assessing the decision-making roles, culture, capabilities, and attitudes of people in a target company—helps acquirers make fundamental go/no-go decisions, determine the price if the deal goes forward, and create an effective and focused integration plan. Indeed, the information gleaned through human due diligence can form the basis for a human capital balance sheet, showing the assets and liabilities of the company in terms of its people.

Integration decisions enabled by human due diligence
- Determining the structure of the organization and resolving conflicts in decision-making processes.
- Setting the tone for the combined culture and establishing a process for migrating to a new culture.
- Filling the top jobs quickly and deciding how to retain other key talent.
- Implementing programs aimed at winning the hearts and minds of employees in the target organization.

Methods and tools
- For a fact-based view of a target company's culture and the strengths and weaknesses of its people, acquirers can draw on organization charts, compensation and promotion processes, job descriptions and responsibilities, employee turnover rates, culture audits, 360-degree feedback, internal satisfaction surveys, and measures of employee loyalty.
- For a more qualitative assessment of people issues and capabilities, acquirers use interviews with key executives, role plays to determine patterns of response to business situations, reviews of how the management team handled prior crises, and interviews with customers and suppliers.

Not every company, of course, wants to retain all its target's managers, and most will need to determine who goes and who stays. Working that out requires the same kind of detailed assessment that goes into any high-level hiring effort. Acquisition team members should gather performance reviews, interview third parties (headhunters and former executives, for instance), and assess the executives' track records. They should probe the executives' leadership styles and evaluate how they have dealt with difficult decisions. Most of all, acquisition team members should simply spend time with their counterparts in the target company, preferably on the target's turf, getting to know them as individuals. The investment bankers who entertain an acquisition team at the target company's facilities will always want team members to spend their time in conference rooms, focusing on the performance story and numbers. But every visit to a target is also a chance to get out and learn firsthand how the organization feels.

The wider the cultural gulf between two companies, the more important direct interaction with the target's management becomes. That's particularly true of mergers involving companies based in different countries. To take another example, a U.S. appliance manufacturer (let's call it Atlantic Appliance) took a quite aggressive—and valuable—approach with an Asian manufacturer (Pacific Appliance) it was considering acquiring. In every key function, senior executives from the two companies got together for intensive, three-day sessions involving business reviews, strategy presentations, question-and-answer periods, and factory and office visits. Participants also dined and socialized together. On one level, the meetings were designed to help the acquirer gather information about Pacific's processes and practices. For example, the program helped Atlantic realize that the merger integration could break down as a result of the very different financial standards used by the two companies. On another level, however, the meetings provided Atlantic with insights into Pacific's management style and culture as well as a sense of the skills and attitudes of key managers. This analysis may well have been the primary benefit of the time spent together, becoming the basis for decisions Atlantic made about which Pacific managers to retain in top jobs and which to let go. It ensured, in other words, that the departure of employees occurred where it would do the least harm and potentially even bring benefits.

So far, our people discussion has focused on the top jobs. But in many acquisitions, the rationale is as much about the rank and file's capabilities as the top managers'. Here, the people-assessment process overlaps with structural human due diligence. The capabilities stocktaking we described earlier tells the acquirer exactly which departments and functions house the talent the acquirer wants to retain. The acquirer can then make judgments about which individuals in those units to keep on. If it is the people in sales who are essential to the acquisition's success, the team should talk to customers about which sales reps are the best, possibly combining this with the cultural interviews we described earlier. If the acquirer is buying research and development capabilities, it needs to bring in outside experts capable of evaluating the target's scientists and engineers. A particularly useful tool for assessing talent at a target is forced ranking. This needs to involve some combination of HR and key senior employees who will be part of the new organization. Using performance reviews and input from senior executives, the acquisition team can usually rank every employee in the critical departments from top to bottom. These results can be cross-checked against individual bonus awards, which are often a good guide to past performance.

Once key people are identified, the acquirer must face the challenge of retaining them. Those at the top may have an ownership stake in the company, which could generate a big payout as a result of the acquisition, and they may feel they can safely leave the company or retire. Even those without an ownership stake may decide it's time to seek greener pastures. To complicate the situation, the acquirer may want to keep some of its new employees over the long term while retaining others only for six months or a year. The best way to solve this puzzle, typically, is to put your cards on the table: Tell people exactly what you're hoping they will do, be it stay for a short while or stay on long term, and design incentives to encourage just that. Nonfinancial rewards and aspirations are important as well. If you can convince people that they'll now be part of a bigger, more exciting organization, they'll be more likely to stay on.

What Will Employees Think About the Deal?

Intimately linked with the question of whom you want to retain is the question of post-merger morale. The success of pretty much any deal (except perhaps those in which the acquirer is really only after a specific physical asset or patent) depends on what the target's employees think about the deal. Are they pleased or are they horrified to be acquired? Are they afraid? Will they actively undermine efforts to change the organization? Their attitudes will determine whether the acquirer can retain key employees, how difficult it will be to acculturate them, and whether they will accept new structures and processes.

If the deal is hostile, of course, you will not be well placed to gauge employee morale. Incumbent management at the target will be telling employees that the deal is a nonstarter and will be bad for the company. For that reason, pulling off a hostile acquisition whose investment thesis is based on the people is extremely challenging. But if the deal is a friendly one, then there's a lot you can do to gauge and even manage the attitudes of the target's people.

The obvious starting point is employee surveys. Most companies keep track of their employee satisfaction levels, and the results of these surveys can tell you a lot about employees' attitudes toward their company. Do they feel that there is a free flow of information up and down the hierarchy? Do they believe that they are rewarded on the basis of merit and hard work? You can also find out which units are happy with the status quo and which are not, thereby indicating where the main communication challenges will lie. Units that are happy with the status quo may resist the changes you propose, while those that are dissatisfied may look on you as a white knight. In addition to reviewing past surveys, you can work with the target to directly survey employees about their attitudes toward your company as an acquirer. And you can monitor industry and employee placement chat rooms to see what's being posted by your employees and by competitors.

As you build a picture of employee attitudes at your target, you will probably want to move beyond surveys to spend time with frontline employees on their coffee breaks and lunch hours, walking through plants and offices, talking with people at the operating level. When, in 2002, Johnson Wax Professional was in negotiations to buy DiverseyLever, part of the consumer goods giant Unilever, CEO Greg Lawton spent more than 100 hours talking individually with Diversey executives. From these conversations, he was able not only to identify members of a new management team before the deal was completed but also to map out a comprehensive program for communicating what the deal would mean for all stakeholders—employees, of course, but also customers, suppliers, and investors. By the time the deal was announced, Lawton and his counterpart at Diversey, Cetin Yuceulug, had prepared a joint vision and values statement, along with a video describing the new company's direction and plans, which they distributed to the company's worldwide staff on the day the deal was announced.

Conducting human due diligence requires both sustained commitment from senior executives and the allocation of the necessary resources. It is particularly hard to do when, as too often happens, executives of a would-be acquirer are hastily responding to an opportunity that has suddenly appeared on their radar screen. There is little time even to create a cogent deal thesis to test, let alone find the time to do the kind of due diligence on people issues that a successful deal entails. But there's another way to go about it. As we have argued, the most successful acquirers have a strategic rationale behind their deals. They build a pipeline of potential acquisitions that fit the rationale, on which they can conduct ongoing due diligence, both financial and human, before any merger opportunities ever arise. (See "Building Deals on Bedrock," HBR, September 2004.) With that kind of approach, acquirers usually have plenty of time and opportunity to pursue thorough human due diligence over a period of months or even years. When formal due diligence kicks off, these acquirers already know a lot about the target, including the strengths and weaknesses of its key people. They have a good idea from the outset of who is going to be the cultural acquirer in the deal, reducing the odds of misunderstandings or culture clashes. Done this way, human due diligence can turn people issues from a potential liability into a solid asset.

How the Best Divest

Companies often sell off businesses when times are hard. Smart CEOs approach divestiture more strategically.

Michael Mankins, David Harding, and Rolf-Magnus Weddigen

In our view, the conditions have been ripe for a renaissance in mergers and acquisitions at least since 2010. Capital is plentiful and cheap. Opportunities abound for profitable growth through deal making. And yet activity has picked up only slowly. The chief reason seems to be that potential sellers are reluctant to divest. Like homeowners hanging on in a tough real estate environment, they want to wait for the market to turn, and sell only when they can get top dollar.

That mindset is almost always a mistake, as this article demonstrates. Companies that are best at divestment don't try to time the market. Rather, they develop a systematic, disciplined approach to divestiture. They ask themselves what they are looking for and why. They determine what they want in their portfolio. A dedicated team then analyzes the company's assets in light of that strategy, determining whether the assets fit with the core business and whether they are worth more to the company than to anyone else. When the company decides to sell, the team plans carefully for de-integration and develops a "story" that makes sense to both buyers and employees. That has always been the path to profitable divestiture, and it continues to be today.

M ost corporations are geared up to buy assets, not sell them—the majority acquire three businesses for every one they divest. So when they decide to sell, many do it at the wrong time or in the wrong manner. Those are expensive mistakes.

Corporations that take a disciplined approach to divestiture not only sharpen their strategic focus on their core but also create nearly twice as much value for shareholders. That's what a Bain & Company study found in an analysis of 7,315 divestitures completed by 742 companies over a 20-year period: An investment of $100 in the average company in 1987 would have been worth roughly $1,000

HBR October 2008

at the end of 2007, but a similar investment made in a portfolio of the "best divestors" would have been worth more than $1,800.

For a good example of effective divestiture, look at the $16 billion forest-products company Weyerhaeuser. Since 2004, it has divested operations totaling more than $9 billion and used the capital raised and the management resources released to transform itself from a traditional pulp-and-paper company into a leader in timber, building materials, and real estate. In the process, Weyerhaeuser has produced some of the highest returns in its sector.

Weyerhaeuser is not alone. Our experience and research show that the most effective divestors follow four straightforward rules: They set up a dedicated team to focus on divesting. They avoid holding on to businesses that are not core to their portfolio—no matter how much cash they may generate. They make robust de-integration plans for the businesses they intend to sell. And they develop a compelling exit story to use internally and externally, taking the buyers' and employees' perspectives very much into account.

Used consistently, these disciplines produce an internal sell-side capability that enables divestors to generate superior returns for their shareholders. In the following pages, we'll explore each of these rules in more detail.

Rule 1: Establish a Dedicated Team

Most firms have sizable corporate development organizations, elaborate acquisition pipelines, and extensive relationships with investment banks, which all drive buy-side activity. In fact, as more companies—particularly private equity firms—have focused on deal-making disciplines, buy-side returns have improved over the past few years. Buyers are now just as likely as sellers to create value—which was far from the case during most of the 1980s and 1990s.

The best divestors approach divestitures with the same level of planning and rigor that their counterparts in corporate development bring to acquisitions. They have established sell-side teams, which are constantly screening their company's portfolio for divestiture candidates and are continually thinking through the timing and implementation steps needed to maximize value. In most cases, teams have standing members with unique skills—such as experience in separating accounting systems, specialized HR expertise, or the ability to set up detailed service-level agreements between the corporation and the divested businesses. They typically develop a divestiture pipeline by screening the company's portfolio (at least annually) and flagging those businesses that may be worth more to others than they are to the company's shareholders and are not core to its long-term strategy.

Textron has embraced this discipline. Ted French, Textron's CFO, has assembled a team with distinctive deal-execution capabilities. Team members maintain a detailed database of potential buyers for the company's businesses—both other corporations (often described as "strategic buyers") and private equity and other financial firms. They also keep data on virtually every transaction that has been completed or contemplated in the markets in which Textron competes. As a result, management has an excellent understanding of the needs of potential buyers and, therefore, the deals that can be done if Textron wishes to put a business up for sale. When an opportunity arises, Textron can act quickly and decisively, minimizing disruptions to its other business units and enabling executives in the target business to focus on making it worth as much as possible to potential buyers.

Since 2001, the Providence, Rhode Island–based conglomerate has sold 41 businesses with more than $4.4 billion in total revenue and acquired 24 businesses with $1.4 billion in sales. In the process, Textron's divestiture expertise has paid handsome dividends for the company's shareholders. Since 2001, the company has produced average shareholder returns that are more than 6% higher than those of its multi-industry peers.

Like Textron, most companies—even those with experienced sell-side teams—maintain relationships with investment banks, which can bring knowledge of potential buyers that even the most experienced seller may not have. They are often aware of potential buyers outside the seller's primary market, for instance, because they work with companies from many industries. Furthermore, the involvement of an experienced third party can be invaluable if a business needs to be split into pieces and sold to several buyers. Still, for the best divestors, investment banks play a clear supporting role. The company determines what businesses will be divested, when, to whom, and how.

Rule 2: Test for Fit and Value

Obviously, it makes the most sense to sell a business while potential acquirers can still extract value from the operations and take steps to reignite profitable growth. Yet our observation is that when faced with the three choices for dealing with an underperforming business—sell, milk, or transform—too many companies become de facto milkers. Unwilling to sell, but unable to support the level of investment required to transform an underperforming business, these companies hold on, often for many years, until the unit has lost much of the value it once had.

To avoid the milking trap and identify the right divestiture targets, the best divestors apply two criteria—fit and value. To determine fit, management asks: Is keeping the business essential to positioning the company for long-term growth and profitability? To judge value, management must work out whether the business is worth more held in the company's portfolio than it is anywhere else.

It takes discipline to apply these tests consistently. In our experience, executives are moved to divest not when it's best for the company but as a reaction to the business cycle. They're most reluctant to sell assets when economic conditions are good and potential asking prices are at their highest, and they can't wait to sell when the economy slows, values fall, and buyers dry up.

By adopting the fit and value tests, companies become far better able to sell at the right time. The benefits of this approach are twofold: Divested assets usually fetch better prices because companies are able to sell on their own terms, and markets are more forgiving of such a strategic readjustment when investors expect the company will grow at a heady pace as a result. Weyerhaeuser's transformation of its pulp-and-paper portfolio at the peak of its business cycle is a clear example of this type of disciplined divesting.

To be a candidate for divestiture, a business must fall short on *both* criteria— that is, it must be neither core to the company's strategy nor naturally more valuable to the company than to anyone else. Some businesses may not be core but can still be managed more profitably by the company than by any other entity: Disney's repurchase of its North American retail stores from The Children's Place is a case in point. Some businesses that are worth more to others should nevertheless be retained to build or sustain a competitive advantage elsewhere in the portfolio: Coca-Cola's continued participation in its heritage fountain

The Smart Way to Divest

Rule 1
Dedicate a team to divestment full time, just as you do with acquisitions.

Rule 2
Establish objective criteria for determining divestment candidates—don't panic and sell for a song in bad times.

Rule 3
Work through all the details of the de-integration process before you divest.

Rule 4
Make sure you can clearly articulate how the deal will benefit the buyer and how you will motivate the unit's employees to stay on until the deal is done.

business, for example, creates distribution and other advantages for the company in its core soft drinks business.

In making divestiture selections, the best companies are studiously unsentimental, sometimes jettisoning businesses with long and storied histories. Take the case of Roche. Starting in 2000, the Swiss pharmaceutical giant sold off its flavors and fragrances, vitamins, and fine chemicals businesses to focus on extending the company's leadership positions in oncology and diagnostics. Parting with those businesses couldn't have been easy. Roche had been a major player in flavors and fragrances since 1963, and the company had pioneered the industrial synthesis of vitamin C back in 1933. In total, the divested businesses represented more than a quarter of Roche's revenue for most of the 1990s.

Continued growth in those businesses would have required substantial investment—which then-CEO Franz Humer and his team believed would be better used to build Roche's position through new medical technology and pharmaceutical innovation. In June 2000, the company spun off its flavors and fragrances interests to the company's shareholders to form Givaudan. In the fall of 2002, Roche announced that it would sell its vitamin and fine chemicals businesses to DSM for more than $2 billion. The idea was to channel the proceeds into expanding its core pharmaceuticals business in Japan, which it was already in the process of doing by acquiring a controlling interest in Chugai.

Private equity firms and conglomerates naturally place great emphasis on value when it comes to determining which businesses to keep. To identify which assets to sell, the management committee at Textron, for example, applies three tests of value to the company's diverse portfolio, which is composed of some 12 divisions and 72 strategic business units (SBUs). For Textron to retain an asset:

- The unit's long-term fundamentals must be sound. The team gauges this by assessing the attractiveness of each SBU's market and the unit's competitive strength within that market.

- Textron must be able to grow the unit's intrinsic value by 15% or more, annually. The team applies this screen by carefully scrutinizing each SBU's business plan each year and challenging its divisional management teams to assess the value-growth potential of each business objectively.

- The unit's revenues must reach a certain threshold. Textron seeks to hold a portfolio of relevant businesses, each with at least $1 billion in revenue. Businesses that are not generating $1 billion or more in sales—and are not likely to reach this watershed within the foreseeable future—are targets for divestiture.

Applying tests like these requires a deep understanding of each business's long-term profitability and growth prospects—as well as the value outsiders are placing (or might place) on similar assets. Private equity firms are masters of the value test, to the point where they occasionally swap businesses among themselves in lieu of cash transactions.

Rule 3: Plan for De-Integration

Once executives have decided to divest a unit, they must determine what type of separation will best meet the company's needs and then carefully think through the implementation steps required to generate the maximum value from the separation.

Divestitures can take two main forms. Many companies choose outright sale, either to strategic buyers or to private equity or other financial buyers. An example of the former is Ford's recent sale of its premium Land Rover and Jaguar auto lines to India's Tata Motors; examples of the latter include The Home Depot's sale in 2007 of HD Supply to a team of private equity firms for $8.5 billion and Weyerhaeuser's sale the same year of its Canadian wholesale building-products distribution centers to Platinum Equity. In other circumstances, a divestor will spin off or carve out the target as a separate entity, with its own shares, as Altria did with its majority interest in Kraft Foods. Each approach has benefits and costs, and the best divestors consider how to structure the deal and to whom they will sell as carefully as they do what units to sell off and when. The sidebar "Making Separation Pay" summarizes the trade-offs involved in those determinations.

Whatever form the divestiture takes, good divestors are meticulous about planning how it will unfold—just as savvy acquirers are diligent about post-merger integration. Divestors start by comprehensively defining the boundaries of any divested business, answering such questions as: Which products and regions will be included? Which customers? Which facilities? They determine which specific assets will be separated from the company and transferred to the divested unit. They have developed tried-and-true methods for dealing with shared overhead costs, common brands, and patents. Cross-company systems and processes are carefully unraveled (or even shared by both companies for a transition period) to ensure effective separation.

Establishing these boundaries is often not easy. Legacy businesses are frequently embedded deeply in the parent, and disentangling asset ownership can become very thorny very quickly. In some situations, moreover, effective divestitures involve retaining close links with the divestor. Bell Canada's recent spin-off of its regional small-business operations and the rural portions of DSL (its

Making Separation Pay

Corporations are not private-equity firms—they are not in the business of buying and selling assets. But they need to be just as savvy about how to structure a divestiture deal and whom to sell to. Here's the best thinking about the "how" and the "who" of divesting.

The How

Once a company has decided that a unit is not vital to its core, it must determine how best to separate it out. That involves answering two important questions:

Do we sell for cash or stock? In most cases, selling a business for cash makes the most sense. There are instances, however, when spinning off a division to shareholders can be a better bet—either because the seller has no use for the cash proceeds (and doesn't want to hold them for fear of becoming a takeover target) or because a spin-off would produce higher after-tax proceeds.

Do we sell the whole business or a piece of it? Most of the time, it's easier to sell a whole business than to break it up into pieces, keeping some and selling others. In some cases, though, selling the whole business is not desirable or not feasible. That was so with Bell Canada's local wire-line business, where the real value lay in separating, and creating a different ownership structure for, the urban and the rural parts of the business.

The Who

Identifying the right buyer for divested assets involves answering two additional questions:

Who will pay the highest price? Typically, the company that makes the best offer is the one that views the property as the most strategic. But sellers can't assume that buyers will intuitively understand their own strategic advantages, nor can sellers count on investment banks to tout the deal's potential effectively. The key to maximizing the sale price is seeing the divested business through the buyer's eyes and tailoring the sales pitch accordingly. This "reverse due diligence" extends to identifying and quantifying potential cost and revenue synergies for potential buyers.

Is one buyer better than another from a strategic standpoint? In the vast majority of cases, selling to the highest bidder will create the most value for the divestor's shareholders. But not always. Had Ford sold its Jaguar and Land Rover brands to an automaker with a wide range of products that overlapped with Ford's core business in many markets, for example, rather than to the less-entrenched Tata Motors, the sale might have exacerbated competitive pressures on Ford's other auto lines. Thus, in deciding whom to sell to, divestors must be careful to account for the competitive threat posed by each potential buyer.

residential wire-line business), in the face of growing competition from cable providers, is a case in point.

The deal had many advantages for both the parent and the spin-off. The new company, Bell Aliant Regional Communications, would focus on rural territories, while Bell Canada would focus on national wireless, as well as on major urban markets where it could sell a broader range of products (voice, data, video, wireless). By combining the scale of Bell Canada's rural operations with those of Aliant (a company Bell Canada only partially owned), the deal would create sufficient scale in Bell Aliant's rural wire-line business. The arrangement would allow Bell Canada to focus on its higher growth wireless operations and reduce its exposure to the slower-growth wire-line business. The new company would attract a better market valuation than when it was buried within Bell Canada, especially merged with Aliant's wire-line business, releasing shareholder value for both Bell Canada and Aliant. Finally, the deal was structured to reap considerable tax advantages, and the proceeds allowed Bell Canada to reduce debt and make a special distribution to shareholders.

The deal made sense for the parties involved, but what about the government agencies and other large national customers that required service in rural areas? What about the shared network assets that underpin telephone service in both urban (Bell Canada) and rural (Aliant) areas? It was easy enough to sell the physical assets that would become Bell Aliant Regional Communications, but the networks that supported them couldn't be ripped out or re-created without prohibitive expense. And what was to become of installation and repair—especially in border areas?

Bell Canada carefully sorted through these particulars. Before announcing the deal, the divestiture team created a detailed plan whereby Bell Canada would continue to provide network functions, billing, call centers, dispatch centers, marketing, and corporate services such as finance, legal, and HR—some services in perpetuity and some for defined transition periods. Aliant would create its own sales force for small and midsize business, markets in which Bell Canada had done less well. Aliant would also gain the freedom to create new wire-line products. Comprehensive legal agreements formalized all of these important points, and a plan was in place well before the day of divestiture.

The plan has borne fruit. Since the beginning of 2007, Bell Aliant stock has outperformed other Canadian regional carriers'. Bell Canada's rigorous divestiture planning has enabled it to create a regionally focused carrier, which has grown by acquiring additional rural assets.

In planning a divestiture, it pays to time the deal to coincide with the use of the proceeds—ideally investing in such things as debt restructuring, share repurchase, or acquisition of a new business adjacent to the company's core. Groupe Danone, for example, announced it was in discussions to sell its biscuits business to Kraft Foods for more than $7 billion in July 2007. Less than two weeks later, the company announced it would buy Royal Numico, the Dutch baby formula and nutrition-bar manufacturer, for $16.8 billion. This near-simultaneous sale and purchase enabled Danone to kill two birds with one stone: It used virtually all of the company's cash on hand, thereby reducing its appeal as a takeover target following the sale of its biscuits unit. It also vaulted itself into a leadership position in the world markets for baby food and clinical nutrition. "Numico has all the characteristics we like," said Antoine Giscard d'Estaing, Danone's then-CFO, on the day of the announcement, "health orientation, extremely good research and development, market leadership and exposure to high-growth markets." Investors viewed the deal favorably as well, quickly bidding up the value of Danone's shares.

Rule 4: Provide a Compelling Logic for Buyers and Employees

The best divestors clearly communicate what's in the deal for all involved. This entails having convincing—and honest—answers to four questions:

- What actions should be taken to improve the profitability of the divestiture candidate or fuel its growth?

- How long will it take the buyer to achieve the deal's full potential value? (The faster an acquirer can realize the increase in value, the more it will be willing to pay for the divested business.)

- How should the value that can be unlocked through divestiture be split between the buyer and the seller?

- How will we motivate and inspire the people in the business to keep it humming along until the deal closes (and beyond)?

Though not strictly a divestiture, Gillette's sale of itself to Procter & Gamble in October 2005 illustrates the payoff that both parties can realize from carefully addressing the first two questions. P&G had been interested in Gillette for years—viewing Gillette's franchise in razors and blades, and its emerging strength in toiletries, as an ideal extension to its own consumer products portfolio. Gillette resisted selling as late as 1999. But after Jim Kilts became Gillette's CEO in 2001, he and his executive team carefully analyzed the potential value to P&G of pushing Gillette's products through P&G's distribution network.

Gillette then provided P&G with a detailed plan for realizing potential synergies on both the cost and revenue side. So compelling was its presentation that it was able to negotiate a price ($57 billion) that allowed Gillette's shareholders to reap all of the potential cost synergies from the transaction. That's because the revenue synergies for P&G were demonstrably large enough to justify the premium it paid to acquire control.

In making a case to buyers, companies need to be forthright about the warts of the business they're selling. In 2007, when Raytheon sold its commercial aircraft unit, RAC (now Hawker Beechcraft), for $3.3 billion to two private equity firms, Onex and GS Capital, management made no effort to downplay the unit's poor performance. Raytheon was careful to acknowledge that any new owner would need to make significant investments in new products and was clear about the unit's poor strategic fit with Raytheon's core government and defense businesses. This honesty made Raytheon's recommendations for ways a buyer could turn the unit around more credible than they would otherwise have been.

A good way to address the question of allocating value is to structure the deal so that both the buyer and the seller win if the divested business is successful. For example, IRS rules allow for tax-free divestiture deals under a reverse Morris trust. The structure of these deals can be complex, but essentially they all amount to the seller's spinning off a business or division to its shareholders, after which the acquiring company merges with the separated entity. The result is that both groups of shareholders own the newly created company, so everyone wins only if it does well. Examples of reverse Morris trust deals include H.J. Heinz's spin-off of North American pet foods, StarKist, and a number of its other businesses to Del Monte in 2002; Disney's 2007 divestiture of ABC Radio to Citadel Broadcasting; and Kraft Foods' deal to divest Post cereals to Ralcorp the same year.

In the Heinz–Del Monte deal, Heinz shareholders ended up owning almost 75% of Del Monte, so the deal created value for Heinz only if Del Monte benefited from its acquisition. Accordingly, Heinz CEO William Johnson was right when he said in the press release announcing the deal: "This transformative transaction is a unique win-win proposition for both companies." Richard Wolford, the CEO of Del Monte, echoed the sound logic for the deal, maintaining: "As this combination develops, Del Monte will be a much stronger company. This will be a company that will have leading brands in a number of important grocery aisles." In short, these deals work because they really do work for both parties.

Of course, structuring the deal well is only part of a winning divestiture story. There is a human narrative that must be carefully managed, as well. Here, a creative approach to compensation and HR policies can help.

At Textron, for example, compensation packages for executives of divested units typically consist of three elements. A completion bonus is paid to the top one or two executives to encourage them to get the deal done successfully. Retention packages are provided to key executives to ensure that they stay put until after the deal is completed. And severance packages reduce the fear of the unknown for all employees. Severance packages typically guarantee compensation for one year after the close of any divestiture but can extend beyond that period. Finally, Textron prohibits its own organization from poaching talent from businesses being divested.

The underlying principle is simple, says CFO Ted French: "Maximize the value of the business first, even if that means that talented executives are separated from Textron. People are treated fairly and rewarded for their contributions. As a result, people really don't mind being sold by us. There are very few other companies that can make that claim."

Beyond developing a compelling logic for divesting a business as it currently exists, sellers can (and often should) take simple steps to boost its performance to produce a credible track record of results before a sale. When Pfizer decided to divest its Adams confectionery business, for instance, the company spent several months reducing the plethora of its offerings and renegotiating supply contracts. This effort improved the performance of the unit, making it more attractive to Cadbury Schweppes, which paid $4.2 billion for Adams in 2003. The combination of a good story and real progress paid off handsomely for Pfizer's shareholders.

Selling a business is rarely a one-off activity. Our research shows that companies that actively manage their divestiture portfolios in a selective and disciplined manner outperform competitors that sit on the sidelines. With time and practice, these companies create an institutional capacity to spot and take advantage of divestiture opportunities whenever they arise. The best have become what we call "divestiture ready"—able to consistently move at the right time and in the right way to create the most value for their shareholders.

The Bipolarity of Change

Major change initiatives provoke wild mood swings, which cloud people's judgment and lead to bad decisions. Companies that have mastered change know how to anticipate those swings and counter the serious risks they create.

Patrick Litre and Kevin Murphy

Looking back over the centuries, it's difficult to grasp the emotional turmoil that Columbus and his sailors must have faced on their voyage into the unknown. Yet the pattern of highs and lows would probably seem familiar to anyone living through a corporate transformation, with its bipolar effects on the participants.

The initial reaction to the proposed journey is invariably skeptical, fearful, resistant. We can't do that. It's too risky, too expensive. We might fall off the face of the earth. Columbus was turned down by the rulers of Portugal, Venice, and Genoa before he found backing for his venture from Spain.

But then the mood begins to shift. Perhaps influential individuals—think Ferdinand and Isabella—sign on. Perhaps the organization's leaders become seduced by the potential benefits. Soon the idea has gained momentum, and people start clamoring to be part of it. What once looked impossible now seems both feasible and desirable.

That's two severe mood swings already, even though no one has yet gone near the water. And the emotional fluctuations don't end there. Once the ships have actually set out—once the initiative is under way—the original negativity returns with a vengeance. Obstacles once again loom large. Gloom sets in, and progress sputters. Like Columbus's sailors, people grow dispirited. They want desperately to turn back.

This down-up-down sequence is remarkably similar whether the journey focuses on cost reduction, organizational restructuring, post-merger integration, or any other major change. (See the exhibit "A Predictable Emotional Pattern.") In some respects, it's a corporate version of the psychological condition known as bipolar disorder, with its patterns of extreme highs and lows. Certainly the results are the same: clouded judgment and poor decisions, the emotional pendulum swinging first one way and then the other. In a merger, for example, deal fever can lead executives to overestimate potential synergies and discount organizational obstacles. But

A Predictable Emotional Pattern

In change programs, cognitive biases intensify the inevitable mood swings.

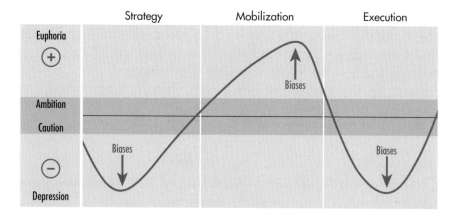

once the deal is done and the integration process begun, reality sets in. Cultural differences and operational challenges now look insurmountable. Some people leave; some customers defect. What once seemed like a great idea now feels misguided.

Organizational psychologists have studied the reasons for these extreme mood swings and the poor decisions that result. In times of stress, they say, people are the prisoners of cognitive biases. They don't see reality clearly, so their judgment is compromised. Different cognitive biases cut in at each stage of a journey, creating a predictable sequence of moods and mindsets as change unfolds. These states of mind affect how people process information, how much weight they assign to particular experiences, how they receive feedback, and a host of other factors that influence judgment and decisions.

It doesn't have to be this way. Some business leaders retain their common sense and wisdom, even in the face of radical change. They recognize that mood swings occur in predictable patterns. They anticipate what's coming, and they help others cope by counteracting the emotional fluctuations and mitigating the accompanying risks. When executives prepare in this fashion, the initiative stays on course and delivers results.

Phase I. Mapping the Journey

When a leader proposes a major new direction in an organization, people usually feel skeptical, even threatened. They don't see the need to change. They can't perceive the possibilities.

In effect, the proponents of change are asking team members to move out of their comfort zone. But the way forward is blocked by cognitive biases that interfere with people's openness to change. *Anchoring*, or relying on familiar reference points, locks them into conventional thought patterns. The *ambiguity effect*, which leads people to favor the known over the unknown, raises fears about the future. *Confirmation bias* encourages them to look for evidence that supports their fears and casts doubt on the possibility of change. When these inevitable biases emerge, people on the leadership team feel uneasy. They tend to cling to incremental ideas rather than embrace more dramatic change. A bricks-and-mortar retailer, for instance, might persuade itself that it is moving rapidly into the digital world because it is offering goods online, when in fact it is far behind the more comprehensive and integrated digital strategies of its competitors.

Loosening these anchors starts with assembling the facts. Data—about the company's situation, what customers are saying, the "size of the prize" to be realized from the change—helps cut through the biases by appealing to people's left-brain, rational side. Another effective tool is co-creating a clear, compelling vision of the future. Change proponents help the leadership team buy into the proposal by activating their right brain and enabling them to *picture* that future New World.

For example, when a health care provider launched a major change effort to improve patient satisfaction, it started with the hospital registration process. In a workshop, the company's leaders jointly developed a powerful metaphor for the vision: a hotel check-in. The efficient yet friendly experience of checking into a hotel captured exactly what they wanted for their patients. And every employee could understand the idea—it changed not just the definition of the process but how people behaved and even the architectural design of the registration area. A powerful metaphor like this not only helps people to visualize the change; it also accelerates the change process. Project teams can now make most decisions without input from top leaders because they have a clear understanding of the future state.

At some point in this process, the idea of the change catches on. The balance tips. Fears vanish, and enthusiasm grows. What once seemed impossible now feels within reach.

Phase II. The Tide Turns

As the emotional tide turns, new cognitive biases reinforce and exaggerate the change in mood. *Confirmation bias* now reinforces people's belief in the possibility of change. So does *pervasive optimism*, or the natural human tendency to believe that we have control of our lives and will be able to achieve what we set out to do. These biases are powerful, and seem to sweep away doubt or disagreement. Team members choose the most optimistic scenarios about the benefits of the new direction. They think they can achieve those goals in the shortest possible time frame.

It's just as important to contain the over-optimism at this stage as it was to counteract the initial pessimism. Overconfidence and unconstrained optimism can cloud return-on-investment calculations. They lead to even deeper pessimism later, when the next mood swing occurs.

How can leadership teams mitigate these risks? One effective tool is to look backward. Using a standardized risk model, teams can analyze what went wrong and what went right in previous change efforts. What were the typical failure modes? What does our organization do well, and what does it do poorly? Benchmarking can be valuable in this context: For example, a database of some 350 companies helps Bain identify the biggest obstacles to change. People naturally expect today's change initiative to play out much like yesterday's, with all the same problems. If you can learn from the past, you can surprise them by doing it better.

It's equally essential to look forward—to immerse the team in the future they have begun to co-create. Asked to think in specific detail about future events, people create a richer, more accurate reality. Leaders can then ask themselves exactly what changes are required and who will be most affected. This kind of analysis highlights the impact of change on specific groups, and has the effect of bringing everyone down to earth.

To anticipate the future, it helps to use a predictive risk model and then to develop an explicit risk-mitigation plan. Fifteen specific risks threaten to disrupt change efforts, such as poor sponsorship and change overload. (See the sidebar "The 15 Questions Every Change Leader Should Ask.") These risks tend to occur in predictable patterns over the life cycle of a change, but only a handful of risks determine success or failure at each stage. A risk assessment enables a company to understand the unique risk profile of an initiative and identify the four or five risks that pose the biggest threats, the sequence in which they will arise, and the tools that will be most effective for containing and managing each one.

For instance, when Merck KGaA, the German chemicals and pharmaceuticals concern, acquired U.S. biotech equipment supplier Millipore, managers drew up a two-by-two chart representing every group in the organization on two dimensions: their importance in achieving the integration goals and the degree of disruption they would experience from the upcoming change. That allowed the leadership team to focus on supporting the people who were most important to the success of the merger, and who faced the greatest risk of serious dislocation. Leaders clarified roles, set priorities, and provided focused change management support to help the integration succeed.

But then, inevitably, the voyage begins. And once more the mood changes. . . .

Phase III. Skirting the Rocks

The initiative has launched. Everyone is supposed to climb on board. But now, somehow, things don't play out as expected. Obstacles appear. Costs mount. The venture is harder than people thought. Some argue that it is time to call a halt and cut losses.

A different set of cognitive biases takes over when people confront real obstacles. Facing reality, most human beings are *loss averse*—they prefer avoiding

The 15 Questions Every Change Leader Should Ask

1. Is our description of success clear and inspiring enough to generate emotional buy-in with our people?
2. Are the proposed solutions appealing to the organization, and will they work in our culture?
3. Are top leaders demonstrating alignment on this change in their communications and actions?
4. Do we have the right leaders who can work effectively as a team, both today and in the future state?
5. Are line managers at all levels actively and visibly reinforcing the adoption of the change?
6. Have we selected credible team members and involved trusted opinion leaders?
7. Do we know who will be most disrupted, and do we have a plan to address resistance and build commitment?
8. Can we develop or acquire the talent and expertise we need for this change?
9. Have we identified the few behaviors that will drive results and the reinforcements to encourage them?
10. Is the program governance designed to make and execute sound, efficient, and timely decisions?
11. Can we deliver the change on time while protecting our business's performance from capacity overload?
12. Do we have goals, metrics, and a system to forecast results and course-correct before it's too late?
13. Are we tuning our organization (structure, culture, incentive system, etc.) to sustain the change?
14. Can we enhance our systems and leverage new technology fast enough to deliver the results on time?
15. Are we designing fast feedback loops to learn and enhance our solutions over time?

losses to acquiring an equal amount of gains. When the going gets rough, they naturally look back toward the familiar harbor they left behind. *Negativity bias,* the tendency for negative events to loom larger than positive ones in people's minds, reinforces that reaction. So does *normalcy bias* (also known as the "ostrich effect"), which refers to the difficulties people have in seeing problems when they are in new situations outside of their normal experience.

This is a critical and time-consuming phase of an initiative. What's at stake, typically, is winning the hearts and minds of employees and helping them change well-worn patterns of behavior. A variety of tools can help to counteract the natural negativity at this stage, but four in particular stand out:

Creating an enrollment cascade. Instead of relying on broadcast communication from the top, change leaders create a companywide dialogue about what is happening. The dialogue rolls out through the ranks: Every individual in the organization hears the plan from his or her direct supervisor and is invited to ask questions and provide feedback on the spot. The story is thus told in the best possible way, by the most credible person, the one with the most influence on an individual employee's work life. The resulting dialogue allows individuals to feel heard and so offers them a greater sense of control. It also sets expectations that are more likely to be realistic. The newly merged Merck Millipore, for example, conducted this kind of structured dialogue throughout the organization—one key to the successful post-merger integration of the two companies.

Preparing leaders at all levels to be sponsors. When people's lives are disrupted, their reactions follow a predictable resistance curve. It is often said that companies at this stage should "communicate, communicate, communicate." That is wrong. Some communication is necessary at the outset. But now, it's more important to listen. Much of the listening inevitably falls to middle managers and supervisors, who will need training in how best to deal with resistance. They can learn, for instance, that resistance is a natural and normal reaction to disruption, a sign of progress rather than a problem to be solved.

Designing positive consequences for behavioral change. Transformations often involve changes in how employees act every day on the job. A company in this situation needs to spell out not only what people should do differently but how they will be reinforced for adopting the new behaviors.

One bank, for instance, invested heavily in a program for cross-selling products to customers. It alerted bank tellers about which customers would be suitable prospects, trained tellers how to sell, and compensated those who successfully cross-sold. It also designed a set of immediate consequences for changed behavior. After witnessing an encounter between a teller and an impatient customer, for example, a platform manager standing nearby would offer encouragement: "You handled that well. You were not defensive. Remember, it's only one in five customers who will buy." That encouraged the teller to continue applying the script—and as he began to sell the new product to more clients, the rise in performance metrics typically encouraged him further. Positive reinforcement of this sort is four times as powerful in changing behavior as "push" activities (such as training) alone.

Encouraging a "red is good" attitude. "Red" in a change process—the identification of a problem area or a risk—is often seen as a negative sign. That's backward: It should be seen as a signal that people are involved, that they care about the initiative's success. Companies we work with often train change agents in every branch and function to look for the highest risks perceived by frontline employees and others on the receiving end of the change. They discuss these concerns right away with local leaders, resolve whatever issues they can, and elevate concerns that need attention at a higher level.

Conclusion: Building a Change Capability

Leaders who try to change an organization are up against some of the deepest attributes of human nature. The mood swings and cognitive biases that accompany change efforts blur people's ability to evaluate a situation and make good decisions. Even smart, experienced leaders sometimes end up making promises that they can't keep, damaging their credibility and eroding trust.

But a company that mounts systematic efforts to identify the risks and counter the biases alters the terms of the equation. Now the change effort is no longer an unfair fight. The obstacles have become predictable and thus manageable. Over time, the company strengthens its change muscles, creating a repeatable model for change. It becomes more adept at managing not just this transformation but the next one as well. In a world of constant change, that equips a company to out-execute its competitors.

Recommended Reading

Bain Books

Blenko, Marcia, Michael C. Mankins, and Paul Rogers. *Decide & Deliver: 5 Steps to Break-through Performance in Your Organization*. Harvard Business Review Press, 2010.

Gadiesh, Orit, and Hugh MacArthur. *Lessons from Private Equity Any Company Can Use*. Harvard Business Press, 2008.

Gottfredson, Mark, and Steve Schaubert. *The Breakthrough Imperative: How the Best Managers Get Outstanding Results*. HarperCollins, 2008.

Harding, David, and Sam Rovit. *Mastering the Merger: Four Critical Decisions That Make or Break the Deal*. Harvard Business School Press, 2004.

Lorsch, Jay W., and Thomas J. Tierney. *Aligning the Stars: How to Succeed When Professionals Drive Results*. Harvard Business School Press, 2002.

Reichheld, Fred. *The Ultimate Question: Driving Good Profits and True Growth*. Harvard Business School Press, 2006.

Reichheld, Frederick F. *Loyalty Rules! How Today's Leaders Build Lasting Relationships*. Harvard Business School Press, 2001.

Reichheld, Fred, with Rob Markey. *The Ultimate Question 2.0: How Net Promoter Companies Thrive in a Customer-Driven World*. Harvard Business Review Press, 2011.

Reichheld, Frederick F., with Thomas Teal. *The Loyalty Effect: The Hidden Force Behind Growth, Profits, and Lasting Value*. Harvard Business School Press, 1996.

Rigby, Darrell. *Winning in Turbulence*. Harvard Business Press, 2009.

Zook, Chris. *Unstoppable: Finding Hidden Assets to Renew the Core and Fuel Profitable Growth*. Harvard Business School Press, 2007.

Zook, Chris. *Beyond the Core: Expand Your Market Without Abandoning Your Roots*. Harvard Business School Press, 2004.

Zook, Chris, and James Allen. *Repeatability: Build Enduring Businesses for a World of Constant Change*. Harvard Business Review Press, 2012.

Zook, Chris, with James Allen. *Profit from the Core: A Return to Growth in Turbulent Times*. Harvard Business Press, 2010.

Articles in *Harvard Business Review* and Related Publications

Winning Strategy

Baveja, Sarabjit Singh, Steve Ellis, and Darrell Rigby. "Taking Advantage of a Downturn." *Harvard Management Update*, September 2002.

Chen, Ann, and Vijay Vishwanath. "Expanding in China." *Harvard Business Review*, March 2005.

Gadiesh, Orit, and James L. Gilbert. "Transforming Corner-Office Strategy into Front-line Action." *Harvard Business Review*, May 2001.

Gadiesh, Orit, and James L. Gilbert. "Profit Pools: A Fresh Look at Strategy." *Harvard Business Review*, May 1998.

Quelch, John A., and David Harding. "Brands Versus Private Labels: Fighting to Win." *Harvard Business Review*, January 1996.

Rigby, Darrell. "Moving Upward in a Downturn." *Harvard Business Review*, June 2001.

Rigby, Darrell, and Chris Zook. "Open-Market Innovation." *Harvard Business Review*, October 2002.

Schwalm, Eric, and David Harding. "Winning with the Big-Box Retailers." *Harvard Business Review*, September 2000.

Vestring, Till, Ted Rouse, and Uwe Reinert. "Making the Move to Low-Cost Countries." *Supply Chain Strategy*, June 2005.

Vishwanath, Vijay, and David Harding. "The Starbucks Effect." *Harvard Business Review*, March 2000.

Zook, Chris. "Finding Your Next Core Business." *Harvard Business Review*, April 2007.

Zook, Chris, and Darrell Rigby. "How to Think Strategically in a Recession." *Harvard Management Update*, November 2001.

Customer Focus

Allen, James, Frederick F. Reichheld, and Barney Hamilton. "Tuning into the Voice of Your Customer." *Harvard Management Update*, October 2005.

Collins, Michael, and Phil Schefter. "The Narrow Path to Victory for B2B Exchanges." *Harvard Management Update*, September 2000.

Reichheld, Frederick F. "The One Number You Need to Grow." *Harvard Business Review*, December 2003.

Reichheld, Frederick F. "Lead for Loyalty." *Harvard Business Review*, July 2001.

Reichheld, Frederick F. "Learning from Customer Defections." *Harvard Business Review*, March 1996.

Reichheld, Frederick F., and W. Earl Sasser, Jr. "Zero Defections: Quality Comes to Services." *Harvard Business Review*, September 1990.

Reichheld, Frederick F., and Phil Schefter. "E-Loyalty: Your Secret Weapon on the Web." *Harvard Business Review*, July 2000.

Rigby, Darrell, and Dianne Ledingham. "CRM Done Right." *Harvard Business Review*, November 2004.

Rigby, Darrell, Frederick F. Reichheld, and Phil Schefter. "Avoid the Four Perils of CRM." *Harvard Business Review*, February 2002.

Operational Excellence

Brenneman, Greg. "Right Away and All at Once: How We Saved Continental." *Harvard Business Review*, September 1998.

Cook, Miles, Pratap Mukharji, Lorenz Kiefer, and Marco Petruzzi. "Working Your Assets to Boost Your Growth." *Supply Chain Strategy*, March 2005.

Gottfredson, Mark, Rudy Puryear, and Stephen Phillips. "Strategic Sourcing: From Periphery to the Core." *Harvard Business Review*, February 2005.

Hansen, Morten T., Nitin Nohria, and Thomas Tierney. "What's Your Strategy for Managing Knowledge?" *Harvard Business Review*, March 1999.

High-Performance Organization

Farkas, Charles M., and Suzy Wetlaufer. "The Ways Chief Executive Officers Lead." *Harvard Business Review*, May 1996.

Gnamm, Joerg, and Klaus Neuhaus. "Leading from the Factory Floor." *Harvard Business Review*, November 2005.

Milway, Katie Smith, Ann Goggins Gregory, Jenny Davis-Peccoud, and Kathleen Yazbak. "Get Ready for Your Next Assignment." *Harvard Business Review*, December 2011.

Rogers, Paul, and Hernan Saenz. "Make Your Back Office an Accelerator." *Harvard Business Review*, March 2007.

Vishwanath, Vijay, and Marcia Blenko. "The Art of Developing Leaders at Kraft." *Harvard Management Update*, November 2004.

Maximum Enterprise Value

Cullinan, Geoffrey, Jean-Marc Le Roux, and Rolf-Magnus Weddigen. "When to Walk Away from a Deal." *Harvard Business Review*, April 2004.

Harding, David, Sam Rovit, and Alistair Corbett. "Three Steps to Avoiding Merger Meltdown." *Harvard Business Review*, March 2005.

Harding, David, and Phyllis Yale. "Discipline and the Dilutive Deal." *Harvard Business Review*, July 2002.

Itoh, Ryoji, and Till Vestring. "Buying into Japan Inc." *Harvard Business Review*, November 2001.

About the Authors

James Allen is co-leader of Bain's Global Strategy practice. He is co-author of *Repeatability: Build Enduring Businesses for a World of Constant Change* (Harvard Business Review Press, 2012) and *Profit from the Core: A Return to Growth in Turbulent Times* (Harvard Business Press, 2010).

Keith Aspinall is a senior advisor in Bain's Global Strategy practice.

Alan Bird is a senior member in Bain's Organization practice and a partner in the firm's London and Johannesburg offices.

Marcia Blenko is a partner in Boston and the former leader of Bain's Global Organization practice. She is co-author of *Decide & Deliver: 5 Steps to Breakthrough Performance in Your Organization* (Harvard Business Review Press, 2010).

Andreas Dullweber is a partner based in Munich, where he leads Bain's Customer Strategy & Marketing practice in EMEA.

Orit Gadiesh, chairman, Bain, is co-author of *Lessons from Private Equity Any Company Can Use* (Harvard Business Press, 2008).

James Gilbert was formerly a partner based in Boston.

Mark Gottfredson is a partner in the Dallas office and the former leader of Bain's Global Performance Improvement practice. He is co-author of *The Breakthrough Imperative: How the Best Managers Get Outstanding Results* (HarperCollins, 2008).

Kara Gruver is the former leader of Bain's Consumer Products practice in the Americas and a partner in the firm's Boston office.

Dan Haas is the former leader of Bain's Private Equity practice in the Americas and a partner in the firm's Zurich office.

David Harding is a partner in the Boston office and co-leader of Bain's Global Mergers & Acquisitions practice. He is co-author of *Mastering the Merger: Four Critical Decisions That Make or Break the Deal* (Harvard Business School Press, 2004).

Tom Holland is a partner in Bain's San Francisco office and a senior member of the firm's Private Equity practice.

Dianne Ledingham is a partner in Boston and a senior member of Bain's Global Customer Strategy & Marketing practice.

Philip Leung is a senior member of Bain's Healthcare practice and is a partner in Shanghai.

Patrick Litre is a partner based in Atlanta and leads Bain's Global Results Delivery capability.

Heidi Locke Simon is a former Bain partner based in San Francisco.

Manny Maceda is a partner in San Francisco and the former leader of Bain's Global Performance Improvement practice.

Michael Mankins leads Bain's Organization practice in the Americas and is a partner in San Francisco. He is co-author of *Decide & Deliver: 5 Steps to Breakthrough Performance in Your Organization* (Harvard Business Review Press, 2010).

Jonathan Mark is a former Bain partner based in Boston.

Rob Markey is a partner in the New York office and leads Bain's Global Customer Strategy & Marketing practice. He is co-author of *The Ultimate Question 2.0: How Net Promoter Companies Thrive in a Customer-Driven World* (Harvard Business Review Press, 2011).

Kevin Murphy is a partner based in Atlanta and a senior member in Bain's Global Results Delivery capability.

Fred Reichheld is a Bain Fellow and author or co-author of *The Ultimate Question 2.0: How Net Promoter Companies Thrive in a Customer-Driven World* (Harvard Business Review Press, 2011); *The Ultimate Question: Driving Good Profits and True Growth* (Harvard Business School Press, 2006); *Loyalty Rules! How Today's Leaders Build Lasting Relationships* (Harvard Business School Press, 2001); and *The Loyalty Effect: The Hidden Force Behind Growth, Profits, and Lasting Value* (Harvard Business School Press, 1996).

Darrell Rigby is a partner in Boston and leads Bain's Global Retail and Global Innovation practices. He is the author of *Winning in Turbulence* (Harvard Business Press, 2009).

Paul Rogers is a partner in London and leads Bain's Global Organization practice. He is co-author of *Decide & Deliver: 5 Steps to Breakthrough Performance in Your Organization* (Harvard Business Review Press, 2010).

James Root leads Bain's Organization practice in Asia-Pacific and is a partner in Hong Kong.

Ted Rouse is a partner in Bain's Chicago office and a co-leader in its Global Mergers & Acquisitions practice, overseeing the firm's post-merger integration activities.

Sam Rovit is a former Bain partner based in Chicago. He is co-author of *Mastering the Merger: Four Critical Decisions That Make or Break the Deal* (Harvard Business School Press, 2004).

Hernan Saenz is a partner in Bain's Dallas and Mexico City offices and a senior member of the firm's Performance Improvement practice in the Americas.

Steve Schaubert, a senior advisor with Bain, is co-author of *The Breakthrough Imperative: How the Best Managers Get Outstanding Results* (HarperCollins, 2008).

Till Vestring is a partner based in Singapore and the former co-leader of the firm's Global Mergers & Acquisitions practice.

Vijay Vishwanath, based in Boston, leads Bain's Global Consumer Products practice.

Rolf-Magnus Weddigen is a partner in Bain's Munich office and is the former leader of the firm's Private Equity and Corporate M&A practices in EMEA.

Chris Zook is a partner and co-leader in the firm's Global Strategy practice. He is author or co-author of *Repeatability: Build Enduring Businesses for a World of Constant Change* (Harvard Business Review Press, 2012); *Profit from the Core: A Return to Growth in Turbulent Times* (Harvard Business Press, 2010); *Unstoppable: Finding Hidden Assets to Renew the Core and Fuel Profitable Growth* (Harvard Business School Press, 2007); and *Beyond the Core: Expand Your Market Without Abandoning Your Roots* (Harvard Business School Press, 2004).

Index

middle markets, 58, 59, 61–63,
68–70
exhibit, 61
Millipore, 270–71
mission, vii–viii
mission-critical projects, 209–10
mixed players, 21
Model T analysis, 145–50, 168
exhibit, 146
morale, employee, 100, 251–52
Morgan Crucible, 159–60, 162
Mosaic Company, 234, 246
motivation, 201–203
Mulally, Alan, 193–94
Mulcahy, Anne, 195
multinationals, 57
China's middle market
pursued by, 70
Chinese challenge to, 60–61
entering middle market
exhibit, 61
in good-enough markets. *See*
good-enough market
using M&A to move into good-
enough market, 62, 68–70
Murphy, Kevin, 267–73

Nabisco, 9, 232
Nanfu, 68–69
National Semiconductor, 33
Navistar International, 144
negativity bias, 272–73
Nestlé, 39, 220
Net Promoter® system, viii, 55, 99,
115–19, 166. *See also* NPS®
Neutrogena, 6
New York Stock Exchange, 244
Newell Rubbermaid, 137, 227–29,
231
Nextel, 137
niche marketing, 6
Nike, 35–36, 37–38, 42, 48, 71, 72
Ningbo Bird, 67
Nintendo, 161
Nissan Diesel, 198
Nokia, 46, 55–56, 67
nonnegotiables, 47, 52, 53–54
normalcy bias, 272
North American (pet foods), 264
Norton, David, 219
NPS® (Net Promoter® score),
115–16, 166
surveys of, 118–19

Ocean's Eleven (film), 210
offensive-defense strategy, 65
Office Depot, 138
Oil of Olay, 5

Olam, 38–40, 43–44, 51–53, 54
Olive Garden, 106–107
Olympics, 210
omnichannel retailing, 83–95
design specifications of, 89
organization of, 93–95
targeting customers in, 90
Onex, 264
online sales. *See* e-commerce
online shopping. *See* e-commerce
operating enterprise, 118
operating profit, 5
operational excellence, viii, 135–71
opportunities, 162
optimism, pervasive, 269–70
optimized automation, tools, and
procedures, 127, 128–29
organizational structure, 189–90
organizations. *See also*
reorganizations
BothBrain® approach in, 71–82
complexity of, 169
culture of. *See* culture,
organizational
decision-driven, 186, 189–200
flexible, 53
high-performance, viii, 175–211
structure of, after merger or
acquisition, 245–46
underperforming, 257
Ornstein, Robert, 73
Oscar Mayer, 5, 10
ostrich effect, 272
outsourcing, 12, 185–86
overperformers, 160, 161, 162

Packard, David, 72, 75
Palm, 137
Paradyne, 217
Parfums Chanel, 75
Parmalat, 66
partnerships, 72, 75–76, 76–79,
186
passives, 166
Peace, John, 225
Peet's, 12
performance
assessing, 208
bonuses and, 220
breakthrough, 43, 155
culture of, 224
decision making and, 175–88,
190–93
diagnosis of, helping new
leadership with, 153–71
evaluating, 210
improvement of, successful
program for, 154–56

by management, 127, 129–30
organizational structure and,
189–90
reorganizations and, 190
strategic differentiation and, 48
targets for, 32
Performance Improvement
Diagnostic℠, x, 153
Permira, 216
pervasive optimism, 269–70
Pets.com, 84
PetSmart, 93
Pfizer, 265
Phelps Dodge, 216
Philip Morris, 232
Pillsbury, 232
Pilot, Michael, 122, 124–25
Pistorio, Pasquale, 46
Pixar Animation Studios, 73,
75–76, 207, 244–45
"planning for opportunity," 237
Platinum Equity, 260
PlayStation, 161
point of arrival, ix
Polet, Robert, 76–77, 78, 80, 81
positive reinforcement, 273
Post (cereals), 6, 232, 264
potential, vii–x
Power Corporation of Canada, 225
"power customers," 115
Prada, Miuccia, 76
predictive risk model, 270
premium brands
in China, 58, 59
customer loyalty and, 8
exhibit, 61
high RMS and, 7–9
as high-road brands, 7–9, 13
innovation and, 6
low RMS and, 6–7
managing portfolio of, 13–14
most profitable strategy for,
5–6
profitability of, 4, 6–7
price wars, 6, 8
pricing
analysis of, 156–60
customer retention and, 109–10
drastic reductions in, 11–12
high-road brands and, 8
industry and, 157–58
market leaders and, 7
sensitivity to, 66
principles, core, 53–54
private-equity (PE) firms, 215–
26, 259
private-label brands, 4, 8
process complexity, 169–70